Reducing Genocide to Law

Could the prevailing view that genocide is the ultimate crime be wrong? Is it possible that it is actually on an equal footing with war crimes and crimes against humanity? Is the power of the word *genocide* derived from something other than jurisprudence? And why should a hierarchical abstraction assume such importance in conferring meaning on suffering and injustice? Could reducing a reality that is beyond reason and words into a fixed category undermine the very progress and justice that such labeling purports to achieve?

For some, these questions may border on the international law equivalent of blasphemy. This original and daring book, written by a renowned scholar and practitioner who was the first Legal Advisor to the UN Prosecutor at The Hague, is a probing reflection on empathy and our faith in global justice.

PAYAM AKHAVAN is Professor of International Law at McGill University in Montreal, Canada. He was the first Legal Advisor to the Prosecutor's Office of the International Criminal Tribunals for the former Yugoslavia and Rwanda at The Hague (1994–2000) and has served with the United Nations in Cambodia, East Timor, and Guatemala. He is also the author of the *Report on the Work of the Office of the Special Advisor of the United Nations Secretary-General on the Prevention of Genocide* (2005), has served as chairman of the Global Conference on the Prevention of Genocide (2007), and is coproducer of the documentary film *Genos.Cide: The Great Challenge* (2009).

CAMBRIDGE STUDIES IN INTERNATIONAL AND COMPARATIVE LAW

Established in 1946, this series produces high quality scholarship in the fields of public and private international law and comparative law. Although these are distinct legal subdisciplines, developments since 1946 confirm their interrelations.

Comparative law is increasingly used as a tool in the making of law at national, regional, and international levels. Private international law is now often affected by international conventions, and the issues faced by classical conflict rules are frequently dealt with by substantive harmonization of law under international auspices. Mixed international arbitrations, especially those involving state economic activity, raise mixed questions of public and private international law, while in many fields (such as the protection of human rights and democratic standards, investment guarantees, and international criminal law) international and national systems interact. National constitutional arrangements relating to "foreign affairs," and to the implementation of international norms, are a focus of attention.

The series welcomes works of a theoretical or interdisciplinary character, and those focusing on the new approaches to international or comparative law or conflicts of law. Studies of particular institutions or problems are equally welcome, as are translations of the best work published in other languages.

General Editors	James Crawford SC FBA *Whewell Professor of International Law, Faculty of Law, University of Cambridge*
	John S. Bell FBA *Professor of Law, Faculty of Law, University of Cambridge*

A list of books in the series can be found at the end of this volume.

Reducing Genocide to Law

Definition, Meaning, and the Ultimate Crime

Payam Akhavan

CAMBRIDGE
UNIVERSITY PRESS

University Printing House, Cambridge CB2 8BS, United Kingdom

Cambridge University Press is part of the University of Cambridge.

It furthers the University's mission by disseminating knowledge in the pursuit of education, learning and research at the highest international levels of excellence.

www.cambridge.org
Information on this title: www.cambridge.org/9781107480056

First published 2012
First paperback edition 2014

A catalogue record for this publication is available from the British Library

ISBN 978-0-521-82441-5 Hardback
ISBN 978-1-107-48005-6 Paperback

Contents

Preface

In July 1995, in the shadow of the shocking mass murder of thousands of Bosnian Muslims in Srebrenica, I sat around a table with colleagues from the Prosecutor's Office of the International Criminal Tribunal for the former Yugoslavia (ICTY). We were called upon to review a draft indictment against the notorious Bosnian Serb leaders President Radovan Karadžić and General Ratko Mladić. Those of us assembled in The Hague on that day were considering for the first time ever whether to charge an accused with the crime of genocide. It had just been a few months since the tribunal had become operational, there was a sense of urgency as the war in Bosnia was still raging, and there was little jurisprudence or academic commentary to guide our deliberations. After all, the Genocide Convention had been adopted only in 1948, after the Judgment of the International Military Tribunal at Nuremberg in 1946, and there had been no international criminal jurisdiction to prosecute such crimes until the ICTY's establishment in 1993. As Legal Advisor, I had prepared an exhaustive Memorandum on the Law of Genocide that analyzed every conceivable source of authority – from the *travaux préparatoires* to UN expert studies – and I was confident I had mastery of the subject. But on that day, as we attempted to reduce the enormity of the horrors unfolding in Bosnia to the strictures of legal reasoning, I felt a profound sense of futility.

For a young international jurist, the excitement of this historic moment was palpable. This was, after all, a unique opportunity to shape an obscure and dormant but fundamentally important field of international law that would go on to revolutionize the discipline in significant ways. This was no less than the resumption of the post-Nuremberg project to establish a permanent penal court that the International Law Commission had been entrusted with, but that had been abandoned in the cynical Cold War era that followed. The "ethnic cleansing" campaign in the former Yugoslavia had prompted the UN Security Council to establish a tribunal as an unprecedented enforcement measure under Chapter VII of the Charter. This unanticipated event, I considered at the time, would surely expedite the establishment of the long-awaited International Criminal Court. My Harvard LLM thesis had lamented as recently as 1990 the conspicuous absence of enforcement mechanisms for the crime of genocide. I could have scarcely imagined then that I would soon have the good fortune of becoming a pioneer in international criminal law at the very beginning of my career.

Juxtaposed with this glorious intellectual enterprise – the defining moment in any jurist's career – were the unspeakable images of human suffering that I had witnessed a few months earlier while serving with the UN in Bosnia. My youthful idealism had collided with scenes from hell. In village after village, I had witnessed wickedness that knew no limits. I came across women with babes in arms murdered in the streets as they attempted to flee, entire families burned alive while sheltering in their basements, the harrowing testimony of children raped in front of their parents, survivors weeping uncontrollably as they sifted through mass graves in search of their loved ones. And the affliction of those unfortunate souls reawakened in my mind the terrible anguish that surrounded my family as we witnessed helplessly the torture and murder of fellow Bahá'ís in the Islamic Republic of Iran after the 1979 revolution. While the distant pursuit of global justice had filled me with a kind of professional hubris, the intimate reality of victims pointed in a very different direction. Instead of the burgeoning war crimes industry and the endless procession of conferences and publications and opportunities for professional advancement, it led to a place where words fail, where legal concepts are found wanting, a place of grief and silence where we are forced to humbly ponder the human condition, ever mindful that it cannot be captured in manageable doctrines and concepts.

To determine whether we should charge genocide or not, I explained to my colleagues with a fluent command of the law that a core element of the crime is a somewhat elusive factor of scale or gravity. Was the evidence sufficient to prove beyond a reasonable doubt – as required by the definition of genocide – that Karadžić and Mladić had the intention to destroy a "substantial part" of the Bosnian Muslim group, or not? The debate wavered from abstract statistical assertions about the numerical proportion of civilian deaths to the gravity of particular incidents in detention camps. Suddenly, amidst this intellectual chaos, a colleague exclaimed: "But this is not the Holocaust!" There was an uncomfortable silence as the weight of those words sank in. Absent a mathematical formula that would determine the threshold of genocide, what exactly qualified the Bosnian atrocities one way or the other? Was this an exercise in legal reasoning, or a comparative survey built on the archetypal image of the Holocaust from which the concept of genocide first emerged? Some colleagues eventually mustered the courage to disagree with the proposition that only Hitler's crimes were worthy of being labeled as the ultimate crime: "This *is* genocide. The atrocities are truly heinous, truly shocking. They are the worst of the worst. What would the victims think if we don't charge genocide?"

The year before, in 1994, as close to one million Tutsis were exterminated in Rwanda, the refusal of United States officials to label the events genocide had caused a storm of controversy. It was as if there was a special power in invoking this word, whether to justify or avoid humanitarian intervention. Most intriguing was the invocation of the term to give victims a measure of recognition that their suffering deserved the hierarchical primacy reserved for genocide. I revisited this issue in relation to the International Criminal Tribunal for Rwanda (ICTR) that had been established in 1994 by the UN Security Council. What, I wondered, if the Tutsis were actually a "social" group and not an ethnic or racial group encompassed by the definition of genocide? Could a charge of genocide fail on such grounds and what would it mean for the victims and the credibility of global justice? I would encounter the issue in yet other countries where I served the UN. In Cambodia in 1997, victims and jurists were full of rage and disbelief to consider that the mass murder of "political" groups by the Khmer Rouge might not qualify as genocide in proceedings before the yet to be established Extraordinary Chamber in the Courts of Cambodia. By contrast, in Guatemala in 1998, the Mayan victims celebrated when the UN Historical Clarification Commission recognized their mass murder as genocide.

Increasingly, I felt something perverse in this discourse, in its privileging of hierarchical abstractions over the far more compelling stories and scenes that had been seared into my memory. The emotional connection with those people and events, it seemed, could be captured only by remaining ineffable, by recognition that taxonomic distinctions and definitions were grossly inadequate in conveying their meaning. The triumphant international law narrative quickly gave way to a more profound reflection on how the legal debate on defining genocide masked other unexplored sensibilities about how the jurist comes to grips with intense suffering and overwhelming emotion. It also implicated my family upbringing – as a child of both eastern and western civilizations, I was steeped in oriental mysticism and a spiritual worldview – with my formal legal education – in the tradition of occidental rationalism and its place of distinction for objective theoretical learning divorced from subjective experience. As I embarked on a scholarly writing project for my doctoral dissertation in those years, there was a great temptation to transform my groundbreaking Memorandum into an authoritative treatise on the law of genocide. The prevalent sense of futility, however, shifted the focus elsewhere. The ambitious jurist had succumbed to that search for answers that is born of existential angst. In straying beyond law, I attempted to convey a truth that could not be contained in carefully regimented chapters and sequential paragraphs, offering the reader a dazzling panoply of intellectual prowess and conceptual wonders. The project that emerged was decidedly not an authoritative treatise, but rather a series of reflections on the encounter between the rationalist credo of law and the ineffability of emotions, viewed through the prism of genocide.

This book was written first and foremost as a means of reckoning with the pursuit of juridical redemption in the face of irredeemable loss. It grapples with both the potentialities and the limitations inherent in law, in search of the boundary between legal reasoning and that other realm of experience where structures built on words and arguments collapse. As such, it embraces jurisprudence and literature, theory and storytelling, in a complex multilayered inquiry that attempts to convey through its medium the message at its core. That the reader must first read patiently through legal doctrine and theory to arrive at the more penetrating but unwieldy chapters is a matter of deliberate choice.

Acknowledgments

This book is based on a dissertation submitted in 2001 for the Doctor of Juridical Sciences degree at Harvard Law School. It was completed under the supervision of Professor Henry Steiner to whom I am indebted for his years of support and guidance. My exceptional reader and enduring mentor, Dean Martha Minow, deserves special gratitude for encouraging me to venture beyond the familiar but narrow understanding of academic writing to explore other paths to knowledge and meaning.

The manuscript first began in 1993 as a Memorandum of Law written at the request of Professor Antonio Cassese of Florence University, then president of the ICTY, whose contributions to jurisprudence and scholarship over the years have been a source of respect and admiration. The streams of thought reflected in the book emerged during my years as Legal Advisor to the Prosecutor's Office of the ICTY (1994–2000), serving under two distinguished jurists, Richard Goldstone and Louise Arbour, and engaging in countless spirited legal debates with colleagues such as William Fenrick, Morten Bergsmo, and Rodney Dixon.

My stint as Visiting Lecturer and Senior Fellow at Yale Law School during the fall 1998 semester, thanks to the support of Professor Harold Koh, and the fruitful exchanges with Michael Reisman and other faculty members were a welcome respite from the intense pressures of work at the ICTY to begin conceptualizing the manuscript. The initial dissertation was completed in the winter of 2001 while I was a Visiting Lecturer and Senior Fellow at the E. M. Meijers Institute of Legal Studies of Leiden University in the Netherlands with the support of the Open Society Institute.

The manuscript's publication was delayed for several years by life circumstances until it was revisited and substantially revised in the

2009–10 academic year, while I served as professor at McGill University Faculty of Law, where I found a splendid home thanks to the tremendous support and friendship of Dean Nicholas Kasirer and Professor Irwin Cotler. Over the years, I have also benefited greatly from those at the forefront of genocide studies, including especially Professor Frank Chalk of Concordia University. Among those that provided inspiration and friendship who are no longer with us, I wish to mention Professor Thomas Franck of New York University, Professor Erik Marcussen of Southwestern University, and Alison des Forges of Human Rights Watch, three extraordinary human beings who left a deep imprint on all those who had the good fortune of knowing them.

The final revision of the new manuscript would not have been possible without the invaluable assistance of my editor Stephen Scher and my research assistant Sam Walker. Both were phenomenal in their professionalism. The patience of Professor James Crawford and Finola O'Sullivan of Cambridge University Press, from the first review of the doctoral dissertation in 2002–03 until submission of the final manuscript in 2010 after seemingly never-ending revision, also merits special mention.

Special gratitude is reserved for all those that inspired a deeper meaning of justice and what it means to survive the unthinkable through their personal example. They include Professor Thomas Buergenthal who first introduced me to the United States Holocaust Memorial Museum, and my sister Esther Mujawayo whose heroic efforts have given a voice to Rwanda's forgotten widows and their children. The courage and sacrifice of another sister, Mona Mahmudnizhad, who on 18 June 1983 was hanged at the age of 16 in Shiraz with nine legendary Iranian Bahá'í women, I shall never forget for, being of the same age and community, all that separated us was the arbitrariness of fate. Of these heroines it can be said that they were truly spiritual giants.

And since this book is about reconciling the distance of our vocation as jurists and scholars with the intimacy of emotions, it is to my family that I dedicate this book, because it is their abiding love that has sustained my hope amidst despair and, after years of confronting death, it was my precious children whose arrival in this world awakened me to the miracle of life.

1   The power of a word

On 19 January 2007, at about noon, Hrant Dink left his office to walk through the bustling streets of Istanbul. Dink was chief editor of *Agos*, an Armenian weekly newspaper. He was a courageous voice for Turkey's dwindling Armenian community, the descendants of those few that remained after the mass murder and deportations of 1915–17. Dink wrote of the constant threats against him by hateful nationalists and how he had thought about leaving the country. But, for him, staying was necessary "out of respect to the thousands of friends in Turkey [who] struggled for democracy and who supported us. We were going to stay and we were going to resist." Alluding to the recurring trauma of exile, he asked: "If we were forced to leave one day, however, [what then]? We were going to set out just as in 1915? Like our ancestors? Without knowing where we were going? Walking the roads they walked? Feeling the ordeal, experiencing the pain? With such a reproach we were going to leave our home-land. And we would go where our feet took us, but not our hearts." As Dink walked through Istanbul's streets that day, 17-year-old Ogun Samast approached him from behind and shot him three times in the head.[1]

What motivated this shocking murder?

The culprit was captured shortly afterward with the murder weapon in hand and confessed.[2] He had never met Dink. The unrepentant youth explained: "I read on the Internet that [Dink] said 'I am from Turkey but Turkish blood is dirty' and I decided to kill him … I do not

---

[1] For an overview, see European Court of Human Rights, *Affaire Dink c. Turquie*, Arrêt, Requêtes nos. 2668/07, 6102/08, 30079/08, 7072/09 et 7124/09 (14 September 2010).

[2] "Armenian Editor Is Slain in Turkey," *New York Times*, 20 January 2007.

regret this."[3] This misconception was based on Dink's earlier conviction by a Turkish court for "insulting Turkishness" under Article 301 of the Turkish Penal Code. His crime? Using the word *genocide* to describe the atrocities of 1915.

How could one word have set this chain of events in motion? Taner Akçam, a Turkish scholar and close friend of Dink, pointed to the irony that, throughout his career, Dink himself had diligently avoided using the dreaded *g* word, preferring to recount the story of his people rather than dwelling on abstract labels. He understood its power. As Akçam recounted in an editorial published in *Agos* prior to the murder:

Just look at [Dink's] writings, look at his talks. You won't find one single instance of the word "genocide," because he never used it. Anytime he was asked if a genocide took place or not, he'd crack a smile. He didn't place a whole lot of importance on which word was necessary to describe what happened. "You call it what you want," he would say. "I know what happened to my people."

I don't recall Hrant ever took an interest in the legal label for the events of 1915. That side of the issue didn't concern him; the human side did. From what I can remember, he even wrote on the subject. "A nation which once lived here is no more. It was pulled out by its roots, like a tree. Their lives here were ended. I can't put into words this human tragedy, this ending of a life." It was words like this that came out of him.

The real question for Hrant, his primary concern, was never about what happened. It was about how to construct a positive future after all the negativity we've seen. I know from our private conversations that he preferred to stay away from the word "genocide" because of the tension it created and because it didn't do very much to resolve the problem.[4]

Apparently, Dink's fatal error occurred when he was pressed in a television interview to respond either "yes" or "no" to whether he thought the events of 1915–17 constituted "genocide." The usually cautious Dink reluctantly admitted that he thought they did. Such was his "crime," one that culminated in his brutal murder.

Sometime in 2003, President George W. Bush was sent a summary of Samantha Power's book, *"A Problem from Hell": America and the Age of Genocide.*[5] This stinging condemnation of the United States' inaction in

[3] "Armenian Editor Killed for Insulting Turks – Report," *Reuters*, 21 January 2007, www.reuters.com/article/idUSL21636786.
[4] Taner Akçam, "Hrant Dink, 301 and a Criminal Complaint," *Agos*, 6 October 2006 [in Turkish].
[5] Samantha Power, *"A Problem from Hell": America and the Age of Genocide* (New York: HarperCollins, 2002).

THE POWER OF A WORD

the face of mass murder throughout the twentieth century details in one chapter the absurd contortions of the administration of President Bill Clinton to avoid using the word "genocide" to describe the unfolding extermination campaign against the Rwandan Tutsis in 1994. In a notorious incident the US State Department spokeswoman Christine Shelly found herself in the ludicrous position of admitting in response to media questions that "acts of genocide" may have taken place though she adamantly refused to characterize the overall situation as a "genocide."[6] A senior administration official explained that this "semantic squirm" was required because "[g]enocide is a word that carries an enormous amount of responsibility."[7] It has been reported that, in the margins of Power's book, Bush penned in large letters "NOT ON MY WATCH."[8]

Some might think that Bush meant he would never again allow the United States to stand idly by as a genocide unfolded, even in a remote African nation where Americans had little interest. But early in 2004, as it became increasingly clear that the events in Darfur, Sudan, constituted a slow-motion annihilation of an entire people, the United States took no concrete action. The Bush administration did, however, improve on the Clinton era in one respect: It proved willing early on to use the word *genocide* to describe the situation. During a visit to the region in September 2004, Secretary of State Colin Powell became the first senior government official of a major power to call the killings in Darfur "genocide."[9] Three months later, the US Congress passed a resolution accusing the government of Sudan of an "orchestrated campaign of genocide in Darfur."[10]

Little was done, however, to effectively halt the ongoing atrocities in Darfur. It is difficult to tell whether this newfound taxonomical accuracy is an improvement. Is it better to not call a genocide "genocide" and do nothing, or is it better to call a genocide "genocide" and still do nothing? As events unfolded, much controversy arose concerning the use of the g word itself, but not concerning the everyday horrors confronted by the victims in Sudan.

---

[6] Peter Ronayne, *Never Again? The United States and the Prevention and Punishment of Genocide Since the Holocaust* (New York: Rowman & Littlefield, 2001), 74.

[7] *Ibid.*, 174.

[8] Samantha Power, "Genocide and America," *New York Review of Books*, 14 March 2002.

[9] "Powell Calls Sudan Killings Genocide," *CNN*, 9 September 2004, www.cnn.com/2004/WORLD/Africa/09/09/sudan.powell/.

[10] Comprehensive Peace in Sudan Act of 2004, Pub. L. No. 108-497, 118 Stat. 4012.

In December 2004, amidst the diplomatic storm following United States accusations of genocide, the United Nations Security Council sent a high-level panel to Darfur in order to ascertain the facts and determine whether genocide had been committed. The commission of inquiry, headed by eminent Italian jurist Antonio Cassese, concluded that the balance of evidence did not point toward a specific genocidal intent on the part of the Sudanese government.[11] The controversy surrounding this finding eclipsed the commission's other conclusion that, irrespective of legal classification, "massive atrocities were perpetrated on a very large scale,"[12] including the destruction of entire villages, mass killings and rape, and widespread forced displacement:

[T]he people of Darfur have suffered enormously during the last few years. Their ordeal must remain at the centre of international attention. They have been living a nightmare of violence and abuse that has stripped them of the very little they had. Thousands were killed, women were raped, villages were burned, homes destroyed, and belongings looted. About 1,8 million were forcibly displaced and became refugees or internally-displaced persons. They need protection.[13]

The commission went to great lengths to stress that its conclusion on the lack of genocidal intent "should not be taken in any way as detracting from the gravity of the crimes perpetrated in that region. International offences such as the crimes against humanity and war crimes that have been committed in Darfur may be no less serious and heinous than genocide."[14] All these subtle admonitions and legal qualifications fell on deaf ears, with newspapers blaring headlines such as "UN Clears Sudan of Genocide in Darfur" and "UN Confusion as Sudan Conflict Is No Longer 'Genocide.'"[15] When, in 2009, a pretrial chamber of the International Criminal Court (ICC) refused to issue an arrest warrant on charges of genocide against Sudanese president Omar Al-Bashir,[16] the controversy deepened further (although the ICC Appeals Chamber ultimately reversed that decision).[17]

---

[11] *Report of the International Commission of Inquiry on Darfur to the United Nations Secretary-General Pursuant to Security Council Resolution 1564 of 18 September 2004* (25 January 2005), www.un.org/news/dh/sudan/com_inq_darfur.pdf.
[12] *Ibid.*, para. 642.   [13] *Ibid.*, para. 626.   [14] *Ibid.*, 4.
[15] David Luban, "Calling Genocide by Its Rightful Name: Lemkin's Word, Darfur, and the UN Report," *Chicago Journal of International Law* 7 (2006): 303, 304.
[16] *Prosecutor v. Omar Hassan Ahmad Al Bashir*, Decision on the Prosecution's Application for a Warrant of Arrest Against Omar Hassan Ahmad Al Bashir (Pre-trial Chamber I, International Criminal Court, 4 March 2009).
[17] *Prosecutor v. Omar Hassan Ahmad Al Bashir*, Judgment on the Appeal of the Prosecutor Against the "Decision on the Prosecution's Application for a Warrant of Arrest

And so, as the immense suffering continued unabated in Darfur, international commissions were established, decisions were rendered, politicians expounded, and jurists and scholars debated whether the horrors of Darfur met the technical definition of genocide. Meanwhile, the "nightmare of violence" continued, unchanged by the word by which it was (or was not) called.

When Russia invaded Georgia in August 2008, the g word was a prominent feature of the propaganda war. This conflict was fueled by a long history of discord – in particular, by Russia's support of ethnic separatists in northern Georgia as a means of destabilizing a former Soviet satellite turned NATO ally. Russia originally justified its invasion by accusing Georgia of "genocide." It was claimed that, in a brief military operation against ethnic Ossetian separatists, Georgian forces had slaughtered over 2,000 civilians in the city of Tskhinvali.[18] The Russian ambassador to the United Nations even compared the situation to the massacres at Srebrenica.[19] *Pravda* claimed that "Georgian troops" had locked Ossetian refugees in a house "and set the house on fire, burning all the people inside alive."[20] Prime Minister Vladimir Putin himself declared that "in one hour" Georgia "wiped ten Ossetian villages from the face of the earth" and that Georgia "used tanks to knock down children and the elderly" and "burnt civilians alive."[21] Russia's foreign minister, Sergei Lavrov, invoked the "responsibility to protect" in justifying the armed attack, claiming that Russia was acting only to "protect the life and dignity of Russian citizens"[22] (most residents of South Ossetia, the affected region of Georgia, had been granted Russian citizenship).

against Omar Hassan Ahmad Al Bashir," Appeals Chamber, International Criminal Court, 3 February 2010).

[18] Sarah E. Mendelson, "An August War in the Caucasus," *Center for Strategic and International Studies – Critical Questions*, 11 August 2008, csis.org/publication/august-war-caucasus.

[19] *Ibid.*

[20] "Georgian Troops Burn South Ossetian Refugees Alive," *Pravda*, 10 August 2008 [in Russian]. Likewise, *Russia Today*, the pro-Kremlin cable news channel, continuously ran the headline "Ossetia Genocide."

[21] "Russia Launches Genocide Probe over S. Ossetia Events," *RIA: Novosti*, 14 August 2008 [in Russian].

[22] Ministry of Foreign Affairs of the Russian Federation, *Interview by Minister of Foreign Affairs of the Russian Federation Sergey Lavrov to BBC*, Moscow (9 August 2008), www.ln.mid.ru/brp_4.nsf/e78a48070f128a7b43256999005bcbb3/f87a3fb7a7f669ebc32574a100262597?OpenDocument; see also International Crisis Group, *Russia vs. Georgia: The Fallout* (Europe Report No. 195, 22 August 2008), 28.

These inflammatory accusations turned out to be wholly false. Indeed, Russia later acknowledged that the number of casualties it had previously reported was vastly inflated and that there were only 133 combat deaths, as confirmed by Amnesty International.[23] Investigations by Human Rights Watch also found no evidence to substantiate the alleged atrocities.[24]

The false accusation of "genocide" was used as the initial cover for a Russian invasion at a time when few in the international community knew what was actually happening on the ground. By invoking the word *genocide*, Russia incited South Ossetian militants who, relying on reports of the mass murder of their people, then engaged in a campaign of ethnic cleansing against a population of 138,000 Georgians.[25] A Human Rights Watch observer in South Ossetia reported that enraged Ossetians referred to reports by "Russian federal TV channels" about "thousands of civilian casualties" to "justif[y] the torching and looting of the ethnic Georgian enclave villages."[26]

These examples reflect the power of the genocide label, which is variously a pretext for murder (as in the story of Hrant Dink), inaction (as in Rwanda and Darfur), and war (as in the Russian invasion of Georgia). Yet it is a label that first emerged in the pursuit of justice and human betterment following the unprecedented horrors of Nazi Germany. How is it that an abstract juridical term that entered our vocabulary only in recent history can wield so much influence, incite so much emotion, and consume so much energy? What accounts for its perception as the ultimate crime?

The story begins with Polish jurist Raphaël Lemkin, a man who lost almost his entire family in the Holocaust. Bewildered by the enormity of the Nazi death machine, British prime minister Winston Churchill had referred to the "Final Solution" as "the crime without a name."[27] It was Lemkin who put a name to this nameless crime by coining the term *genocide*. In *Axis Rule in Occupied Europe*, which he completed in 1943 during his exile in the United States, he wrote that "[n]ew conceptions

[23] Amnesty International, *Civilians in the Line of Fire* (2008), 65 (citing "Death Toll in South Ossetia a Tenth of Initial Russian Claims," *Australian*, 22 August 2008).
[24] Human Rights Watch, *Up in Flames: Humanitarian Law Violations and Civilian Victims in the Conflict over South Ossetia* (2009), 71–73.
[25] Amnesty International, *Civilians in the Aftermath of War: Georgia–Russia One Year After* (7 August 2009) (based on UNHCR data).
[26] Human Rights Watch, *Up in Flames*, 74.
[27] Leo Kuper, *Genocide: Its Political Use in the Twentieth Century* (London: Penguin, 1981), 12.

require new terms." He used *genocide* to refer to "the destruction of a national or of an ethnic group. This new word ... is made from the ancient Greek word *genos* (race, tribe) and the Latin *cide* (killing), thus corresponding in its formation to such words as tyrannicide, homicide, infanticide, etc."[28]

Lemkin made genocide into a coherent, manageable concept, and the postwar consensus against Nazi crimes provided the political will to adopt an international treaty. Thanks largely to Lemkin's tireless lobbying efforts, on 9 December 1948 the UN General Assembly adopted the Convention on the Prevention and Punishment of the Crime of Genocide. The assembly president, Herbert Evatt of Australia, triumphantly announced that "the supremacy of international law had been proclaimed and a significant advance had been made in the development of international criminal law."[29] But this euphoria was not shared by the likes of Hartley Shawcross, the illustrious British prosecutor at Nuremberg, who considered the term *genocide* superfluous. It was, he claimed, "already generally recognized as a crime punishable by law and was simply a new word to describe a particular form of murder ... While making no significant contribution to international law ... [the convention] might delude people into thinking that some great step forward had been taken whereas in reality nothing at all had been changed."[30] In 1955, the eminent jurist Hersch Lauterpacht remarked that, "to a considerable extent, the Convention amounts to a registration of protest against past misdeeds of individual savagery rather than to an effective instrument of their prevention or repression."[31] This portentous sentiment proved to be right. Despite the convention's forceful condemnation of genocide, it would have little impact on the sordid Cold War culture of impunity that followed.

The twentieth century, called by some the "Century of Genocide,"[32] nearly ended without a single conviction for the "ultimate crime."

---

[28] Raphaël Lemkin, *Axis Rule in Occupied Europe: Laws of Occupation, Analysis of Government, Proposals for Redress* (Washington, DC: Carnegie Endowment for International Peace, 1944), 79.

[29] UN GAOR, 3rd Sess., 19th plen. mtg. at 852, UN Doc. A/PV.179 (1948).

[30] UN GAOR, 3rd Sess., 6th Cmte., 64th mtg., UN Doc. A/C.6/SR.64 (1948); Hirad Abtahi and Philippa Webb, eds., *The Genocide Convention: The Travaux Préparatoires*, vol. II (Leiden and Boston: Martinus Nijhoff, 2008), 1307.

[31] Lassa Oppenheim, *International Law: A Treatise*, vol. I, 8th edn., ed. Hersch Lauterpacht (London: Longman, 1955), 75.

[32] See, for example, Samuel Totten, William Parsons, and Israel Charny, eds., *Century of Genocide: Critical Essays and Eyewitness Accounts* (New York: Routledge, 2004).

But on 2 September 1998, exactly half a century after the convention was adopted, the Senegalese judge Laity Kama of the International Criminal Tribunal for Rwanda (ICTR) issued the following conviction against a Rwandan mayor who had organized the systematic rape of Tutsi women: "The accused, Jean-Paul Akayesu, you are declared guilty of genocide."[33] The decision was hailed by UN secretary-general Kofi Annan as "a landmark decision in the history of international criminal law ... [that] brings to life, for the first time, the ideals of the Genocide Convention."[34]

Since then, jurisprudence and commentary on genocide have proliferated on the international stage, and this "crime of crimes" has gripped the imagination of many concerned with the progress of humankind. At the International Criminal Tribunal for the former Yugoslavia (ICTY), two men have been found guilty of aiding and abetting genocide,[35] and two others for committing genocide,[36] all in relation to the massacre at Srebrenica. Another two men, Radovan Karadžić and Ratko Mladić, are currently on trial for genocide.[37] In addition, the War Crimes Chamber in Bosnia-Herzegovina, based in Sarajevo, has found nine individuals guilty of genocide,[38] and a further four convictions have been rendered in German courts.[39] Beyond criminal law, the Bosnian genocide has received judicial treatment in civil suits before

---

[33] Power, "A Problem from Hell," 486; see Akayesu, Trial Judgement (ICTR, 2 September 1998). Shortly thereafter, on 14 December 1999, the International Criminal Tribunal for the former Yugoslavia rendered its first judgment on the crime of genocide in the Jelisić case, although the accused was acquitted in this instance: Jelisić, Trial Judgement (ICTY, 14 December 1999).

[34] Statement by the UN Secretary-General Kofi Annan on the Occasion of the Announcement of the First Judgment in a Case of Genocide by the International Criminal Tribunal for Rwanda, UN Doc. PR/10/98/UNIC (1998).

[35] Krstić, Appeals Judgement (ICTY, 19 April 2004). The second individual is Drago Nikolić, one of the seven accused in the Popović case (see n. 36).

[36] Popović, Trial Judgement (ICTY, 10 June 2010).

[37] See International Criminal Tribunal for the former Yugoslavia, The Cases, www.icty.org/action/cases/4.

[38] See Court of Bosnia-Herzegovina, Verdicts of Section I, www.sudbih.gov.ba/?opcija=sve_presude&odjel=1&jezik=e. A number of other trials have taken place in lower Bosnian courts. See Human Rights Watch, Still Waiting: Bringing Justice for War Crimes, Crimes Against Humanity, and Genocide in Bosnia and Herzegovina's Cantonal and District Courts (July 2008).

[39] Nikola Jorgić, Federal Constitutional Court, 2BvR 1290/99, 12 December 2000; Novislav Djajić, Bavarian Appeals Court, 23 May 1997, 3 St 20/96 (both are cited in Krstić, Trial Judgement [ICTY, 2 August 2001], para. 589). The two others are Maksim Sokolović, Bundesgerichtshof, Third Criminal Senate, 21 February 2001, 3 StR 372/00; Đurađ Kušljić, Bundesgerichtshof, 21 February 2001, 3 StR 244/00.

American and Dutch courts,[40] as well as the landmark 2007 case of the International Court of Justice (ICJ) in the *Bosnia v. Serbia* case (finding Serbia responsible for failing to prevent genocide in Srebrenica).[41] With respect to the Rwandan genocide, the ICTR has convicted thirty-six individuals of genocide or incitement to genocide,[42] and thousands of additional cases are the subject of domestic proceedings in Rwanda before the traditional *gacaca* courts.[43] Rwandan *génocidaires* have also been convicted in domestic courts in other countries, including Canada[44] and Belgium.[45] The ICC has yet to prosecute anyone for genocide, although it has issued an arrest warrant on such charges against President Omar Al-Bashir of Sudan. There are also four defendants accused of genocide in trials before the Extraordinary Chambers of the Courts of Cambodia.[46] Several other lesser-known genocide trials, of varying success and credibility, have taken place in various domestic jurisdictions in recent decades.

This prolific jurisprudence has infused the Genocide Convention with an unprecedented vitality and relevance that would have been unimaginable until the past decade or so. What was dismissed for so long as a merely symbolic condemnation of Nazi crimes has been transformed into the normative foundation for a burgeoning corpus of international criminal law, arousing the keen interest of academics and practitioners alike. Scholarship on the legal aspects of genocide, dormant for many years, has experienced a resurgence as courts continue to explore the legal complexities of genocide, providing ample material for academic analysis and debate.[47]

---

[40] *Doe v. Karadžić*, No. 93 Civ. 878 (S.D.N.Y.); *Kadić v. Karadžić*, No. 93 Civ. 1163 (S.D.N.Y.); see also Mike Corder, "Dutch Court Upholds UN Immunity in Srebrenica Case," Associated Press, 30 March 2010.

[41] *Application of the Convention on the Prevention and Punishment of the Crime of Genocide* (Bosnia and Herzegovina v. Serbia and Montenegro) (International Court of Justice, 26 February 2007).

[42] See International Criminal Tribunal for Rwanda, *Status of Cases*, http://69.94.11.53/ENGLISH/cases/status.htm.

[43] Human Rights Watch, *Law and Reality: Progress in Judicial Reform in Rwanda* (2008).

[44] *R. v. Munyaneza*, 2009 QCCS 2201 (22 May 2009).

[45] "Rwandans Sentenced over Genocide," *BBC News*, 29 June 2005, news.bbc.co.uk/2/hi/africa/4635637.stm.

[46] See Extraordinary Chambers in the Courts of Cambodia, *Case Information*, www.eccc.gov.kh/english/case002.aspx.

[47] The leading scholarly works include William Schabas, *Genocide in International Law: The Crime of Crimes*, 2nd edn. (Cambridge: Cambridge University Press, 2009); Larry May, *Genocide: A Normative Account* (Cambridge: Cambridge University Press,

Despite these commendable legal developments and the growing scholarship on genocide, there is still a sense of chagrin in attempting to reconcile the rationalist credo of judicial proceedings and academic commentary with the irrationality and unspeakability of this heinous crime. As Hannah Arendt remarked after the Nuremberg Tribunal delivered its judgment, "The Nazi crimes ... explode the limits of the law; and that is precisely what constitutes their monstrousness. For these crimes, no punishment is severe enough ... This guilt, in contrast to all criminal guilt, oversteps and shatters any and all legal systems."[48] The scale and gravity of organized mass murder, the seeming inscrutability of the perpetrators' cruelty, and the unimaginable suffering of the victims overwhelm our conventional capacity for dispassionate legal analysis. As George Steiner rightly observes, transgressions such as the Holocaust "defy the ordering of common sense. They seem to be just on the other side of reason. They are extra-territorial to analytic debate."[49] Yet, reducing genocide to law calls for exactly such an ordering, in which the crime is examined, measured, analyzed, and evaluated. Judicial encounters with such radical evil thus provide a valuable glimpse into whether and how something so irrational and intensely emotional can be translated into the strictures of legal idiom. Understanding this tension and what it says about our self-conception and ability to deal with moral challenges is the theme of this book. The crime of genocide provides an especially valuable case to study because of its purported preeminence as the ultimate crime.

In the imagination of jurists, there is perhaps no crime that can compare to genocide. The ICTR has designated it as the "crime of crimes,"[50] and scholars such as William Schabas have maintained that, in the hierarchy of crimes, genocide "belongs at the apex of the pyramid."[51] Others have variously called it "the most heinous international

2010); Paola Gaeta, ed., *The UN Genocide Convention: A Commentary* (Oxford: Oxford University Press, 2009); and John Quigley, *The Genocide Convention: An International Law Analysis* (Aldershot, UK: Ashgate, 2006).

[48] "Letter to Karl Jaspers," in *Hannah Arendt/Karl Jaspers: Correspondence 1926–1969*, eds. Lotte Kohler and Hans Saner, trans. Robert Kimber and Rita Kimber (New York: Harcourt Brace Jovanovich, 1992), 51, 54.

[49] George Steiner, *No Passion Spent: Essays 1978–1995* (New Haven: Yale University Press, 1996), 346–47.

[50] Kambanda, Trial Judgement (ICTR, 4 September 1998), para. 16.

[51] Schabas, *Genocide in International Law*, 10–11.

offense,"[52] "the most horrible and atrocious of crimes ... the supreme negation of civilization and solidarity,"[53] "the worst of all [crimes],"[54] and "the ultimate crime."[55] Perhaps this privileged distinction reflects our intuitive understanding that genocide represents "the work of *homo sapiens* at its worst."[56] But, could it be that the prevailing wisdom that genocide is the ultimate crime is wrong? Or that this perception of the crime is a gross oversimplification of a far more complex issue? And could it be that emphasizing the distinctiveness of genocide may actually undermine the very progress and justice that international law intends to achieve? For some, these questions may border on the international law equivalent of blasphemy. But, as this book attempts to convey, they are questions essential to a better understanding of our faith in global justice.

The exploration of this theme must first consider whether genocide is, in fact, the ultimate crime. It cannot simply be presumed that its taxonomic prominence in moral discourse translates into greater gravity within the confines of international law. Is it possible, instead, that this "crime of crimes" is actually on an equal footing with other serious international offenses such as war crimes and crimes against humanity? And, even if it is a more serious crime, what are the concrete legal consequences of such a distinction? Or is the power of the word *genocide* derived from something other than jurisprudence? Even if we reach the conclusion that it does represent the pinnacle of evil, it still remains to be considered why a hierarchical abstraction assumes such importance in our discourse on suffering and injustice. What is the potential, and limitation, of a mere word in conveying a reality so overwhelming that it is unspeakable? And why should it matter if one word is more important than another?

What follows is a series of probing reflections on these important questions. Let us begin by considering: What is so ultimate about being the ultimate crime?

[52] Steven R. Ratner and Jason S. Abrams, *Accountability for Human Rights Atrocities in International Law: Beyond the Nuremberg Legacy* (New York: Oxford University Press, 1997), 43.
[53] *Yearbook of the International Law Commission 1994*, vol. I, 214, para. 21.
[54] Ibid., 208, para. 41.
[55] Benjamin Whitaker, *Revised and Updated Report on the Question of the Prevention and Punishment of the Crime of Genocide*, UN Doc. E/CN.4/Sub.2/1985/6 (1985).
[56] Stephen T. Davis, "Genocide, Despair, and Religious Hope: An Essay on Human Nature," in John K. Roth, ed., *Genocide and Human Rights: A Philosophical Guide* (Basingstoke: Palgrave Macmillan, 2005), 35.

2   The taxonomy of crimes

In 1971, in two separate incidents in the US state of Georgia, Ehrlich Anthony Coker raped two young women. He stabbed one to death and left the other, a 16-year-old girl, to die in a wooded area after bludgeoning her with a club.[1] Coker was sentenced to forty-eight years' imprisonment,[2] but just a year and a half later he managed to escape from the state prison in Waycross, Georgia. On 2 September 1974, at approximately 11 p.m., he entered the house of Allen and Elnita Carver through an unlocked door. He then grabbed a kitchen knife, forced Mr. Carver into the bathroom, and tied him up. He then turned his attention to the 16-year-old Mrs. Carver, who had given birth to the couple's son only three weeks prior. Brandishing the knife and yelling, "You know what's going to happen to you if you try anything, don't you?," Coker raped the young Mrs. Carver. Coker then made his escape in the Carvers' car, taking Mrs. Carver with him. Eventually, Mr. Carver was able to free himself and call the police. Soon after, Coker was found and arrested. Mrs. Carver had survived the ordeal.[3]

At trial, Ehrlich Coker was found guilty of escape, armed robbery, motor vehicle theft, kidnapping, and rape. On the count of rape, the jury returned a sentence of death by electrocution.[4] At the time, Georgia was one of only three US states authorizing the death penalty for rape in certain aggravating circumstances: where the rape was committed by an ex-felon, committed in the course of a capital felony, or carried out in an "outrageously or wantonly vile, horrible or inhuman" manner. Coker's death sentence derived from the first two criteria. The jury, it seems, felt that Coker – a serial rapist, murderer, and obvious

---

[1] *Coker v. Georgia*, 433 U.S. 584 (1987).
[2] *Ibid.*   [3] *Ibid.*, 587.   [4] *Ibid.*, 588.

12

danger to the public – deserved no less than a complete and irrevocable excision from society.

Proportionality and the purposes of punishment

The point of departure in grasping the distinction of genocide as the "ultimate crime" is to ask what makes one crime more serious than another. Is rape as serious as murder? Is genocide worse than crimes against humanity or war crimes? After all, if genocide first emerged as a juridical concept, shouldn't its meaning and potency be derived from its gravity in international law? Determining a hierarchy of crimes – even to ordinary crimes such as murder and rape in domestic law – has left many a jurist perplexed. Comparing the gravity of international crimes is even more perplexing, given the complexity of their elements.

The landmark 1977 case of *Coker v. Georgia* provides a valuable illustration of such an exercise in establishing a hierarchy of crimes, and a useful point of contrast with the debate concerning the gravity of genocide relative to other international crimes. Upon being convicted and sentenced to death for the rape of Mrs. Carver, Ehrlich Coker lodged a number of appeals, and the matter was finally brought before the US Supreme Court. The justices had to decide whether the application of the death penalty for rape was constitutional. The Eighth Amendment of the US Constitution,[5] the court said, barred "not only those punishments that are 'barbaric' [or 'cruel and unusual'] but also those that are 'excessive' in relation to the crime committed." It presented the following test:

> [A] punishment is "excessive" and unconstitutional if it (1) makes no measurable contribution to acceptable goals of punishment and hence is nothing more than the purposeless and needless imposition of pain and suffering; or (2) is grossly out of proportion to the severity of the crime. A punishment might fail the test on either ground.[6]

More specifically, could Coker's execution be seen as a means of promoting the goal of deterrence or that of retribution – historically, two of the most important goals of punishment – and could it also be seen as proportional to the particular crime that he had committed? In

---

[5] The Eighth Amendment reads: "Excessive bail shall not be required, nor excessive fines imposed, nor cruel and unusual punishments inflicted."
[6] *Coker v. Georgia*, 592.

particular, the court had to consider whether rape was of comparable gravity to murder and thus justified imposing the death penalty. The measure of gravity was thus inextricably linked with the proportionate punishment – the more serious the crime, the more severe the punishment. This fundamental principle applies with the same force in international criminal law as it does in domestic law. Understanding the logic of this principle requires an exploration of the purposes of punishment – namely, deterrence and retribution.

Deterrence

Deterrence is based on the assumption that the prospective criminal is a rational calculator who exercises choice. Punishment is intended to influence his cost-benefit calculus in deciding whether a crime really will "pay."[7] Deterrence reflects a utilitarian view of criminal justice, first championed by the influential eighteenth-century English philosopher Jeremy Bentham. Revolted by cruel punishments, including torture, under the law of retaliation (*lex talionis*), utilitarian thought maintained that punishment was an evil that could be justified only if it contributed to concrete social objectives. As George Fletcher puts it, Bentham's "rationale of punishment"[8] is one that "finds the justification for criminal sanctions in the *good* that they engender. The predicted *benefits* of condemning the particular defendant as a criminal and depriving him of his liberty outweigh the *costs* imposed on the imprisoned convict and his or her family."[9] The deterrence rationale comprises both "general deterrence" – in that punishing one criminal is assumed to dissuade others from committing the same crime – as well as "special deterrence," which aims at preventing the same criminal from reoffending.[10]

---

[7] See, for example, Isaac Ehrlich, "Crime, Punishment, and the Market for Offenses," *Journal of Economic Perspectives* 10 (1996): 43 (supporting the mainstream view of deterrence theory that punishment restrains criminals because they are rational cost-benefit calculators).

[8] Jeremy Bentham, *The Rationale of Punishment* (London: Robert Heward, 1830).

[9] George P. Fletcher, *Basic Concepts of Criminal Law* (New York: Oxford University Press, 1998), 30.

[10] For the sake of expedience, I am leaving aside two other rationales for punishment, which are typically considered to fall under the deterrence view: rehabilitation (that is, punishment will "cure" the offender's criminal impulses) and incapacitation (that is, confinement prevents the offender from posing a threat to anyone). Broadly speaking, the individualized nature of rehabilitation and incapacitation implies that they can be said to fall under special deterrence.

A "pure" deterrence rationale allows unlimited discretion in sentencing. Any punishment, no matter how severe, is considered appropriate as long as it prevents more harm than it causes. This view, like all "pure" utilitarian rationales, has been criticized for its disregard of moral constraints,[11] as well as for its dehumanization of the criminal such that he is no longer a moral agent but is "to be made to suffer merely in order to intimidate others from disobeying the law."[12] Fletcher himself was discomfited by this idea, reminding us that "[a]s the National Socialists well knew in controlling inmates in slave labor camps, occasionally hanging an innocent person effectively deters disobedience by other inmates."[13] Some critics have even rejected the possibility that deterrence is achievable, citing empirical studies to the effect that varying the severity of punishment has little effect on recidivism or even on crime rates generally.[14]

Irrespective of these criticisms, at the very least the deterrence rationale compels the stratification of crimes based on some notion of comparable gravity and proportionate sentencing. Richard Posner observes: "If the maximum punishment for murder is life imprisonment, we may not want to make armed robbery also punishable by life imprisonment, for then armed robbers would have no additional incentive not to murder their victims."[15] In other words, punishment should be apportioned according to the importance of the social interest that is threatened, with the aim of establishing effective disincentives for committing particular crimes. Even if we may not know exactly *by how much* sentences should vary, it is at least certain that the penalties should increase as we ascend the hierarchy of crimes.[16]

---

[11] H. L. A. Hart, *Punishment and Responsibility* (Oxford: Clarendon Press, 1968), 8–9.

[12] Andrew von Hirsch and Andrew Ashworth, *Proportionate Sentencing: Exploring the Principles* (Oxford: Oxford University Press, 2005), 15.

[13] George Fletcher, *Rethinking Criminal Law* (Boston and Toronto: Little, Brown, 1978), 415.

[14] See, for example, Andrew von Hirsch, Anthony E. Bottoms, Elizabeth Burney, and P.-O. Wikstrom, *Criminal Deterrence and Sentence Severity: An Analysis of Recent Research* (Oxford, UK: Hart, 1999), and P. Robinson and J. Darley, "Does Criminal Law Deter? A Behavioural Science Investigation," *Oxford Journal of Legal Studies* 24 (2004): 173. In Britain, the Home Office recently released a report stating: "The almost invariable conclusion of the large amount of research which has been undertaken ... is that it is hard to show any effect that one type of sentence is more likely than any other to reduce the likelihood of reoffending, which is high for all" (UK Home Office, *The Sentence of the Court*, 5th edn., 1990).

[15] Richard Posner, "An Economic Theory of Criminal Law," *Columbia Law Review* 85 (1985): 1193, 1210–11.

[16] David Dolinko, "Three Mistakes of Retributivism," *UCLA Law Review* 39 (1992): 1623 (arguing that, within retributive theory, the principle of proportionality requires

Retribution

Unlike deterrence, retribution does not look to the social utility of punishment. It is based, instead, on the moral theory that, in exercising free will, those who consciously make evil choices are "blameworthy" and "deserve" punishment. As its foremost proponent, Immanuel Kant, would say, punishment is a "categorical imperative"[17] for wrongdoing, irrespective of its social utility. Retributive proportionality is historically rooted in *lex talionis*, derived from the biblical command that "[i]f any harm follows, then you shall give life for life, eye for eye, tooth for tooth, hand for hand, foot for foot, burn for burn, wound for wound, stripe for stripe."[18] Thus, punishment is atonement or expiation for crimes, a restoration of the disturbed equilibrium of the moral universe.[19] Rather than focusing on the social utility of prevention, proportionality in this context reflects the degree of moral turpitude or evil attached to particular conduct. In the past, retributive proportionality assumed varying forms of corporal punishment to expunge evil, but is expressed in modern criminal law through graduated sentencing.[20]

Determining what punishment a criminal intrinsically "deserves" requires a distinction between two general principles of criminal law. Fletcher, in a comprehensive comparative survey of such principles, describes these as *wrongdoing* and *culpability*, respectively.[21]

Wrongdoing, according to Fletcher, is not a "categorical attribute" but "a matter of degree," entailing judgment as to "the intrinsic quality of [the perpetrator's] deed."[22] It is a somewhat intuitive measure of the degree of moral opprobrium that a particular act deserves. It seems obvious that "a greater degree of wrongdoing justifies greater punishment"; few would disagree, for example, that culpable homicide

only that sentences increase as the gravity of the crime increases, but does not provide a starting point or quantify the increasing increments of punishment).

[17] Immanuel Kant, *The Metaphysics of Morals*, trans. Mary Gregor (Cambridge: Cambridge University Press, 1991), 141.

[18] Exodus 21:23–21:27.

[19] G. W. F. Hegel, *The Philosophy of Right*, trans. T. M. Knox (Oxford, UK: Clarendon Press, 1962), 69 (arguing that punishment negates the wrong and vindicates the right) [originally published 1820].

[20] See, for example, Michel Foucault, *Discipline and Punish: The Birth of the Prison*, trans. Alan Sheridan (New York: Pantheon, 1977) (describing the evolution of punishment from the reenactment of evil on the human body in medieval times to the modern institution of imprisonment).

[21] Fletcher, *Rethinking Criminal Law*.

[22] Ibid., 458.

is a greater wrong than petty theft and that greater punishment is therefore warranted.[23] But in complex cases, as Fletcher points out, "Determining the degree of wrongdoing is obviously a subtle problem of moral judgment"[24] that assumes the possibility of arriving at some form of "consensus on a scale of relative wrongdoing."[25] Factors to be taken into consideration include the "importance of the violated or threatened social interest," as well as "the proximity or the degree of danger to that interest"[26] – essentially the same idea as was discussed earlier in relation to Posner's views on deterrence – about the need to assign different punishments for murder and robbery.[27] Ultimately, Fletcher notes, determining the degree of wrongdoing is "patently an evaluative and irreducibly political issue."[28]

Determining the "just dessert" of the offender requires consideration of a second factor – namely *culpability*, or the blameworthiness of the perpetrator. For Fletcher, *culpability* refers to "the principle of moral attribution": whether a crime can fully be considered to be imputed upon the accused, even if there is no doubt he caused the offense. For example, although every homicide shares a similar objective component – the killing of a human being – the blame we attach to the perpetrator will rightly depend on the particular circumstances. The killer may have pulled the trigger with malice or have acted recklessly, showing an indifference to the value of human life; the death may have been a pure accident; or the killer may have been a minor or someone with a mental disability. Each of these killers deserves a different degree of moral condemnation. For the victim's family, the end result is the same, but the perpetrator's responsibility for the wrongdoing varies with each case. Thus, the degree of wrongdoing, which takes into account the act itself and, when appropriate, its larger social and political context, sets the maximum level of punishment, whereas the actor's degree of culpability for that wrongdoing will determine whether the maximum penalty or something less should be applied.[29]

A hierarchy of crimes

As set forth above, both deterrence and retributive theories require a hierarchy, or ordering, of crimes, with corresponding degrees of

---

[23] *Ibid.*, 461.   [24] *Ibid.*, 458.
[25] *Ibid.*, 461.   [26] *Ibid.*   [27] See p. 15
[28] Fletcher, *Rethinking Criminal Law*, 461.   [29] *Ibid.*, 462.

punishment. In the language of deterrence, the level of "wrongdoing" reflects the importance of the violated or threatened social interest, and in the language of retribution theory, the "intrinsic gravity" of the crime – though as Fletcher notes, even retributive theory needs, in complex cases, to take into account the social or other interests at stake.

In considering whether murder is more serious than rape, or whether genocide is more serious than war crimes, there is an important distinction between a category of wrongdoing, or the gravity of crimes *in abstracto*, and the perpetrator's culpability or individual circumstances. Whereas the latter requires a case-by-case analysis, consideration of genocide's distinction as the ultimate crime implicates the existence of an abstract, normative hierarchy of crimes. It is, after all, this presumed privileged status that gives rise to its power as a word. But how can it be said that one type of wrongdoing is categorically more serious than another – irrespective of the factual circumstances of each particular case?

Returning to *Coker v. Georgia*, what did the US Supreme Court say about whether Coker could be sent to the electric chair for rape – a punishment typically reserved for murderers? The court, faced with deciding whether rape could ever be considered as grave as murder (and thus as deserving the death penalty), issued a divided judgment, thereby highlighting the difficulty of constructing an abstract hierarchy among crimes.

Two of the nine justices – William J. Brennan, Jr., and Thurgood Marshall – simply restated their already well-known view that the death penalty should be abolished in all cases. Of the remaining seven justices, four engaged in an abstract comparison of the two crimes and arrived at the conclusion that the lesser gravity of rape required imposition of a less severe punishment than murder. Their analysis represents the best attempt at a dispassionate, objective ranking of the crimes:

We do not discount the seriousness of rape as a crime. It is highly reprehensible, both in a moral sense and in its almost total contempt for the personal integrity and autonomy of the female victim and for the latter's privilege of choosing those with whom intimate relationships are to be established. Short of homicide, it is the "ultimate violation of self." It is also a violent crime because it normally involves force, or the threat of force or intimidation, to overcome the will and the capacity of the victim to resist. Rape is very often accompanied by physical injury to the female and can also inflict mental and psychological damage. Because it undermines the community's sense of security, there is public injury as well.

Rape is without doubt deserving of serious punishment; but in terms of moral depravity and of the injury to the person and to the public, it does not compare with murder, which does involve the unjustified taking of human life. Although it may be accompanied by another crime, rape by definition does not include the death of or even the serious injury to another person. The murderer kills; the rapist, if no more than that, does not. Life is over for the victim of the murderer; for the rape victim, life may not be nearly so happy as it was, but it is not over and normally is not beyond repair. We have the abiding conviction that the death penalty, which "is unique in its severity and irrevocability," is an excessive penalty for the rapist who, as such, does not take human life.[30]

For the three dissenting justices, the matter was not so straightforward. In the joint dissent of Chief Justice Warren E. Burger and Justice William Rehnquist, the analysis focused on deterrence in relation to the death penalty for rape, which Georgia allowed in certain instances. The aim of the death penalty was, they argued, to deter "criminal activity which consistently poses serious danger of death or grave bodily harm."[31] And as the opinion bluntly stated: "It is, after all, not irrational – nor constitutionally impermissible – for a legislature to make the penalty more severe than the criminal act it punishes in the hope it would deter wrongdoing."[32]

Finally, a fourth strand of reasoning was presented in the partial dissent by Justice Lewis F. Powell, Jr., who rejected what he termed the "simplistic all-or-nothing views of the plurality."[33] Powell argued that a hierarchical assumption about the relative gravity of rape versus murder was inappropriate, from the viewpoints of both wrongdoing and culpability:

[T]he plurality draws a bright line between murder and all rapes – regardless of the degree of brutality of the rape or the effect upon the victim. I dissent because I am not persuaded that such a bright line is appropriate ... "[There] is extreme variation in the degree of culpability of rapists." The deliberate viciousness of the rapist may be greater than that of the murderer. Rape is never an act committed accidentally. Rarely can it be said to be unpremeditated. There also is wide variation in the effect on the victim. The plurality opinion says that "[l]ife is over for the victim of the murderer; for the rape victim, life may not be nearly so happy as it was, but it is not over and normally

---

[30] *Coker v. Georgia*, 597–98 (footnotes and citation omitted).
[31] *Ibid.*, 620.   [32] *Ibid.*, 619.   [33] *Ibid.*, 602 note 1.

is not beyond repair." But there is indeed "extreme variation" in the crime of rape. Some victims are so grievously injured physically or psychologically that life is beyond repair.

Thus, it may be that the death penalty is not disproportionate punishment for the crime of aggravated rape.[34]

Powell's nuanced view is shared by numerous distinguished commentators, including US president Barack Obama, who supports the availability of the death penalty in cases of child rape.[35] Obama's opinion was prompted by a case decided two decades after *Coker* – the 2008 case of *Kennedy v. Louisiana*, in which the court, in reasoning similar to *Coker*, struck down the death penalty for raping a child.[36] Although the application of *Coker* to the rape of children, and not just to the rape of adult women, had previously been in question, *Kennedy* authoritatively extended the prohibition against the death penalty for rape to all cases of rape; from now on, the death penalty would be available only for intentional homicide and some crimes against the state, such as treason.

The *Kennedy* judgment covered much the same ground as *Coker*, and its 5–4 split demonstrates, moreover, that the juridical stratification of evil is no less complicated today than it was in 1977. In particular, the dissenting justices struggled to comprehend how anyone could doubt that "in the eyes of ordinary Americans, the very worst child rapists – predators who seek out and inflict serious physical and emotional injury on defenseless young children – are the epitome of moral depravity."[37] This viewpoint is forcefully illustrated in the compelling example set forth by Justice Samuel A. Alito, Jr.:

With respect to the question of moral depravity, is it really true that every person who is convicted of capital murder and sentenced to death is more morally depraved than every child rapist? Consider the following two cases. In the first, a defendant robs a convenience store and watches as his accomplice shoots the storeowner. The defendant acts recklessly, but was not the

---

[34] *Ibid.*, 603 (crossreference omitted).
[35] "Justices Bar Death Penalty for the Rape of a Child," *New York Times*, 26 June 2008. The article quotes Obama as follows: "I think that the rape of a small child, 6 or 8 years old, is a heinous crime, and if a state makes a decision under narrow, limited, well-defined circumstances, that the death penalty is at least potentially applicable, that does not violate our Constitution." He added that the Supreme Court should have set conditions for imposing the death penalty for the crime, "but it basically had a blanket prohibition, and I disagree with the decision."
[36] *Kennedy v. Louisiana*, 128 S.Ct. 2641 (2008).
[37] *Ibid.*, 2676 (Alito, J., dissenting).

triggerman and did not intend the killing. In the second case, a previously convicted child rapist kidnaps, repeatedly rapes, and tortures multiple child victims. Is it clear that the first defendant is more morally depraved than the second?[38]

Alito's query is all the more compelling when considering the especially gruesome facts of the *Kennedy* case itself. As even the majority was at pains to point out, Kennedy's "crime was one that cannot be recounted in these pages in a way sufficient to capture in full the hurt and horror inflicted on his victim or to convey the revulsion society, and the jury that represents it, sought to express by sentencing petitioner to death."[39] The judgment recounts in excruciating detail the horrifying aftermath of the crime:

When police arrived at petitioner's home between 9:20 and 9:30 a.m., they found L. H. [Kennedy's 8-year-old stepdaughter] on her bed, wearing a T-shirt and wrapped in a bloody blanket. She was bleeding profusely from the vaginal area …

L. H. was transported to the Children's Hospital. An expert in pediatric forensic medicine testified that L. H.'s injuries were the most severe he had seen from a sexual assault in his four years of practice. A laceration to the left wall of the vagina had separated her cervix from the back of her vagina, causing her rectum to protrude into the vaginal structure. Her entire perineum was torn from the posterior fourchette to the anus. The injuries required emergency surgery.[40]

Thus the seemingly simple question – is murder more serious than rape? – quickly becomes an exceedingly complex inquiry for the jurist, who must engage in a multilayered analysis. Most important is a choice of punishment that best serves the purposes of both deterrence and retribution, based on the metaphysical "gravity" of the deed as determined both by logic and by societal consensus. A confounding factor, of course, is that the true horror of some crimes is simply too difficult to quantify, too odious to categorize, as it overwhelms our senses and our ability for rational and dispassionate judgment. Although it would seem possible to create a rough normative hierarchy based on the proportionality principle, such stratification will sometimes elude us since reasonable persons can and will disagree about what punishment fits a specific case. The case is all the more difficult when comparing genocide with

[38] *Ibid.* (citation omitted).
[39] *Ibid.*, 2645 (opinion of the court).   [40] *Ibid.*, 2646.

other international crimes, given the complex definitions and elements of those offenses.

Stigma and proportionality in punishment

In constructing a hierarchy among crimes, another important consideration is that focusing exclusively on the severity of punishment – for example, the length of a prison sentence – disregards the significance of the opprobrium that society feels toward particular transgressions. Irrespective of the length of imprisonment, the stigma attached to a crime may itself constitute a form of punishment. The very term *crime* and associated terms such as *guilt, innocence, blame,* and *responsibility* carry far-reaching moral connotations that are unique to the discourse of criminal law. The shame and condemnation associated with these terms form an essential distinction between criminal and other forms of liability. H. L. A. Hart expresses this point by noting that "[w]hat distinguishes a criminal from a civil sanction and all that distinguishes it, it is ventured, is the *judgment of community condemnation* which accompanies and justifies its imposition."[41] This idea of "criminal tainting" reflects, in part, the deeply held view that particular crimes occupy specific, immovable levels on a scale of gravity.

Similar to criminal tainting, but more recently developed, is the principle of *fair labeling* in the criminal law.[42] This concept demands that our criminal justice system record convictions that accurately describe the nature and magnitude of the wrongdoing. To take the simplest case, the law should obviously not call a thief a murderer. It should also differentiate between different kinds of murder, such as first-degree, second-degree, manslaughter, and so on. Taken to an extreme, the fair-labeling principle may well require that offenses be stipulated in more detail, such that someone stealing a loaf of bread might be convicted of "theft of a loaf of bread," as opposed to simply

---

[41] H. L. A. Hart, "The Aims of the Criminal Law," *Law and Contemporary Problems* 23 (1958): 401, 404 (emphasis added).

[42] The concept is said to have been pioneered by Andrew Ashworth (A. Ashworth, "The Elasticity of Mens Rea," in Colin Tapper, ed., *Crime, Proof, and Punishment: Essays in Memory of Sir Rupert Cross* [London: Butterworths, 1981]), and the term to have been coined by Glanville Williams (G. Williams, "Convictions and Fair Labelling," *Cambridge Law Journal* 42 (1983); see also James Chalmers and Fiona Leverick, "Fair Labelling in Criminal Law," *Modern Law Review* 71 (2008): 217; Andrew Ashworth, *Principles of Criminal Law*, 5th edn. (New York: Oxford University Press, 2006), 88.

"theft." Another type of argument draws attention to using the right vocabulary. For example, it might be contended that the crime of rape should be called "rape," not "sexual assault" (as in Canada), because the term *rape* carries with it the degree of moral turpitude that the rapist deserves.[43] The point of fair labeling is that it recognizes that the labels we use have their own communicative power – independent of the punishment itself – and that, out of fairness both to the criminal and to the public, the criminal law should accurately describe what it condemns. An employer reviewing the job application of an ex-felon, for example, might feel better about hiring him if the charge on his record is not vague or ominous; and a victim might feel wronged if the linguistic construction of a crime lets the criminal's full moral turpitude go unnoticed.

The ICTY case of *Prosecutor v. Erdemović* provides a good illustration of how criminal tainting or fair labeling can influence the judges' perception. In that case the ICTY Appeals Chamber addressed whether duress was available as a defense when the underlying offense for a war crime or crime against humanity was murder.[44] The majority opinion was that, for considerations of policy, duress should merely reduce *culpability* but not excuse the *wrongdoing* of murder; that is, duress should be a factor in mitigating punishment but not a ground for excluding liability. Nevertheless, in response to the majority's pragmatic view that any injustice resulting from the rejection of that defense could be resolved through mitigation of punishment at the sentencing phase, the chamber's president, Antonio Cassese, argued in a vigorous dissent that even if a "minimum" or "token penalty" were imposed, the taint of criminality would not thereby be removed (and would potentially be continued unfairly, despite the duress under which the person was found to have acted):

[T]he purpose of criminal law ... is to punish behavior which is *criminal*, i.e., morally reprehensible or injurious to society, not to condemn behaviour which is "the product of coercion that is truly irresistible" or the choice of the lesser of two evils. No matter how much mitigation a court allows an accused, the fundamental fact remains that if it convicts him, it regards his behavior as *criminal*, and considers that he should have behaved differently.[45]

---

[43] See Chalmers and Leverick, "Fair Labelling in Criminal Law."
[44] Erdemović, Appeals Judgement (ICTY, 7 October 1997).
[45] *Ibid.*, para. 48 (separate and dissenting opinion of Cassese, J., footnote omitted).

This sensibility is also reflected in, for instance, the case of *Queen v. Finta*, in which the Supreme Court of Canada placed considerable emphasis on criminal tainting and fair labeling when considering the relative gravity of crimes in relation to the requirement of proportionality. Imre Finta, a commander of the gendarmarie in Szeged, Hungary, during World War II, was accused of participating in the deportation of Jews to Nazi concentration camps. The court held that, in the case of an accused convicted of murder as a crime against humanity or war crime, one must consider not only the condemnation that "will result upon a conviction for the domestic offence" (that is, murder), but also the "additional stigma and opprobrium that will be suffered by an individual whose conduct has been held to constitute crimes against humanity or war crimes."[46] Upon conviction for an international crime,

the accused will be *labeled* a war criminal and will suffer the particularly heavy public opprobrium that is reserved for these offences. Further the sentence which will follow upon conviction will reflect the high degree of moral outrage that society very properly feels toward those convicted of these crimes.[47]

Thus, beyond sentencing, the label of a *war criminal* itself was regarded by the Supreme Court of Canada as a distinct and separate expression of the proportionality of the punishment in relation to the crime.

The significance of stigma must be appreciated in light of the sociopedagogical function of the criminal justice process. For instance, Martha Minow observes that, irrespective of imprisonment, subjection to a criminal trial may itself be a form of punishment, especially in the context of mass atrocities:

A trial in the aftermath of mass atrocity ... should mark an effort between vengeance and forgiveness. It transfers the individuals' desires for revenge to the state or official bodies. The transfer cools vengeance into retribution ... The trial itself steers clear of forgiveness, however. It announces a demand not only for accountability and acknowledgment of harms done, but also for unflinching punishment. At the end of the trial process, after facts are found and convictions are secured, there might be forgiveness of a legal sort: a suspended sentence, or executive pardon, or clemency in light of humanitarian concerns. Even then, the process has exacted time and agony from, and rendered a kind of punishment for defendants.[48]

---

[46] *The Queen v. Finta*, [1994] 1 SCR 701, at 815.
[47] *Ibid.* (emphasis added).
[48] Martha Minow, *Between Vengeance and Forgiveness* (Boston: Beacon, 1998), 26.

Michel Foucault explains the significance of the criminal justice process in light of the shift away from *lex talionis* in modern legal systems. He points out that the rejection of public torture and execution in modern penal systems – or the progressive move from "punishment-as-spectacle" to "trial-as-spectacle" – has entailed a reapportionment of emphasis from the execution of punishment to the more constrained spectacle of legal process:

[I]n punishment-as-spectacle a confused horror spread from the scaffold; it enveloped both executioner and condemned; and, although it was always ready to invert the shame inflicted on the victim into pity or glory, it often turned the legal violence of the executioner into shame. Now the scandal and the light are to be distributed differently; *it is the conviction itself that marks the offender with the unequivocally negative sign: the publicity has shifted to the trial, and to the sentence*; the execution itself is like an additional shame that justice is ashamed to impose on the condemned man; so it keeps its distance from the act, tending always to entrust it to others, under the seal of secrecy ... Those who carry out the penalty tend to become an autonomous section; justice is relieved of responsibility for it by a bureaucratic concealment of the penalty itself.[49]

This shift toward legal process and the concomitant concealment of physical punishment underscores the significance of stigma and abstract hierarchies in the apportionment of moral blameworthiness, irrespective of sentencing. Thus, the gravity of the crime and the attendant moral opprobrium are themselves significant elements of punishment in the criminal justice process. For instance, the public views a person convicted as a *murderer* with greater reprehension than a person convicted as a mere *thief*. Similarly, as discussed in Chapter 3, the conception of genocide as the ultimate crime may entail a unique stigma, irrespective of differential sentencing in relation to the other core international crimes.

The historical evolution from corporal punishment to legal process that Foucault describes also demonstrates the somewhat artificial distinction between retribution and deterrence. In this regard Johannes Andenæs's conception of "general prevention" is especially instructive insofar as it directly links the flow of "moral propaganda" from the criminal justice process to the transformation of social values and behavior.[50] This fusion of moral condemnation through the spectacle

---

[49] Foucault, *Discipline and Punish*, 9–10 (emphasis added).
[50] Johannes Andenæs, *Punishment and Deterrence* (Ann Arbor: University of Michigan Press, 1974).

of legal process with objectives of deterrence merges the traditional divide between retributive and utilitarian theories of punishment. Andenæs points out that, beyond the cost–benefit calculus associated with the conscious fear of punishment, there is yet another, more subtle, dimension of general prevention that operates to prevent wrongful conduct by instilling "unconscious inhibitions against crime" or "a condition of habitual lawfulness."[51] He suggests that the expression of social disapproval through the legal process may influence moral self-conceptions such that "illegal actions will not present themselves consciously as a real alternative to conformity, even in situations where the potential criminal would run no risk whatsoever of being caught."[52]

Ranking crimes in a form of hierarchy is a difficult and complex task, even if considered solely in terms of stigma rather than differential sentencing. Nonetheless, the principle of proportionality mandates such an exercise in the stratification of wrongdoing – however arbitrary it may seem – given its fundamental importance to coherent conceptions of justice. If the simple comparison of gravity between rape and murder in *Coker* gives rise to such controversy and uncertainty, how does it compare with the far more complex designation of genocide as the ultimate crime?

---

[51] *Ibid.*, 950. Andenæs distinguishes this broader concept of general prevention from special and general deterrence as follows:

> The effect of the criminal law and its enforcement may be *mere deterrence*. Because of the hazards involved, a person who contemplates a punishable offense might not act. But it is not correct to regard general prevention and deterrence as one and the same thing. The concept of general prevention also includes the *moral or socio-pedagogical* influence of punishment. The "messages" sent by law and the legal processes contain factual information about what would be risked by disobedience, but they also contain proclamations specifying that it is *wrong* to disobey.
>
> In other words, general prevention consists of both deterrence through fear of punishment and the moral influence of punishment as an expression of social disapproval.

[52] *Ibid.*, 36.

3 The core elements of international crimes

On 22 April 1915, German troops stationed on the Ypres Salient in Belgium made the first concerted use of a new weapon. Its inventor was to call it a "higher form of killing."[1] The weapon was chlorine gas.[2] At exactly five o'clock in the afternoon, a red flare arced across the sky, providing the signal to open the cocks on nearly 6,000 poison canisters that had been secretly buried along the front lines. The prevailing winds carried 168 metric tons of chlorine gas in a massive white and yellow-green cloud toward the Allied trenches. Panic and confusion ensued. The front collapsed.[3] Chemical warfare had come to World War I and would soon be used by the Allies as well.

The British poet Wilfred Owen later described the horrific effects of chemical warfare in his 1917 poem "Dulce et Decorum Est" (which continues "pro patria mori": "How sweet and fitting it is to die for one's country"):

Gas! Gas! Quick, boys! – An ecstasy of fumbling,
Fitting the clumsy helmets just in time;
But someone still was yelling out and stumbling
And flound'ring like a man in fire or lime ...
Dim, through the misty panes and thick green light,
As under a green sea, I saw him drowning.
In all my dreams, before my helpless sight,
He plunges at me, guttering, choking, drowning.

---

[1] "In no future war will the military be able to ignore poison gas. It is a higher form of killing" (Professor Fritz Haber, 1919, quoted in Tim Cook, *No Place to Run: The Canadian Corps and Gas Warfare in the First World War* [Vancouver: UBC Press, 1999], 59.)

[2] Jonathan B. Tucker, *War of Nerves: Chemical Warfare from World War I to Al-Qaeda* (New York: Pantheon, 2006), 13–15.

[3] *Ibid.*

If in some smothering dreams you too could pace
Behind the wagon that we flung him in,
And watch the white eyes writhing in his face,
His hanging face, like a devil's sick of sin;
If you could hear, at every jolt, the blood
Come gargling from the froth-corrupted lungs,
Obscene as cancer, bitter as the cud
Of vile, incurable sores on innocent tongues, –
My friend, you would not tell with such high zest
To children ardent of some desperate glory
The old Lie: Dulce et decorum est
Pro patria mori.[4]

By some estimates, the use of poison gas in World War I claimed nearly a hundred thousand lives in addition to a million casualties.[5]

Now consider a different crime, this time from Nazi Germany during World War II. The accused – a German man and his alleged lover – conspired to denounce the man's Jewish wife to the Gestapo. Their sole motive was to rid themselves of the wife, who had refused to agree to a divorce. Upon her denunciation, the victim was deported to Auschwitz, where she died from malnutrition. The perpetrators, known only as P and Mrs. K, were arrested after the war and brought before the Supreme Court of the British Zone.[6]

Which one of these two international crimes is "worse"? The use of poison gas, deployed on the battlefield, is a war crime. The embittered husband and his accomplice, by contrast, were convicted of crimes against humanity for contributing, if only in a limited way and for purely personal motives, to the systemic persecution of Jews. And both offenses qualify, in the words of the ICC Statute, as the "most serious crimes of concern to the international community as a whole"[7] – namely, war crimes, crimes against humanity, and genocide.

Notwithstanding the seriousness of all these international crimes, the ICTY Trial Chamber in the *Blaškić* case opined that a

---

[4] Quoted from Cook, *No Place to Run*, 7–8.
[5] L. F. Haber, *The Poisonous Cloud: Chemical Warfare in the First World War* (Oxford: Oxford University Press, 1986), 239–43.
[6] *Decision of the Supreme Court for the British Zone from 9 November 1948*, S. StS 78/48, in *Justiz und NS-Verbrechen*, vol. II, 498–99 (cited in *Tadić*, Appeals Judgement [ICTY, 7 May 1997], para. 257).
[7] Under Article 5 of the ICC Statute, the court's jurisdiction is limited to such crimes. It should be noted that the ICTY and ICTR Statutes do not contain such a requirement, although the violations must nevertheless be "serious" (under Article 1 of both tribunals' Statutes).

hierarchy of crimes seems to emerge from the case-law of the ICTR ... The following hierarchy of crimes falling under the jurisdiction of the Tribunal may therefore be compiled:

(1) "The crime of crimes": genocide
(2) Crimes of an extreme seriousness: crimes against humanity
(3) Crimes of a lesser seriousness: war crimes[8]

Are we then to believe that our moral outrage should be greater toward the man who arranges for the racially motivated killing of his wife rather than toward the widespread use of poison gas resulting in thousands of horrible, torturous deaths? The two crimes differ dramatically in kind and quantity; nevertheless, international criminal law places them in different conceptual categories and, if the *Blaškić* Trial Chamber is correct, even suggests that their evil can be graded and ranked. As set forth below, however, the jurisprudence on this issue is considerably more complex and conflicted than it might appear from *Blaškić*.

The previous chapter considered the difficulties of ranking rape versus murder. The gradation of crimes and assignment of proportionate punishments are even more complicated and controversial with respect to international crimes. The foregoing example illustrated that an estranged husband's decision to eliminate his wife by exploiting a policy of persecution may qualify as a crime against humanity. Likewise, in appropriate circumstances, and when committed with the requisite intention, rape can constitute an act of genocide.[9] In contrast, mass murder of soldiers with poison gas remains "merely" a war crime. As discussed below, the complex elements of these international crimes make a determination of comparative gravity far more difficult than the already contentious comparison between the relatively simple crimes of rape and murder.

Unlike ordinary crimes under domestic law – for example, murder or rape – the grading of the core international crimes is a complex undertaking. These crimes are not "specific offences"[10] but rather

---

[8] Blaškić, Trial Judgement (ICTY, 3 March 2000), para. 800 (footnote omitted). The Trial Chamber is referring here to the hierarchy of the ICTR, while noting that no such hierarchy has been established at the ICTY and that seriousness must be assessed based on the "circumstances of the case" (para. 802).

[9] See 000–000 for discussion of the *Akayesu* case (where genocide is found to have been perpetrated by rape).

[10] See, for example, Kupreškić, Trial Judgement (ICTY, 14 January 2000), para. 697.

"sets of crimes." It is not the underlying crime of murder or rape, for example, that qualifies particular conduct as an international crime. Rather, it is the context within which such acts are committed that transforms them from ordinary crimes into international crimes. Consequently, it is not possible to compare the proportional gravity of international crimes *in abstracto* in the same manner as domestic crimes – as in *Coker v. Georgia*, where the Supreme Court discussed the differences between the crimes of murder versus rape. The exact same underlying act – for instance, murder or rape – can variously qualify as a war crime, crime against humanity, or genocide, depending only on the context within which it was committed. In other words, context may be all that stands between an ordinary, domestic crime and the "most serious crimes of concern to the international community as a whole."[11] By the same token, any hierarchy among the core international crimes would be the product of comparing their different contextual elements.

In brief, these contextual elements are as follows: armed conflict as a material element of war crimes; widespread or systematic attack against a civilian population as a mental and material element of crimes against humanity; and an intent to destroy a group as a mental element of genocide.[12] What is immediately apparent is that the *mens rea* is essential to defining the contextual elements of international crimes. In particular, in international criminal law the same *actus reus* can be categorized quite differently by varying the *mens rea*. As a general principle of criminal law, individual liability is determined by two factors: the objective *character or harmfulness* of the act itself (e.g., robbery, rape, or killing) and the *intention* of the accused. As previously noted, however, within both retribution and deterrence theories, it is primarily the subjective or mental elements of crimes, rather than their objective or material elements, that attach specific degrees of gravity to conduct, and that consequently determine the degree of punishment to be imposed. For example, a killing might be accidental, a crime of opportunity, planned carefully in advance, carried out in an especially vicious or sadistic way, and so on.[13] Broadly similar considerations apply to understanding the differing contexts and thus the

[11] ICC Statute, Article 5.
[12] The terms *material* and *mental* are used to refer, respectively, to the *objective* and *subjective* elements, or the *actus reus* and *mens rea*, of a crime.
[13] See George P. Fletcher, *Rethinking Criminal Law* (Boston and Toronto: Little, Brown, 1978), 504–14.

relative gravity of the core international crimes. An examination of
these contextual elements demonstrates why the task of constructing
a hierarchy among these offenses is especially challenging.

War crimes

War crimes, the oldest of international crimes, are defined as violations of the laws and customs of war – which in contemporary times
are most often referred to as international humanitarian law. This
body of law, which regulates armed conflict, consists not just of cus-
tom, but also includes numerous treaties, the most prominent of them
being the 1949 Geneva Conventions. The purpose is to strike a balance
between military necessity and humanitarian imperatives, an idea
that found its first notable expression in the 1863 Lieber Code (the
main precursor to the Hague Conventions and later developments),
issued to Union troops by President Abraham Lincoln at the height of
the US Civil War.[14]

Nexus with armed conflict

Common Article 2 of the Geneva Conventions provides that its humanitarian law provisions are applicable to "all cases of declared war or any
other armed conflict between two or more of the High Contracting
Parties … [including] all cases of partial or total occupation of the territory of a High Contracting Party." Common Article 3 simply applies
to any "armed conflict not of an international character occurring in
the territory of one of the High Contracting Parties." *Armed conflict* is
a technical term designating, in the words of the ICTY, "a resort to
armed force between States or protracted armed violence between
governmental authorities and organized armed groups or between
such groups within a State."[15] It is the existence of armed conflict that
makes humanitarian law applicable to a particular state or territory,
transforming otherwise ordinary crimes into war crimes. By contrast,
the law does not apply in cases of internal disturbance or other violence not amounting to armed conflict.

Not every crime committed in a territory affected by armed conflict is
a war crime. As the ICTY Trial Chamber noted in the *Tadić* Jurisdiction

[14] Louise Doswald-Beck and Sylvain Vité, "International Humanitarian Law and
Human Rights Law," *International Review of the Red Cross* 293 (30 April 1993): 94.
[15] Tadić, Jurisdiction Decision (ICTY, 2 October 1995), para. 70.

Decision, a "nexus" must be established between the offense and the armed conflict itself.[16] Beyond that, the physical act of a war crime can vary considerably, from forcibly displacing civilians to using prohibited weapons against combatants. The requirement of a "nexus" is far from stringent. It does not require a precise geographic or temporal link, and also does not require the act to have been taken on behalf of, or in furtherance of, a plan or policy of one of the belligerent parties: "The only question ... is whether the offences were closely related to the armed conflict as a whole."[17] Whereas the

armed conflict need not have been causal to the commission of the crime ... the existence of an armed conflict must, at a minimum, have played a substantial part in the perpetrator's ability to commit it, his decision to commit it, the manner in which it was committed or the purpose for which it was committed.[18]

Protected person status

In distinguishing between domestic and international crimes, a further requirement is that the victim of a war crime must enjoy "protected" status under humanitarian law. Although humanitarian law also prohibits the wanton destruction or plunder of civilian property and the use of prohibited weapons, the international criminal tribunals are primarily concerned with crimes committed against civilians or other persons *hors de combat*, defined as "protected persons."

In the "grave breaches" provisions of the 1949 Geneva Conventions, the term *protected persons* is a technical designation referring to those "in the hands of a Party to the conflict or Occupying Power *of which they are not nationals*."[19] This definition reflects the strict application of the "grave breaches" provisions only to armed conflicts that are international in character (that is, between two states). ICTY jurisprudence emphasizes, however, that "this provision is directed to the protection of civilians to the maximum extent possible" and that "its applicability [is not] dependent on formal bonds and purely legal relations."[20]

---

[16] *Ibid.*, paras. 67–70; see also Stakić, Appeals Judgement (ICTY, 22 March 2006), para. 342; Kunarac, Appeals Judgement (ICTY, 12 June 2002), para. 55.

[17] Tadić, Trial Judgement (ICTY, 7 May 1997), para. 573.

[18] Kunarac, Appeals Judgement (ICTY, 12 June 2002), para. 58.

[19] See, for example, Article 4(1) of the Geneva Convention [No. IV] Relative to the Protection of Civilian Persons in Time of War (12 August 1949), 6 UST 3516, 75 UNTS 287 (emphasis added).

[20] Tadić, Appeals Judgement (ICTY, 15 July 1999), para. 168.

Furthermore, Article 3 Common to the 1949 Geneva Conventions, which applies to noninternational armed conflicts, broadly confers protection on all persons who are "taking no active part in the hostilities, including members of armed forces who have laid down their arms and those placed *hors de combat* by sickness, wounds, detention, or any other cause."[21] Consequently, with respect to internal armed conflicts, the victim's nationality is not a relevant consideration in defining war crimes.

Mens rea

In determining whether a violation of international humanitarian law has occurred, the ICTY requires that the perpetrator "knew or should have been aware that the victim was taking no active part in the hostilities when the crime was committed."[22] A soldier who knowingly kills a civilian is guilty of a war crime, but if he genuinely mistakes that civilian for a soldier, then it is a justified, combat-related killing. The moral reprehensibility of the conduct stems from the perpetrator's awareness of factual circumstances: ones indicating that the victim does not bear arms and therefore poses no military threat that would justify killing him, either in self-defense or in order to weaken enemy forces. The ICTY further requires "awareness of *factual* circumstances establishing the armed conflict and its (international or internal) character."[23] Earlier jurisprudence held that the definition of armed conflict must "be applied objectively, irrespective of the subjective views of the parties involved in the conflict."[24] The 1949 Geneva Conventions consider the character of armed conflict only with regard to the "scope of application" of humanitarian law rather than *mens rea*.

There is also no such requirement for war crimes under Article 8 of the ICC Statute. The ICC Elements of Crimes, however, includes both "the nexus with armed conflict" and "protected person status" as part of the requisite *mens rea*. Beyond the objective requirement that the "conduct took place in the context of and was associated with

---

[21] See, for example, Article 3 of the Fourth Geneva Convention.
[22] Boškoski and Tarčulovski, Appeals Judgement (ICTY, 19 May 2010), para. 66.
[23] Naletilić, Appeal Judgement (ICTY, 3 May 2006), para. 119.
[24] Akayesu, Trial Judgement (ICTR, 2 September 1998), para. 624; see also Semanza, Trial Judgement (ICTR, 15 May 2003), para. 357; see also, for example Yugoslavia and Rwanda to the Ongoing Work on Elements of Crimes in the Context of the ICC," *American Society of International Law, Proceedings of the 94th Annual Meeting* (2000), 285.

an international armed conflict" and the objective classification of victims as persons "protected" under the 1949 Geneva Conventions, the Elements of Crimes contains a further requirement that the "perpetrator was *aware* of the factual circumstances that established that protected status" and "*aware* of factual circumstances that established the existence of an armed conflict."[25] These subjective elements are qualified: The perpetrator does not need either to conduct a "legal evaluation" of the existence of an armed conflict or to consciously distinguish between international and internal armed conflict. He must simply be aware that the crime "took place in the context of and was associated with" an armed conflict.[26]

Under Article 9 of the ICC Statute, the Elements of Crimes is a nonbinding interpretive tool that does not apply in the event of an inconsistency with the definition of the crimes as contained in Articles 6 to 8 of the Statute.[27] ICC judges therefore still enjoy the discretion to disregard the Elements of Crimes by deeming it inconsistent with the 1949 Geneva Conventions – and, by extension, with Article 8 of the ICC Statute – in the form of an expanded *mens rea* requirement for war crimes. That said, the ICC has recently indicated that it will not easily deviate from the stipulations contained in the Elements of Crimes.[28] Furthermore, although "[t]he question as to what extent the existence of an armed conflict and its nature should be reflected in the *mens rea*

---

[25] ICC Elements of Crimes, Article 8.

[26] *Ibid.* Unlike the ICC Elements of Crimes, *Naletilić* requires awareness of the character of armed conflict (see n. 23). ICTY jurisprudence is similar, however, because there is no requirement of a "legal evaluation" of the character of armed conflict. In *Kordić and Čerkez*, the Appeals Chamber stated:

> The *nullum crimen sine lege* principle does not require that an accused knew the specific legal definition of each element of a crime he committed. It suffices that he was aware of the factual circumstances, e.g. that a foreign state was involved in the armed conflict. It is thus not required that *Kordić* could make a correct legal evaluation as to the international character of the armed conflict. (Kordić, Appeals Judgement [ICTY, 17 December 2004], para. 311).

[27] Article 9(l) of the ICC Statute provides: "Elements of Crimes shall assist the Court in the interpretation and application of [its competence *ratione materiae*]." Furthermore, Article 21(1)(a) provides that, in terms of applicable law, the court shall apply in "the first place, this Statute, Elements of Crimes and its Rules of Procedure and Evidence." Article 9(3), however, stipulates that the "Elements of Crimes … shall be consistent with this Statute," thus reinforcing the implicit primacy of the latter in the event of inconsistency.

[28] See 47, in this respect, for discussion of Prosecutor v. Bashir, Decision on the Prosecution's Application for a Warrant of Arrest Against Omar Hassan Ahmad Al Bashir (ICC, 4 March 2009).

of the accused proved highly controversial" in the ICC Statute's *travaux préparatoires*, the ICTY has held that "the existence of an armed conflict or its character has to be regarded, in accordance with the principle of *in dubio pro reo*, as ordinary elements of a [war] crime under customary international law."[29]

Crimes against humanity

The contextual element of crimes against humanity revolves around an indeterminate factor of "scale and gravity."[30] Crimes against humanity, unlike war crimes, need not be committed in armed conflict: They are simply crimes that, whether committed in wartime or not, rise to a level of seriousness requiring the intervention of international law. The threshold elaborated in the jurisprudence, and now widely accepted, is that an otherwise ordinary crime becomes a crime against humanity when it is committed as "part of a widespread and systematic attack directed against a civilian population." The practical definition of this contextual requirement remains elusive, however, because it raises, in effect, the question whether particular atrocities are of such a scale or gravity that they "shock the conscience of mankind."

No armed conflict requirement

Crimes against humanity were originally considered to be limited, like war crimes, to acts committed in armed conflict. Under Article 6(c) of the Charter of the International Military Tribunal, often referred to as the Nuremberg Charter, crimes against humanity had to be committed "in connection with or in execution of" war crimes or crimes against peace.[31] The "nexus with armed conflict" was a means of restricting the scope of this relatively novel concept and its unprecedented intrusion into the sacrosanct domain of state sovereignty and domestic jurisdiction. This requirement significantly limited the scope of protection provided by international criminal law. In effect, if massive or systematic human rights violations were committed outside armed conflict,

---

[29] Naletilić, Appeal Judgement (ICTY, 3 May 2006), para. 120.
[30] See, for example, Kupreškić, Trial Judgement (ICTY, 14 January 2000), para. 543 (noting that "the essence of [crimes against humanity] is a systematic policy of a certain scale and gravity directed against a civilian population").
[31] Agreement for the Prosecution and Punishment of the Major War Criminals of the European Axis, annex, 8 August 1945, 59 Stat. 1544, 82 UNTS 280.

they would not fall within the reach of crimes against humanity. At Nuremberg, as Samantha Power has pointed out, the

court treated aggressive war ("crimes against peace"), or the violation of another state's sovereignty, as the cardinal sin and prosecuted only those crimes against humanity and war crimes committed *after* Hitler crossed an internationally recognized border. Nazi defendants were thus tried for atrocities they committed during but not before World War II. By inference, if the Nazis had exterminated the entire German Jewish population but never invaded Poland, they would not have been liable at Nuremberg.[32]

This disquieting peculiarity in the early definition of crimes against humanity no longer holds true, though it still finds expression in the ICTY Statute. Article 5 (pertaining to crimes against humanity) requires a nexus with armed conflict, "whether internal or international in character." The analogous Article 3 of the ICTR Statute, however, does not require such an element. This apparent inconsistency was resolved in the *Tadić* case, where the ICTY Appeals Chamber opined, by way of *obiter dicta*, that,

as the Prosecutor points out, customary international law may not require a connection between crimes against humanity and any conflict at all. Thus, by requiring that crimes against humanity be committed in either internal or international armed conflict, the Security Council may have defined the crime in Article 5 more narrowly than necessary under customary international law.[33]

The Appeals Chamber thus concluded that it "is now a settled rule of customary international law that crimes against humanity do not require a connection to international armed conflict."[34] Coming on the eve of negotiations leading to the adoption of the ICC Statute, this precedent played a significant role in emancipating crimes against humanity from a potential legal nexus with armed conflict. The inclusion of such an element in the ICC Statute was considered but then rejected: The "precedent of the statute of the ad hoc Tribunal for Rwanda and the recent decision of the ad hoc Tribunal for the former Yugoslavia in the *Tadić* case" were post-Nuremberg developments that "militated in favor of the exclusion of any requirement of an armed conflict."[35]

---

[32] Samantha Power, "A Problem from Hell": America and the Age of Genocide (New York: HarperCollins, 2002), 49.

[33] Tadić, Jurisdiction Decision (ICTY, 2 October 1995), para. 141.

[34] *Ibid.*

[35] See *Report of the Ad Hoc Committee on the Establishment of an International Criminal Court*, UN GAOR, 50th Sess., Supp. No. 22, UN Doc. A/50/22, para. 79 (1995).

Thus, Article 7 of the ICC Statute does not contain any reference to a nexus with armed conflict in its definition of crimes against humanity, such that this offense applies to any atrocity that is of sufficient scale or gravity.

Widespread or systematic attack

A fundamental distinction between ordinary crimes and crimes against humanity is the requirement of a certain scale and gravity. Article 7 of the ICC Statute stipulates that the acts underlying crimes against humanity (for example, murder) must be committed "as part of a widespread or systematic attack directed against a civilian population." In drafting Article 7, delegates "attributed particular importance to the general criteria for crimes against humanity to distinguish such crimes from ordinary crimes under national law and to avoid interference with national court jurisdiction with respect to the latter."[36] It is their large-scale or exceptional gravity – and not the inhumane nature of isolated or random acts of murder, rape, and so on – that is central to the legal character of crimes against humanity. The International Law Commission has remarked that the "hallmarks of such crimes lie in their large-scale and systematic nature. The particular forms of unlawful acts (murder, enslavement, deportation, torture, rape, imprisonment etc.) are less crucial to the definition [than] factors of scale and deliberate policy."[37]

Both the ICTY and the ICTR have interpreted the phrase "part of a widespread or systematic attack directed against a civilian population" as containing four distinct elements: (1) there must be a "widespread or systematic attack"; (2) the attack must be directed against a civilian population; (3) the accused's act must form part of that attack; and (4) the accused must know that his act formed part of the attack (mens rea).[38]

---

[36] See *Report of the Preparatory Committee on the Establishment of an International Criminal Court*, UN GAOR, 51st Sess., Supp. No. 22, UN Doc. A/51/22, para. 84 (1996).

[37] See *Report of the International Law Commission on the Work of Its Forty-third Session*, GAOR, 46th Sess., Supp. No. 10, UN Doc. A/46/10, at 265 (1991).

[38] The ICTY's latest expression of this test can be found in Popović, Trial Judgement (ICTY, 10 June 2010), paras. 749–58. To much the same effect, see Bagosora, Trial Judgement (ICTR, 18 December 2008), para. 2165. The jurisprudence of both tribunals tends to vary in how the elements are grouped and thus whether there are four or five elements. It should also be noted that by Statute the ICTR requires additionally that the attack must be committed on "national, political, ethnical, racial or religious grounds." It is clear that requirement is a jurisdictional one unique to the ICTR Statute – similar to the ICTY Statute's requiring the existence of

An "attack" consists of conduct involving the commission of acts of violence or mistreatment.[39] The phrase *widespread or systematic* excludes random or isolated acts. The term *widespread* has been interpreted as referring to a multiplicity of victims, although it may comprise either "the cumulative effect of a series of inhumane acts or the singular effect of an inhumane act of extraordinary magnitude."[40] *Systematic* refers to "the organized nature of the acts of violence and the improbability of their random occurrence."[41]

The ICC Statute expressly requires that crimes against humanity constitute "a course of conduct involving the multiple commission" of the enumerated acts "pursuant to or in furtherance of a State or organizational policy to commit such attack."[42] ICTY jurisprudence seemingly contradicts this requirement by stating that "a plan or policy is not a legal element of a crime against humanity though it may be evidentially relevant in proving that an attack was directed against a civilian population and that it was widespread or systematic."[43] Although the existence and scope of this requirement remain controversial,[44] it may be noted that the ICTY *Kupreškić* Trial Judgement held that, despite the lack of a formal policy requirement,

[t]he need for crimes against humanity to have been at least tolerated by a State, Government or entity is also stressed in national and international case-law. The crimes at issue may also be State-sponsored or at any rate may be part of a governmental policy or of an entity holding *de facto* authority over a territory.[45]

The ICC Elements of Crime in Article 7 similarly stipulates that the requirement of a policy may, "in exceptional circumstances, be

---

an armed conflict – and was "not intended to alter the definition of Crimes Against Humanity in international law": Kamuhanda, Trial Judgement (ICTR, 22 January 2004), para. 671; see also Akayesu, Appeals Judgement (ICTR, 1 June 2001), para. 469.

[39] Kunarac, Appeals Judgement (ICTY, 12 June 2002), paras. 85–86.
[40] Blagojević and Jokić, Trial Judgement (ICTY, 17 January 2005), para. 545; Blaškić, Trial Judgement (ICTY, 3 March 2000), para. 206 (citing with approval from *Yearbook of the International Law Commission 1996*, vol. II, pt. 2, at 47 [*Report of the Commission to the General Assembly on the Work of Its Forty-eighth Session*]).
[41] Kunarac, Appeals Judgement (ICTY, 12 June 2002), para. 94.
[42] Article 7(2)(a).
[43] Blaškić, Appeals Judgement (ICTY, 29 July 2004), para. 120; Kunarac, Appeals Judgement (ICTY, 12 June 2002), para. 98.
[44] See, for example, William Schabas, "State Policy as an Element of International Crimes," *Journal of Criminal Law and Criminology* 98 (2008): 953 (arguing that the ICTY should have found a policy requirement in customary international law).
[45] Kupreškić, Trial Judgment (ICTY, 14 January 2000), para. 522.

implemented by a deliberate failure to take action, which is consciously aimed at encouraging such attack."[46] The divergence between
the ICTY–ICTR and the ICC definition may thus be somewhat artificial insofar as both require a "deliberate attempt to target a civilian
population."[47]

Against a civilian population

The second requirement for crimes against humanity – that the attack
be "directed against a civilian population" – simply means that the
civilian population must be the "primary object of the attack."[48] In
defining a *civilian* in the context of an armed conflict, recourse may be
had to the laws of war.[49]

Nexus with the attack

The third requirement – that the accused's act must form part of the
attack – requires a nexus between the accused's act and the attack,
thus excluding random or isolated crimes.[50]

Mens rea

Most importantly, the final requirement of crimes against humanity
concerns *mens rea*: The accused must have deliberately acted in the context of a widespread or systematic attack. Unlike the required nexus
with armed conflict in the case of war crimes (though note the indeterminacy in relation to the ICC Elements of Crimes), this requirement
about acting in the context of a widespread or systematic attack cannot be analyzed exclusively in objective terms. Article 7 of the ICC
Statute expressly requires that the accused have "knowledge of the
attack," whereas this requirement is implicit in the ICTY and ICTR
Statutes and is clarified in jurisprudence. The requisite *mens rea* for
crimes against humanity thus comprises (1) the *intent* to commit the
underlying offense (for example, murder), coupled with (2) *knowledge*
of the broader context in which that offense occurred.[51] Knowledge of
that broader context does not mean that the accused must individually

---

[46] ICC Elements of Crimes, 5 note 6, www.icc-cpi.int/NR/rdonlyres/9CAEE830–38CF-
41D6-AB0B-68E5F9082543/0/Element_of_Crimes_English.pdf.
[47] Tadić, Trial Judgement (ICTY, 7 May 1997), para. 653 (emphasis added).
[48] Kunarac, Appeals Judgement (ICTY, 12 June 2002), para. 91.
[49] *Ibid.*; Galić, Trial Judgement (ICTY, 5 December 2003), para. 144.
[50] Kunarac, Appeals Judgement (ICTY, 12 June 2002), paras. 99–101.
[51] Kordić, Appeals Judgement (ICTY, 17 December 2004), para. 99.

commit multiple or methodical crimes; a single act can potentially be considered a crime against humanity. All that is required is subjective awareness that that single act was being committed in the broader context of a widespread or systematic attack against a civilian population.[52] In other words, it is the knowledge of the accused that his acts occur in the broader context of a widespread or systematic attack that transforms an underlying ordinary crime of murder or rape, for example, into the more serious category of crimes against humanity. The ICTY Appeals Chamber has suggested that it is this element of *mens rea* that defines crimes against humanity as "crimes of a special nature to which a greater degree of moral turpitude attaches than to an ordinary crime."[53]

If the above (general) intent and awareness can be established, the specific motives of the accused in committing the act in question are irrelevant and may even be purely personal.[54] The *mens rea* of crimes against humanity does not require that the accused "share the purpose or goal behind the attack."[55] The accused may even seek to target only the victim and not the civilian population, as long he knows that his crime occurred as part of the broader attack.[56] The ICTY notes that his knowledge of the broader attack may be quite general and incomplete, rather than detailed,[57] and Article 7 of the ICC Elements of Crimes reiterates this position while noting that "[i]n the case of an emerging widespread or systematic attack against a civilian population, the intent clause ... indicates that this mental element is satisfied if the perpetrator intended to further such an attack."[58] This intent requirement, so stated, is obviously not precisely defined, leaving it uncertain exactly what level of knowledge is required, and the ICTY even stresses that the "evidence of knowledge on the part of the accused depends on the facts of a particular case; as a result, the manner in which this legal element may be proved may vary from case to case."[59]

---

[52] See, for example, Tadić, Trial Judgement (ICTY, 7 May 1997), para. 649.
[53] Tadić, Appeals Judgement (ICTY, 15 July 1999), para. 271.
[54] Kunarac, Appeals Judgement (ICTY, 12 June 2002), para. 103; Kordić, Appeals Judgement (ICTY, 17 December 2004), para. 99.
[55] Kunarac, Appeals Judgement (ICTY, 12 June 2002), para. 103.
[56] Kordić, Appeals Judgement (ICTY, 17 December 2004), para. 99.
[57] Kunarac, Appeals Judgement (ICTY, 12 June 2002), para. 102.
[58] ICC Elements of Crimes, 5.
[59] Blaškić, Appeals Judgement (ICTY, 29 July 2004), para. 126.

Comment: definitional uncertainties

This indeterminacy is compounded by the elusive nature of the "widespread or systematic" criterion, the first of the four requirements for crimes against humanity. Although presented as an objective criterion (as are all but the fourth requirement, which concerns *mens rea*), the ICTY has observed that the "quantitative criterion is not objectively definable as witnessed by the fact that neither international texts nor international and national case-law set any threshold starting with which a crime against humanity is constituted."[60] Determining what scale and gravity are sufficient for crimes against humanity cannot fail to be subjective. How is it possible, in practice, to determine what constitutes "widespread or systematic"? Does the "multiplicity of victims" refer to one hundred or one thousand? Does a systematic attack refer to ten, one hundred, or one thousand incidents of a similar nature? Does the term *course of conduct* imply a temporal frame? If so, does it consist of one day, one week, one month, or one year? Do the responses to these questions differ depending on the characteristics of the victimization (for example, would there be a lower numerical, methodical, or temporal threshold if the underlying crime was murder rather than deportation)?

There are obviously no hard-and-fast answers to these questions. How one responds to them will ultimately depend upon a moral or emotional response to the scale and gravity of the crimes in question and on an intuitive perception of the threshold beyond which ordinary domestic crimes or war crimes become crimes against humanity. It was, after all, the immense magnitude and systematic character of the Holocaust that led to the incorporation of crimes against humanity in the Nuremberg Charter. As Egon Schwelb observed, the "unprecedented record of crimes committed by the Nazi régime and the other Axis Powers, not only against Allied combatants but also against the civilian populations of the occupied countries and of the Axis countries themselves, made it necessary to provide that these crimes also should not go unpunished."[61] Even prior to the adoption of the Nuremberg Charter, the UN War Crimes Commission made it clear that the underlying basis of crimes against humanity was an exceptional degree of

---

[60] Blaškić, Trial Judgement (ICTY, 3 March 2000), para. 207.
[61] Egon Schwelb, "Crimes Against Humanity," *British Yearbook of International Law* 23 (1946): 178, 185.

moral turpitude, justifying this then-revolutionary intrusion against state sovereignty:

Only crimes which either by their magnitude and savagery or by their large number or by the fact that a similar pattern was applied at different times and places, *endangered the international community or shocked the conscience of mankind*, warranted intervention by States other than that on whose territory the crimes had been committed, or whose subjects had become their victims.[62]

Despite the considerable development and elaboration of crimes against humanity since Nuremberg, the view that this category is based on a shock factor remains essentially the same in contemporary jurisprudence. In the *Kambanda* case, for instance, the ICTR Trial Chamber noted that crimes against humanity and genocide "are crimes which particularly shock the collective conscience."[63] The technical term *widespread or systematic attacks against a civilian population* is an attempt to give some legal precision and certainty to the morally potent, but ambiguous, phrase "shocks the conscience of mankind." In the words of the Trial Chamber in the *Tadić* case, "The *reason* that crimes against humanity so *shock the conscience of mankind* and warrant intervention by the international community is *because* they are not isolated, random acts of individuals but rather result from a deliberate attempt to target a civilian population."[64]

Genocide

Mens rea

Genocide, as has been repeatedly mentioned, is often described as unique in its particular brand of evil. The contextual element of the crime of genocide, however, is closely related to, although distinct from, the crime against humanity of persecution.[65] *Persecution* is "the intentional and severe deprivation of fundamental rights contrary to international law by reason of the identity of the group or collectivity."[66]

---

[62] United Nations War Crimes Commission, *History of the United Nations War Crimes Commission and the Development of the Laws of War* (London: HMSO, 1948), 179 (emphasis added).

[63] Kambanda, Trial Judgement (ICTR, 4 September 1998), para. 14.

[64] Tadić, Trial Judgement (ICTY, 7 May 1997), para. 653 (emphasis added).

[65] See, for example, *United States v. Josef Altstoetter (Justice Case)*, Trials of War Criminals Before the Nuremberg Military Tribunals Under Control Council Law No. 10, vol. III (1949), 983 (where the US Military Tribunal held that genocide was "the prime illustration of a crime against humanity").

[66] ICC Statute, Art. 7(2)(g).

Unlike other crimes against humanity, persecution requires a discriminatory intent and encompasses a broad range of acts.[67] The primary distinction with genocide is that persecution does not have a requirement of special intent, or *dolus specialis*, to destroy a group. As observed in the *Kupreškić* case:

Both persecution and genocide are crimes perpetrated against persons that belong to a particular group and who are targeted because of such belonging ... While in the case of persecution the discriminatory intent can take multifarious inhumane forms and manifest itself in a plurality of actions including murder, in the case of genocide that intent must be accompanied by the intention to destroy, in whole or in part, the group to which the victims of the genocide belong. From the viewpoint of *mens rea*, genocide is an extreme and most inhuman form of persecution. To put it differently, when persecution escalates to the extreme form of wilful and deliberate acts designed to destroy a group or part of a group, it can be held that such persecution amounts to genocide.[68]

There are two essential parts to the mental element of genocide. First, unlike persecution, the crime of genocide requires that the intended victim be the group "as such," not just its individual members. In other words, genocide "differs from the crime of persecution in which the perpetrator chooses his victims because they belong to a specific community but does not necessarily seek to destroy the community as such."[69] Second, whereas under Article 7 of the ICC Statute persecution may be directed against "any identifiable group or collectivity,"[70] the crime of genocide is restricted to "a national, ethnical, racial or religious group."[71] Thus, political and social groups, for instance, are excluded from protection under the crime of genocide.

---

[67] Stakić, Appeals Judgement (ICTY, 22 March 2006), para. 327; Kupreškić, Appeals Judgement (ICTY, 23 October 2001), para. 98.

[68] Kupreškić, Trial Judgement (ICTY, 14 January 2000), para. 636; see also Brdjanin, Trial Judgement (ICTY, 1 September 2004), para. 699.

[69] Jelisić, Trial Judgement (ICTY, 14 December 1999), para. 79.

[70] In fact, both the ICTY and ICTR Statutes explicitly restrict the crime against humanity of persecution to "political, racial and religious grounds" (Article 5(h) of the ICTY Statute; Article 3(h) of the ICTR Statute). Unlike the ICTY and ICTR Statutes, however, Article 7(1)(h) of the ICC Statute refers to "any identifiable group or collectivity," includes new grounds such as "national, ethnic, cultural, ... [and] gender," and contains the illustrative formulation of "other grounds that are universally recognized as impermissible under international law," thus representing a progressive development of this crime in contrast to prior customary law.

[71] Convention on the Prevention and Punishment of the Crime of Genocide, Article II.

The *mens rea* required for genocide is qualitative and often some-what confused. There is a subtle, but vital, distinction between the *scope* of intent, which requires that one intend to destroy a group as such, and the *degree* of intent, which refers to a hierarchy of culpable mental states such as *dolus eventualis, dolus generalis,* and *dolus specialis.* The centrality of the *degree* of intent to this crime has been under-scored in both the ICTR and the ICTY. "Genocide is unique because of its element of *dolus specialis* (special intent)."[72] It is this *mens rea* that "gives genocide its speciality and distinguishes it from an ordinary crime and other [international crimes]"[73] and that makes it the "crime of crimes."[74]

In order to describe this special intent, terms from different legal systems have been used interchangeably in the jurisprudence of the ICTR and the ICTY, leading to further confusion. The essential point is that there must be an "intent to destroy" as distinct from the intent to carry out the underlying acts that may, in fact, result in such destruc-tion.[75] It is not sufficient that the accused "*knows* that his acts will, inevitably or ... probably, result in the destruction of the group in ques-tion"; rather, the accused must "*seek* the destruction in whole or in part of a group." Put another way,

an accused could not be found guilty of genocide if he himself did not share the goal of destroying in part or in whole a group even if he knew that he was contributing to or through his acts might be contributing to the partial or total destruction of a group.[76]

As long as the accused acts with the requisite intent, his motives are irrelevant. Even if he wants to destroy the group, in whole or in part, for personal reasons not shared with the other perpetrators, he may

---

[72] Kambanda, Trial Judgement (ICTR, 4 September 1998), para. 16; see also Akayesu, Trial Judgement (ICTR, 2 September 1998), para. 498; Krstić, Appeals Judgement (ICTY, 19 April 2004), para. 20.

[73] Jelisić, Trial Judgement (ICTY, 14 December 1999), para. 66.

[74] Kambanda, Trial Judgement (ICTR, 4 September 1998), para. 16; see also *Application of the Convention on the Prevention and Punishment of the Crime of Genocide* (Bosnia and Herzegovina v. Serbia and Montenegro) (International Court of Justice, 26 February 2007), para. 187; *Prosecutor v. Bashir*, Decision on the Prosecution's Application for a Warrant of Arrest Against Omar Hassan Ahmad Al Bashir (International Criminal Court, 4 March 2009), para. 139.

[75] For a useful review of the jurisprudence, along with an attempt to reconcile the varying expressions of this intent to destroy, see Kai Ambos, "What Does 'Intent to Destroy' in Genocide Mean?," *International Review of the Red Cross* 91 (2009): 833.

[76] Jelisić, Trial Judgement (ICTY, 14 December 1999), paras. 85–86.

still be deemed to have the requisite intent.[77] In other words, genocide is a "goal-oriented"[78] crime. Awareness that such destruction would result is not the equivalent of "intent to destroy."[79] In this respect, the *dolus specialis* standard is more exacting than the mere "knowledge" of the context of an attack required for crimes against humanity.

This standard of special intent implies that liability for genocide can attach even if the destruction of a group is not realized. As the ICTR Trial Chamber observed in the *Akayesu* case:

> Contrary to popular belief, the crime of genocide does not imply the actual extermination of a group in its entirety, but is understood as such once any one of the acts mentioned [that is, "killing members of the group," "causing serious bodily or mental harm to members of the group," and so on] is committed with the specific intent [to destroy a group].[80]

Accordingly, the crime of genocide is intent- rather than result-oriented in terms of its relationship to harm. Unlike crimes against humanity and the associated requirements, both objective and subjective, concerning a widespread or systematic attack, the *consummation* of a crime of genocide requires the satisfaction only of a subjective component together with a *single* successful act in execution of the crime.[81] Thus, at least in theory, killing a single victim could qualify as genocide.

This intent-oriented standard caused some concern among delegates in the negotiations leading to the adoption of the ICC Statute at the 1998 Rome Conference. These delegates succeeded in introducing a new objective element into the crime – apparently to remove isolated or trivial acts from the scope of genocide.[82] The Elements of Crimes

---

[77] Jelisić, Appeals Judgement (ICTY, 5 July 2001), para. 71; Simba, Appeals Judgement (ICTR, 27 November 2007), paras. 88, 269.

[78] See Ambos, "What Does 'Intent to Destroy' in Genocide Mean?," 835.

[79] See Krstić, Appeals Judgement (ICTY, 19 April 2004), para. 134; Blagojević and Jokić, Trial Judgement (ICTY, 17 January 2005), para. 656; Brdjanin, Trial Judgement (ICTY, 1 September 2004), para. 695; *Application of the Convention on the Prevention and Punishment of the Crime of Genocide* (Bosnia and Herzegovina v. Serbia and Montenegro) (International Court of Justice, 26 February 2007), para. 187.

[80] Akayesu, Trial Judgement (ICTR, 2 September 1998), para. 497.

[81] Such consummation should not be confused with inchoate crimes such as "attempt to commit genocide" or "direct and public incitement to commit genocide." See, for example, ibid., para. 562.

[82] For a critical account of the American draft of the Elements that resulted in the introduction of this new element, see, for example, William A. Schabas, "Follow Up to Rome: Preparing for Entry into Force of the International Criminal Court Statute," *Human Rights Law Journal* 20 (1999): 157, 163–64.

for Article 6 of the ICC Statute requires, in addition to the intent to destroy a group and the mental and material element (see next section) of the underlying act, that the "conduct took place in the context of a manifest pattern of similar conduct directed against that group or was conduct that could itself effect such destruction."[83] In other words, the ICC Elements of Crimes appears to exclude the possibility of the "lone génocidaire." The introduction of an objective requirement of a "manifest pattern of similar conduct" seems to merge genocide more closely with crimes against humanity insofar as isolated or random acts by perpetrators need to be linked to a broader "widespread or systematic attack" against a civilian population.

The ICTY has explicitly departed from the ICC Elements of Crimes and held that genocide does not require that the perpetrator participate in a widespread and systematic attack against a civilian population.[84] It has held, moreover, that "the existence of a plan or policy is not a legal ingredient of the crime of genocide."[85] The ICTY has based this position on its review of customary law and, in particular, on the observation that the drafters of the 1948 Genocide Convention "did not deem the existence of an organization or a system serving a genocidal objective as a legal ingredient of the crime. In so doing, they did not discount the possibility of a lone individual seeking to destroy a group as such."[86] In this respect the ICC Elements of Crimes thus amends and restricts the scope of genocide as envisaged in both international conventional and customary law.

The further requirement of the ICC Elements of Crimes that the "conduct could itself effect such destruction" is somewhat ambiguous, although it appears to exclude from the ambit of genocide "impossible attempts" that are not likely to succeed, even if they are committed with the requisite intent. In its recent decision to issue an arrest warrant against Sudanese president Omar Al-Bashir, the ICC attempted to settle this ongoing "controversy."[87] The court recognized that

---

[83] ICC Elements of Crimes, Art. 6.

[84] Krstić, Appeals Judgement (ICTY, 19 April 2004), para. 223.

[85] *Ibid.*, para. 225; Jelisić, Appeals Judgement (ICTY, 5 July 2001), para. 48; Simba, Appeals Judgement (ICTR, 27 November 2007), para. 260; Popović, Trial Judgement (ICTY, 10 June 2010), paras. 826–30.

[86] Jelisić, Trial Judgement (ICTY, 14 December 1999), para. 100.

[87] "The Majority is aware that there is certain controversy as to whether this contextual element should be recognized": *Prosecutor v. Bashir*, Decision on the Prosecution's Application for a Warrant of Arrest Against Omar Hassan Ahmad Al Bashir (International Criminal Court, 4 March 2009), para. 125.

for the case law of the ICTY and the ICTR, the crime of genocide is completed by, *inter alia*, killing or causing serious bodily harm to a *single individual* with the intent to destroy in whole or in part the group to which such individual belongs. As a result, according to this case law, for the purpose of completing the crime of genocide, it is irrelevant whether the conduct in question is capable of posing any concrete threat to the existence of the targeted group, or a part thereof.[88]

In the context of interpreting the ICC Statute, however, the court maintained that to consider the Elements of Crimes as "fully discretionary"[89] would be inconsistent with both the intent of the drafters[90] and the *nullum crimen sine lege* principle.[91] The court could therefore derogate from the Elements only in the case of an "irreconcilable contradiction" between it and the Statute.[92] Not finding one with respect to the provisions on genocide, the majority held that

the crime of genocide is only completed when the relevant conduct presents a concrete threat to the existence of the targeted group, or a part thereof. In other words, the protection offered by the penal norm defining the crime of genocide – as an *ultima ratio* mechanism to preserve the highest values of the international community – is only triggered when the threat against the existence of the targeted group, or part thereof, becomes concrete and real, as opposed to just being latent or hypothetical.[93]

The conclusion that there was no contradiction between the Elements and the Statute was informed by the following:

[T]he definition of the crime of genocide, so as to require for its completion an actual threat to the targeted group, or a part thereof, is (i) not *per se* contrary to article 6 of the Statute; (ii) fully respects the requirements of article 22(2) of the Statute that the definition of the crimes "shall be strictly construed and shall not be extended by analogy" and "[i]n case of ambiguity, the definition shall be interpreted in favour of the person being investigated, prosecuted or convicted"; and (iii) is fully consistent with the traditional consideration of the crime of genocide as the "crime of the crimes."[94]

Thus, as is clear from this explanation, the ICC found that including a "concrete threat" as part of the crime of genocide was justified primarily by the need to maintain a privileged status for genocide within the

---

[88] *Ibid.*, para. 119 (footnotes omitted) (emphasis added).
[89] *Ibid.*, para. 131.   [90] *Ibid.*, paras. 129–30.
[91] *Ibid.*, para. 131.   [92] *Ibid.*, para. 128.
[93] *Ibid.*, para. 124 (footnotes omitted).
[94] *Ibid.*, para. 133 (footnotes omitted).

hierarchy of crimes. That this interpretation departs from the precedents set by the ICTY and the ICTR does not seem to have unduly troubled the ICC majority.[95]

Trivial or limited acts are excluded from the scope of genocide, however, by the requirement that the intent be to destroy a group "in whole or in part." The ICTY Appeals Chamber has held that in view of the Genocide Convention's objective "to deal with mass crimes, it is widely acknowledged that the intention to destroy must target at least a *substantial* part of the group,"[96] with a substantial part being considered either "a large majority of the group in question or the most representative members of the targeted community."[97] As the Appeals Chamber in *Krstić* explained:

The numeric size of the targeted part of the group is the necessary and important starting point, though not in all cases the ending point of the inquiry. The number of individuals targeted should be evaluated not only in absolute terms, but also in relation to the overall size of the entire group. In addition to the numeric size of the targeted portion, its prominence within the group can be a useful consideration. If a specific part of the group is emblematic of the overall group, or is essential to its survival, that may support a finding that the part qualifies as substantial within the meaning of Article 4.[98]

Accordingly, ICTY jurisprudence includes, in the alternative, both a *quantitative* and a *qualitative* criterion. Of course, the qualitative criterion – with its assumption that a group's leaders may be central to a group's viability – involves implicit and arguably controversial value judgments as to the relative worth of the group's "ordinary" members.

Another important qualification in the definition of genocide is that genocidal intent may be confined to a limited geographic zone or, as stipulated by the ICJ, it "is not necessary to intend to achieve the complete annihilation of a group from every corner of the globe."[99]

---

[95] This particular issue was not under appeal in the ICC Appeals Chamber's review of the Trial Chamber's decision concerning the prosecutor's request for an arrest warrant. See *Prosecutor v. Bashir*, Judgement on the Appeal of the Prosecutor Against the "Decision on the Prosecution's Application for a Warrant of Arrest Against Omar Hassan Ahmad Al Bashir" (International Criminal Court, 3 February 2010).

[96] Jelisić, Trial Judgement (ICTY, 14 December 1999), para. 82; Krstić, Appeals Judgement (ICTY, 19 April 2004), para. 12.

[97] Jelisić, Trial Judgement (ICTY, 14 December 1999), para. 82.

[98] Krstić, Appeals Judgement (ICTY, 19 April 2004), para. 12.

[99] *Application of the Convention on the Prevention and Punishment of the Crime of Genocide* (Bosnia and Herzegovina v. Serbia and Montenegro) (International Court of Justice, 26 February 2007), para. 199.

These formulations are useful in attempting to define an essential ingredient of genocide – the intended destruction of a group "in whole or in part" – but in practice it is not possible to reliably determine what constitutes "in part." As with crimes against humanity, the elements of scale and gravity are indeterminate, with the consequence that this threshold matter involves an inherently subjective judgment.

By way of illustration, consider the ICTY's *Popović* and *Krstić* cases. Several individuals were convicted of committing genocide at Srebrenica, where between 7,000 and 8,000 Bosnian Muslim men and boys were systematically murdered.[100] "Muslims of eastern Bosnia" were considered a substantial part of "the entire [target] group, Bosnian Muslims."[101] The Muslim community of Srebrenica was said to number approximately 40,000,[102] and the total Muslim population of Bosnia-Herzegovina was around 1.4 million.[103] The ICTY noted that, even though the Bosnian Muslims of Srebrenica and the eastern enclaves comprised only a "small percentage" of the overall Muslim population of Bosnia, "the import of the community is not appreciated solely by its size" and that the "Srebrenica enclave was of immense strategic importance to the Bosnian Serb leadership":

(1) [T]he ethnically Serb state they sought to create would remain divided and access to Serbia disrupted without Srebrenica; (2) most Muslim inhabitants of the region had, at the relevant time, sought refuge in the Srebrenica enclave and the elimination of the enclave would accomplish the goal of eliminating the Muslim presence in the entire region; and (3) the enclave's elimination despite international assurances of safety would demonstrate to the Bosnian Muslims their defenselessness and be "emblematic" of the fate of all Bosnian Muslims.[104]

This analysis, albeit persuasive, shows just how many complex judgments may have to be made about the social, cultural, political, and economic aspects of a given situation.

Actus reus

The material element helps frame the mental element by defining the scope of the term *destroy*. The definition of genocide requires that acts

[100] Krstić, Trial Judgement (ICTY, 2 August 2001), para. 84.
[101] Popović, Trial Judgement (ICTY, 10 June 2010), para. 865.
[102] Krstić, Appeals Judgement (ICTY, 19 April 2004), para. 15.
[103] *Ibid.*, para. 15 note 27.
[104] Popović, Trial Judgement (ICTY 10 June 2010), para. 865; Krstić, Appeals Judgement (ICTY, 19 April 2004), paras. 15–16.

intended to destroy the group be those enumerated under paragraphs (a) to (e) of Article II of the Genocide Convention.

UN General Assembly Resolution 96(1) of 1946 defined *genocide* as "a denial of existence of entire human groups, as homicide is the denial of the right to live of individual human beings."[105] During preparatory work for the Genocide Convention, the delegates considered but rejected an expansive definition that, in addition to *physical* and *biological* destruction, encompassed *cultural* destruction. The definition was eventually restricted to physical and biological destruction – with one possible exception[106] – cumulatively referred to as "material" destruction.[107]

The most unambiguous form of physical destruction is "[k]illing members of the group" under Article II, paragraph (a), of the convention. In contrast to *immediate death* through killing, paragraph (c) essentially refers to *slow death*: "[d]eliberately inflicting on the group conditions of life calculated to bring about its physical destruction."[108] In the *Akayesu* case, the ICTY Trial Chamber construed this category as involving "methods of destruction by which the perpetrator does not immediately kill the members of the group, but which, ultimately, seek their physical destruction."[109] These methods may include "subjecting a group of people to a subsistence diet, systematic expulsion from homes and the reduction of essential medical services below minimum requirement."[110] Both immediate and "slow" death clearly fall within genocide's category of physical destruction.

Paragraph (b) of the Genocide Convention – "causing serious bodily or mental harm to members of the group" – is less clear-cut. The ICTR has adopted a broad interpretation: In addition to "acts of torture," it includes a wide range of "inhumane or degrading treatment, and persecution without limiting itself thereto."[111] Similarly, the ICC Elements of Crimes contains an explanatory note to the effect that such harm "may include, but is not necessarily restricted to, acts of torture, rape,

---

[105] General Assembly Resolution 96 (11 December 1946).
[106] See 52 on "transferring children" as "cultural" rather than "biological" destruction.
[107] See, for example, *Report of the International Law Commission on the Work of Its Forty-eighth Session*, GAOR, 51st Sess., Supp. No. 10, UN Doc. A/51/10, 90–91 (1996).
[108] See *Draft Convention on the Crime of Genocide*, UN Doc. E/447 (1947), 25, where the term *slow death* was used to describe this form of physical destruction.
[109] Akayesu, Trial Judgement (ICTR, 2 September 1998), para. 505.
[110] *Ibid.*, para. 506.   [111] *Ibid.*, para. 504.

sexual violence or inhuman or degrading treatment."[112] As the ICTR Trial Chamber remarked in the *Muvunyi* case: "Trial Chambers at the Tribunal have tended to interpret the term [*destroy*] broadly so that it not only entails acts that are undertaken with the intent to cause death but also includes acts which may fall short of causing death."[113]

Given the open-endedness of this comment from *Muvunyi*, it is not surprising that the criminal tribunals have been inconsistent and unpredictable in determining what constitutes destruction for the purposes of genocide. For instance, in the seminal *Akayesu* judgment, the ICTR Trial Chamber considered rape and sexual violence as a means of inflicting "serious bodily and mental harm" with the intent to destroy the Tutsis in Rwanda.[114] By contrast, in the *Popović* case, the ICTY Trial Chamber held that "forcible transfer does not constitute in and of itself an underlying act of genocide"[115] even if "in some circumstances forcible transfer can be an underlying act that causes serious bodily or mental harm, in particular if the forcible transfer operation was attended by such circumstances as to lead to the death of the whole or part of the displaced population."[116] In other cases, however, the ICTY Trial Chamber has stated that "[s]ystematic expulsion from homes" may be a means of inflicting conditions of life calculated to bring about destruction under Article 2(c) of the Genocide Convention.[117] Moreover, the ICJ has held that systematic "massive mistreatment, beatings, rape and torture causing serious bodily and mental harm during the Bosnian conflict and, in particular, in the detention camps" fulfill the material element of Article 2(b) of the Genocide Convention.[118] The range of acts

---

[112] ICC Elements of Crimes, 2 note 3.

[113] Muvunyi, Trial Judgement (ICTR, 12 September 2006), para. 482.

[114] Akayesu, Trial Judgement (ICTR, 2 September 1998), paras. 733–34.

[115] Popović, Trial Judgement (ICTY, 10 June 2010), para. 843.

[116] *Ibid.*, para. 813; see also Krstić, Appeals Judgement (ICTY, 19 April 2004), para. 33; Blagojević and Jokić, Appeals Judgement (ICTY, 9 May 2007), para. 123; *Application of the Convention on the Prevention and Punishment of the Crime of Genocide* (Bosnia and Herzegovina v. Serbia and Montenegro) (International Court of Justice, 26 February 2007), para. 190.

[117] See, for example, Brdjanin, Trial Judgement (ICTY, 1 September 2004), para. 691; Stakić, Trial Judgement (ICTY, 31 July 2003), para. 517; Akayesu, Trial Judgement (ICTR, 2 September 1998), para. 506; Popović, Trial Judgement (ICTY, 10 June 2010), para. 815.

[118] *Application of the Convention on the Prevention and Punishment of the Crime of Genocide* (Bosnia and Herzegovina v. Serbia and Montenegro) (International Court of Justice, 26 February 2007), para. 319; see also Brdjanin, Trial Judgement (ICTY, 1 September 2004), para. 690 (citing the following as examples of acts that inflict serious bodily or mental harm for the purpose of genocide: "torture, inhumane

mentioned in the jurisprudence underscores that the legal definition of *genocide* is so broad (and indeterminate) that it is difficult to describe – notwithstanding the archetypal image of the Holocaust – what a typical genocide actually "looks like." This is because it is the *mens rea* of genocide that makes it unique, not its physical manifestation.

There are two further means of perpetrating genocide under Article II of the Genocide Convention. Biological destruction through "[i]mposing measures intended to prevent births within the group" – paragraph (d) – is construed by the *Akayesu* case as "sexual mutilation, the practice of sterilization, forced birth control, separation of the sexes and prohibition of marriages."[119] Such measures can be mental as well as physical.[120] With respect to "[f]orcibly transferring children of the group to another group" – paragraph (e) – it should be noted that, although the International Law Commission characterizes it as "biological" destruction, it may more appropriately constitute a form of "cultural destruction."[121]

The elusiveness of the categories

It is evident that, unlike crimes such as rape and murder, war crimes, crimes against humanity, and genocide do not exist in watertight conceptual categories. In many instances, the same conduct can qualify as

---

    or degrading treatment, sexual violence including rape, interrogations combined with beatings, threats of death, and harm that damages health or causes disfigurement or serious injury to members of the targeted national, ethnical, racial or religious group").

[119] Akayesu, Trial Judgement (ICTR, 2 September 1998), para. 507; see also Rutaganda, Trial Judgement (ICTR, 6 December 1999), para. 53.

[120] Rutaganda, Trial Judgement (ICTR, 6 December 1999), para. 53; Akayesu, Trial Judgement (ICTR, 2 September 1998), para. 508; Popović, Trial Judgement (ICTY, 10 June 2010), para. 818.

[121] See, for example, *Report of the International Law Commission on the Work of its Forty-eighth Session*, GAOR, 51st Sess., Supp. No. 10, UN Doc. A/51/10, at 91 (1996), for the view that forcible transfer of children constitutes "biological" destruction. But see *Draft Convention on the Crime of Genocide*, UN Doc. E/447 (1947), 6–7, where "forced transfer of children to another human group" is included under the category of "cultural destruction" defined as destroying "the specific characteristics of the group." This act was interpreted as representing the "disappearance of the group as a cultural unit" (at page 27), as distinct from its physical or biological destruction. During the preparatory work for the convention, there were differing views as to the nature of destruction contemplated by paragraph (e) of Article II. See, for example, UN GAOR, 3rd Sess., 6th Cmte., 82nd mtg., UN Doc. A/C.6/SR.82 (1948).

two or more of the core international crimes. A good example is the *Akayesu* case, in which the accused was said to have spearheaded a campaign of systematic rape of Tutsi girls and women in the municipality where he was the *bourgmestre*.[122]

Consider the following, harrowing testimony:

According to Witness PP, who then went to Kinihira herself, the three women were forced by the Interahamwe to undress and told to walk, run and perform exercises "so that they could display the thighs of Tutsi women." All this took place, she said, in front of approximately two hundred people. After this, she said the women were raped. She described in particular detail the rape of Alexia by Interahamwe who threw her to the ground and climbed on top of her saying "Now, let's see what the vagina of a Tutsi woman feels like." According to Witness PP, Alexia gave the Interahamwe named Pierre her Bible before he raped her and told him, "Take this Bible because it's our memory, because you do not know what you're doing." Then one person held her neck, others took her by the shoulders and others held her thighs apart as numerous Interahamwe continued to rape her – Bongo after Pierre, and Habarurena after Bongo. According to the testimony, Alexia was pregnant. When she became weak she was turned over and lying on her stomach, she went into premature delivery during the rapes. Witness PP testified that the Interahamwe then went on to rape Nishimwe, a young girl, and recalled lots of blood coming from her private parts after several men raped her. Louise was then raped by several Interahamwe while others held her down, and after the rapes, according to the testimony, all three women were placed on their stomachs and hit with sticks and killed.

The brutality of these acts leaves one speechless, without words to capture either the unbearable cruelty of the perpetrators or the unimaginable suffering of the victim. And yet that is exactly what is required of judges whose task it is to channel facts into one or more categories of wrongdoing by application of legal reasoning.

In connection with the rapes described above and other inhumane acts, including murder – for which the accused was found liable – the ICTR Trial Chamber found Akayesu guilty of both crimes against humanity *and* genocide. Later, the Appeals Chamber found that his acquittal on war crimes charges was based upon an error of law.[123]

---

[122] See Akayesu, Trial Judgement (ICTR, 2 September 1998), paras. 157ff.

[123] Akayesu, Appeals Judgement (ICTR, 1 June 2001), paras. 444–45 (holding that the Trial Chamber incorrectly applied a "public agent or government representative test" to war crimes).

Therefore, Akayesu was guilty of all *three* core international crimes *on the same set of facts*:

- The war crimes conviction with respect to the rapes would have been based, in part, upon Article 4(2)(e) of Additional Protocol II to the Geneva Conventions, which prohibits "outrages upon personal dignity, in particular humiliating and degrading treatment, rape, enforced prostitution and any form of indecent assault."
- The conviction for crimes against humanity was partially entered on the basis of a widespread and systematic attack comprising acts of rape under Article 3(g) of the ICTR Statute (which refers to "other inhumane acts").
- The rapes constituted genocide under the Genocide Convention's prohibition against "causing serious bodily or mental harm to members of the group," as reflected in Article 2(b) of the ICTR Statute.

The *Akayesu* Trial Chamber explained these multiple convictions without reference to the comparative gravity of the crimes:

Having regard to its Statute, the Chamber believes that the offences under the Statute – genocide, crimes against humanity, and violations of Article 3 common to the Geneva Conventions and of Additional Protocol II – have different elements and, moreover, are intended to protect different interests. The crime of genocide exists to protect certain groups from extermination or attempted extermination. The concept of crimes against humanity exists to protect civilian populations from persecution. The idea of violations of article 3 common to the Geneva Conventions and of Additional Protocol II is to protect non-combatants from war crimes in civil war. These crimes have different purposes and are, therefore, never co-extensive. Thus it is legitimate to charge these crimes in relation to the same set of facts.[124]

Following this line of reasoning – and rejecting, in effect, the view of the ICTR Trial Chamber in *Kambanda* (as cited in *Blaškić*) that genocide is the "crime of crimes" and that it is, by the same token, more "serious" than the other international crimes[125] – the Trial Chamber maintained that no one type of international crime is inherently "more serious than another." In other words, the ICTR Statute does not "establish a hierarchy of norms, but rather all three offences are presented on an equal footing."[126]

---

[124] Akayesu, Trial Judgement (ICTR, 2 September 1998), para. 469.
[125] Kambanda, Trial Judgement (ICTR, 4 September 1998); see 83–84.
[126] Akayesu, Trial Judgement (ICTR, 2 September 1998), para. 470.

Thus, the comprehensive analysis of the contextual requirements still leaves unanswered a fundamental question: Is genocide the "crime of crimes," or is it just another international crime? What can be gleaned from further analysis of its stigma and the sentencing practice of tribunals? And against the absolute horrors described in Witness PP's testimony, should we really be concerned with such legal abstractions and hierarchies at all?

4   A hierarchy of international crimes?

On 12 July 1995, after a campaign of relentless artillery shelling against civilians, Serb forces captured the Bosnian Muslim enclave of Srebrenica, where an estimated 40,000 terrified victims of "ethnic cleansing" had sought refuge. In the days that followed, some 8,000 men were singled out and summarily executed, and their bodies dumped in mass graves. On 2 August 2001, the ICTY Trial Chamber in the *Krstić* case concluded that this mass murder qualified as "genocide."[1] Referring to this atrocity as "an unspeakable human evil,"[2] the judgment described the tragic fate of the victims:

Almost to a man, the thousands of Bosnian Muslim prisoners captured, following the takeover of Srebrenica, were executed. Some were killed individually or in small groups by the soldiers who captured them and some were killed in the places where they were temporarily detained. Most, however, were slaughtered in carefully orchestrated mass executions, commencing on 13 July 1995, in the region just north of Srebrenica. Prisoners not killed on 13 July 1995 were subsequently bussed to execution sites further north of Bratunac, within the zone of responsibility of the Zvornik Brigade. The large-scale executions in the north took place between 14 and 17 July 1995.

Most of the mass executions followed a well-established pattern. The men were first taken to empty schools or warehouses. After being detained there for some hours, they were loaded onto buses or trucks and taken to another site for execution. Usually, the execution fields were in isolated locations. The prisoners were unarmed and, in many cases, steps had been taken to minimise resistance, such as blindfolding them, binding their wrists behind their backs with ligatures or removing their shoes. Once at the killing fields, the men were taken off the trucks in small groups, lined up and shot. Those who

---

[1] Krstić, Trial Judgement (ICTY, 2 August 2001), para. 598.
[2] *Ibid.*, para. 70.

survived the initial round of gunfire were individually shot with an extra round, though sometimes only after they had been left to suffer for a time. Immediately afterwards, and sometimes even during the executions, earth moving equipment arrived and the bodies were buried, either in the spot where they were killed or in another nearby location.

At several of the sites, a few wounded people survived by pretending to be dead and then crawled away. The Trial Chamber heard from some of these survivors about their ordeals. It also heard from a member of the [Bosnian Serb Army] who participated in one of the largest executions, which took place on 16 July 1995.[3]

Among the Army of Republika Srpska soldiers responsible for this mass execution, the only one to testify for the prosecution was Dražen Erdemović – a 24-year-old ethnic Croat married to an ethnic Serb. His earlier 1996 trial was an anomaly. Far from being an enthusiastic *génocidaire*, his was a case of an unwitting warrior – from a mixed marriage, enmeshed in an ethnic war – who found himself in the wrong place at the wrong time:

On 16 July 1995, he was sent with other members of his unit to the Branjevo collective farm near Pilica, north-west of Zvornik. Once there, they were informed that later that day Muslim men from 17 to 60 years of age would be brought to the farm in buses. The men were unarmed civilians who had surrendered to the members of the Bosnian Serb army or police after the fall of the United Nations "safe area" at Srebrenica. Members of the military police took the civilians off the buses in groups of ten and escorted them to a field next to the farm buildings, where they were lined up with their backs to a firing squad. The men were then killed by Drazen Erdemovic and other members of his unit with the help of soldiers from another brigade.[4]

Unlike other defendants, Erdemović had voluntarily confessed to his crimes and repeatedly expressed remorse. Before the Trial Chamber, he testified that he had initially disobeyed orders to shoot the victims but was left with no choice after his commander threatened to kill him:

Your Honour, I had to do this. If I had refused, I would have been killed together with the victims. When I refused, they told me: "If you're sorry for them, stand up, line up with them and we will kill you too." I am not sorry for myself but for my family, my wife and son who then had nine months, and I could not refuse because then they would have killed me.[5]

---

[3] *Ibid.*, paras. 67–69.
[4] Erdemović, Sentencing Judgement (ICTY, 29 November 1996), para. 2.
[5] *Ibid.*, para. 10.

At his initial trial, he pleaded guilty to both crimes against humanity and war crimes, but the Trial Chamber decided to sentence him solely for crimes against humanity because war crimes had been charged only in the alternative.[6] This decision would inadvertently lead to the ICTY's first consideration of whether one crime should result in a higher sentence than the other on account of its greater gravity.

On appeal, it emerged that Erdemović may not have properly understood the difference between pleading guilty to crimes against humanity rather than solely to war crimes. In its first full proceeding, the ICTY Appeals Chamber considered *proprio motu* (that is, on its own initiative) whether the defendant had entered an "informed" plea of guilty and whether he had, in particular, appreciated "the distinction between the alternative charges [of war crimes and crimes against humanity] and the consequences of pleading guilty to one rather than the other."[7] The Appeals Chamber went on to hold that if he had "been properly apprised of the less serious charge and his entitlement to plead to it, we have grave doubts that he would have continued to plead guilty to the more serious charge."[8] The case was remitted to a new trial chamber, and Erdemović entered a new plea of guilty, but this time only to war crimes. Consequently, his initial sentence was reduced from ten to five years[9] – not because the facts had changed, but merely because of the different categorization of the crime.

Coming as it did in the earliest days of ICTY jurisprudence, the *Erdemović* case raised for the first time the question of whether crimes against humanity are more serious than war crimes, and more generally whether the most serious international crimes are on an equal footing or not. Beyond stigma, the most determinate expression of relative gravity between such crimes is differentiation in sentencing. It follows that, if one crime is more serious than the other, it should result in greater punishment, proportionate to the added moral blameworthiness. Absent sentencing tariffs in international law, however, and considering the substantive overlap between the crimes, what followed in

---

[6] *Ibid.*, para. 3.

[7] Erdemović, Appeals Judgement, Joint Separate Opinion of Judge McDonald and Judge Vohrah (ICTY, 7 October 1999), para. 19. On this particular point, the joint separate opinion takes the same position as the majority opinion; only one of the five judges (Judge Li) dissented on this point. See Erdemović, Appeals Judgement (ICTY, 7 October 1999), para. 20.

[8] Erdemović, Appeals Judgement, Joint Separate Opinion of Judge McDonald and Judge Vohrah (ICTY, 7 October 1999), para. 26.

[9] Erdemović, Sentencing Judgement (ICTY, 5 March 1998).

subsequent decisions was a complex, conflicted, and at times confused debate as to the existence and character of a normative hierarchy. The principles that emerged would have a lasting impact on how we ascertain and compare the gravity of different types of atrocities. They indicate that, despite its conception as the "crime of crimes," genocide is not so clearly the most serious crime. Despite some contrary views, the weight of judicial opinion does not deem genocide to be categorically more serious than either war crimes or crimes against humanity. At best, sentencing practice indicates that, where the facts are exactly the same, genocide results in higher punishment than other crimes, on account of its gravity. Viewed from this perspective, genocide does not seem to merit the great distinction that is often attributed to it.

Principles of sentencing

Gravity of crime and individual circumstances as factors in sentencing

Can greater punishment indicate the relative heinousness of a crime? Making such a determination is complicated by the fact that, unlike sentencing tariffs in national penal codes, the statutes of the ICTY, ICTR, and ICC do not generally stipulate differing minimum or maximum penalties corresponding to different crimes. The ICTY and ICTR Statutes simply provide that the penalty imposed "shall be limited to imprisonment"[10] (thereby excluding the death penalty, forced labor, and similar punishments). Although the "general practice regarding prison sentences" in former Yugoslavia and Rwanda respectively shall be considered,[11] the jurisprudence clarifies that "a Trial Chamber's discretion in imposing sentence is not bound by any maximum term of imprisonment applied in a national system."[12] Article 77(1) of the ICC Statute provides some further guidance but does not differentiate between crimes. It simply states that the court may impose

    (a) Imprisonment for a specified number of years, which may not exceed a maximum of 30 years; or

    (b) A term of life imprisonment when justified by the extreme gravity of the crime and the individual circumstances of the convicted person.

[10] ICTY Statute, Art. 24(1); ICTR Statute, Art. 23(1).
[11] ICTY Statute, Art. 24(1); ICTR Statute, Art. 23(1).
[12] Tadić, Judgement in Sentencing Appeals (ICTY, 26 January 2000), para. 21.

Article 77(2) further provides that, in addition to imprisonment, the court may order the payment of a fine or the "forfeiture of proceeds, property and assets derived directly or indirectly from that crime."

Although the courts' statutes do not, in the context of penalties, specifically differentiate among crimes, the statutes do all provide that the courts should "take into account such factors as the gravity of the crime and the individual circumstances of the convicted person."[13] These provisions resemble the two-step approach to sentencing by national courts for ordinary crimes discussed in Chapter 2 – namely, a combination of the gravity of the crime defined by a specific category of wrongdoing, and culpability defined by the perpetrator's individual circumstances.[14] Nevertheless, since the statutes, unlike their national counterparts, establish no mandatory sentences, it is difficult to ascertain the weight given to the gravity of the crime versus the individual circumstances of the convicted person in relation to any particular sentence. In short, the courts have very broad judicial discretion in sentencing,[15] which gives rise to less quantifiable and less predictable results.

The Rules of Procedure and Evidence of all three tribunals provide further guidance on the factors to be considered in sentencing. These factors include the degree of participation and culpability of the accused, the particular means employed to execute the crime, and even, *inter alia*, the "age, education, social and economic condition of the convicted person."[16] These factors do not relate to the gravity of the crime as defined by specific categories of wrongdoing, however, and in any event they are neither exhaustive nor obligatory.[17] The sentencing practices of tribunals indicate that certain factors are applied with greater consistency than others. In particular, the rank or authority of

---

[13] ICTY Statute, Art. 24(2); ICTR Statute, Art. 23(2); ICC Statute, Art. 78(1).

[14] See 17–22; Andrea Carcano, "Sentencing and the Gravity of the Offence in International Criminal Law," *International and Comparative Law Quarterly* 51 (2002): 583.

[15] Akayesu, Appeals Judgement (ICTR, 1 June 2001), para. 416; see also Krstić, Appeals Judgement (ICTY, 19 April 2004), para. 242: "The jurisprudence of the ICTY and ICTR has ... generated a body of relevant factors to consider during sentencing. The Appeals Chamber has emphasised, however, that it is 'inappropriate to set down a definitive list of sentencing guidelines for future reference,' given that the imposition of a sentence is a discretionary decision."

[16] ICC Rules on Procedure and Evidence, Rule 145; see also the ICTY and ICTR Rules of Procedure and Evidence, Rule 101.

[17] See generally William A. Schabas, "Sentencing by International Tribunals: A Human Rights Approach," *Duke Journal of Comparative & International Law* 7 (1997): 461.

a convicted person within the relevant political or military hierarchy is almost always considered, pointing to a "fairly strong and positive relationship between power and punishment."[18] Another factor is whether the accused has cooperated with the prosecution or entered a guilty plea, either of which usually results in a lighter sentence.[19] But, once again, these factors do not correspond to the gravity of the crime as such.

In addition to these listed factors, numerous others have been identified in jurisprudential literature. Scholars James Meernik and Kimi King, in an empirical study of ICTY cases, found the following aggravating factors cited by judges: magnitude of crimes, zeal, heinousness, duration of crimes, discriminatory intent, vulnerability of victims, youth of victims, abuse of trust or personal authority, failure to punish those committing crimes, intimidation of witnesses/courtroom demeanor, and personal gain. By contrast, mitigating factors mentioned in judgments include "guilty pleas," "co-operation," "remorse," "surrendered," "no prior criminal record," "assisted victims," "not active participant," "family," "youth," "old age," "not a present threat," "redeemable," "subordinate rank," "prison would be far away," "context of actions," "co-operation with defense counsel," and "post-conflict conduct."[20] Again, these factors do not seem to correspond to the gravity of crimes *in abstracto*.

There is some question as to whether these aggravating and mitigating factors are a third type of measurement to be used during sentencing, or if they are already encompassed in the "individual circumstances of the convicted person." Robert Sloane, in reference to the ICTR, explains that individual circumstances

effectively [mean], or [overlap] almost entirely with, aggravating and mitigating circumstances under Rule 101. At times, the Tribunal describes certain sentencing facts under the heading "individual circumstances," but these serve no independent function in the determination of sentence

---

[18] James Meernik and Kimi King, "The Sentencing Determinants of the International Criminal Tribunal for the Former Yugoslavia: An Empirical and Doctrinal Analysis," *Leiden Journal of International Law* 16 (2003): 717, 739.

[19] *Ibid.* Rule 101(B)(ii) of the Rules of Procedure and Evidence in both tribunals specifically provides for these as mitigating factors. See also Nikolić, Appeals Judgement (ICTY, 4 February 2005), para. 89 (noting the "special context of a plea agreement").

[20] Meernik and King, "The Sentencing Determinants of the International Criminal Tribunal for the Former Yugoslavia: An Empirical and Doctrinal Analysis."

except insofar as the Tribunal finds them to be aggravating or mitigating. "Gravity," by contrast, does – at least in theory.[21]

In view of broad judicial discretion and myriad factors considered, the categorization of sentencing factors can prove to be an elusive task. For example, the gravity of a crime and individual circumstances may overlap. In such instances, the ICTY Appeals Chamber "considers that factors which a Trial Chamber takes into account as aspects of the gravity of the crime cannot additionally be taken into account as separate aggravating circumstances, and *vice versa* … [D]ouble-counting for sentencing purposes is impermissible."[22] Judges may assess gravity and aggravating circumstances together,[23] however, and they may assess a factor "which normally would be taken into account in … gravity … as an aggravating factor."[24]

At most, it can be said that "in the vast majority of cases," gravity "establish[es] a high baseline" for sentencing, whereas "adjustments to and individualization of the sentence virtually all take place at the level of 'individual circumstances.'"[25] That is, although individual circumstances are always taken into account in sentencing, the gravity of the crime is a more significant factor. This central importance of gravity is reflected by its characterization as the "sentencing lodestar,"[26] "litmus test for the appropriate sentence,"[27] "deciding factor,"[28] "primary consideration,"[29] and "cardinal feature"[30] in sentencing. Nonetheless, the gravity of crimes corresponds to the factual circumstances in which specific crimes are actually committed by the convicted person and not to a category of wrongdoing *in abstracto*.

The purposes of punishment in international criminal law

Sentencing in international criminal justice is determined not only by the gravity of crimes and individual circumstances, but also by

[21] Robert D. Sloane, "Sentencing for the 'Crime of Crimes': The Evolving 'Common Law' of Sentencing of the International Criminal Tribunal for Rwanda," *Journal of International Criminal Justice* 5 (2007): 713, 722.

[22] Deronjić, Appeals Judgement (ICTY, 20 July 2005), paras. 106–07.

[23] *Ibid.*, para. 107.

[24] Vasiljević, Appeals Judgement (ICTY, 25 February 2004), para. 157.

[25] Sloane, "Sentencing for the 'Crime of Crimes,'" 722.

[26] *Ibid.*

[27] Akayesu, Appeals Judgement (ICTR, 1 June 2001), para. 413.

[28] Nahimana, Appeals Judgement (ICTR, 28 November 2007), para. 1060.

[29] Čelebići, Appeals Judgement (ICTY, 20 February 2001), para. 731.

[30] Plavšić, Sentencing Judgement (ICTY, 27 February 2003), para. 25.

retribution and deterrence[31] – the two primary purposes of punishment in domestic law.[32] These factors add a further element of complexity in determining the comparative seriousness of international crimes. As discussed in Chapter 2, imposing punishment in proportion to the degree of wrongdoing has a central place both in retributive theories based on moral blameworthiness and in utilitarian theories based on objectives such as deterrence. If one crime is more serious than another, it should receive greater punishment, whether to justify the additional moral stigma or to create a disincentive for greater wrongdoing. The tribunals have given great weight to deterrence in that putting an end to impunity is the leitmotif of international criminal law. However, while deterrence is a primary justification for punishing international crimes, it seems to have little influence on the determination of individual sentences.

With respect to *special* deterrence (that is, preventing an individual from reoffending), tribunals have expressed doubt as to its relevance in the context of prosecuting mass atrocities before international criminal tribunals. The ICTY Trial Chamber in *Kunarac* explained that

special deterrence, as a general sentencing factor, is generally of little significance before this jurisdiction. The main reason is that the likelihood of persons convicted here ever again being faced with an opportunity to commit war crimes, crimes against humanity, genocide or grave breaches is so remote as to render its consideration in this way unreasonable and unfair.[33]

With respect to *general* deterrence, it is virtually impossible for judges to decide how best to deter future international crimes in determining a sentence, especially given the lack of empirical research on the subject.[34] Would prolonging the sentence of a convict by ten years better prevent genocide from recurring in a particular country in

---

[31] Tadić, Sentencing Judgement (ICTY, 11 November 1999), para. 9 ("retribution and deterrence serv[e] as the primary purposes of sentence"); see also Furundžija, Trial Judgement (ICTY, 10 December 1998), para. 288; Deronjić, Sentencing Judgement (ICTY, 30 March 2004), para. 142; Rutaganda, Trial Judgement (ICTR, 6 December 1999), para. 456; Serushago, Sentencing Judgement (ICTR, 5 February 1999), para. 20.

[32] See 13–17.

[33] Kunarac, Trial Judgement (ICTY, 26 February 2001), para. 840.

[34] Shahram Dana, "Genocide, Reconciliation and Sentencing in the Jurisprudence of the ICTY," in Ralph Henham and Paul Behrens, eds., *The Criminal Law of Genocide: International, Comparative and Contextual Aspects* (Aldershot, UK: Ashgate, 2007), 259 (noting that the "most significant [challenge to determining 'the role of sentencing'] is lack or insufficiency of empirical data linking punishment to the prevention of genocide").

the future? Or, perhaps, would a lesser sentence better contribute to national reconciliation? These complex questions may be beyond the competence of the trial judge within the confines of a judicial proceeding. Consequently, general deterrence remains an important purpose of international criminal punishment but carries little weight in the determination of individual sentences.[35]

In ICTY jurisprudence, for instance, "judgments simply cite deterrence as a sentencing principle but draw no particular connection between deterrence and the sentence imposed."[36] As the Appeals Chamber in *Nikolić* stated:

While it is undisputed that [deterrence] plays "an important role in the functioning of the Tribunal," the Trial Chamber's duty remains to tailor the penalty to fit the individual circumstances of the accused and the gravity of the crime. By doing so, Trial Chambers contribute to the promotion of the rule of law and respond to the call from the international community to end impunity, while ensuring that the accused are punished solely on the basis of their wrongdoings and receive a fair trial.[37]

It has also been argued that there is a special place in international criminal law for Johannes Andenæs's theory of "general prevention,"[38] or what the ICTY has called "affirmative prevention."[39] That international criminals are seen to be punished is of "communicative" or "expressive" significance[40] for members of society, given the special moral stigma attached to such crimes. As explained by the Appeals Chamber in *Kordić*, "the sentence seeks to internalise these rules and

---

[35] The *Kunarac* Trial Chamber curiously implied that general deterrence was a kind of aggravating factor increasing all sentences, but that, "in the circumstances of the present case, the Trial Chamber considers that increasing the terms of imprisonment because of general deterrence is unnecessary in light of the length of the sentences dictated by the inherent gravity of the offences": Kunarac, Trial Judgement (ICTY, 26 February 2001), para. 857.

[36] Allison Danner, "Constructing a Hierarchy of Crimes in International Criminal Law Sentencing," *Virginia Law Review* 87 (2001): 415, 448.

[37] Nikolić, Appeals Judgement (ICTY, 4 February 2005), para. 45.

[38] See 25–26.

[39] Kordić, Appeals Judgement (ICTY, 17 December 2004), paras. 1073, 1080–88 ("[T]he sentence seeks to internalise these rules [of humanitarian international law] and the moral demands they are based on in the minds of the public. The reprobation or stigmatisation associated with a sentence is closely related to the purpose of affirmative prevention. Similarly, putting an end to impunity for the commission of serious violations of international humanitarian law refers to affirmative prevention").

[40] Danner, "Constructing a Hierarchy of Crimes," 489.

the moral demands they are based on in the minds of the public."[41] This dynamic is distinct from general deterrence in that it is not *fear* of punishment that prevents further atrocities, but rather a kind of pervasive moral suasion that leads to habitual lawfulness by instilling subliminal inhibitions against international crimes.

Other, less persuasive factors have also influenced sentencing in the international context. The jurisprudence of the ICTY identifies, for example, individual rehabilitation and national reconciliation. Rehabilitation is distinct from, but related to, special deterrence in that it is aimed at transforming a criminal into a law-abiding person.[42] Reconciliation might also be a factor in sentencing – by way of mitigation, in order to promote healing and the restoration of social normalcy. In *Plavšić*, for example, the former president of Republika Srpska pleaded guilty to the crime against humanity of persecution. According to the ICTY, the guilty plea had a crucial role in "establishing the truth" – which, "together with acceptance of responsibility for the committed wrongs, will promote reconciliation … in Bosnia and Herzegovina and the region as a whole."[43] Thus, Plavšić was sentenced to a mere eleven years' imprisonment in Sweden despite the gravity of the crimes.[44]

Yet other purposes of international criminal law include establishing a historical record, meeting the demands of victim communities, delegitimizing nationalist regimes and racist ideologies, and maintaining a lasting peace.[45] These myriad justifications have led one scholar to point to "an identity crisis in international punishment" and an ever shifting list of factors that both complicates the task of international judges and "undermines the principle of equal treatment."[46]

The diversity and complexity of factors relevant to sentencing in international criminal law – including the gravity of a crime based on factual circumstances, the individual circumstances of a convicted person, and consideration of the multiple objectives of punishment – lead to uncertain and potentially inconsistent sentencing, rendering the task of comparing the relative seriousness of international crimes especially difficult. In particular, absent sentencing tariffs, the

---

[41] Kordić, Appeals Judgement (ICTY, 17 December 2004), para. 1080; Nikolić, Sentencing Judgement (ICTY, 18 December 2003), para. 139.

[42] Dana, "Genocide, Reconciliation and Sentencing," 261.

[43] Plavšić, Sentencing Judgement (ICTY, 27 February 2003), para. 80.

[44] Dana, "Genocide, Reconciliation and Sentencing," 267.

[45] Ibid., 262–64.   [46] Ibid., 264.

practice of a "global sentence" for multiple crimes obscures the relative weight of the factors considered. As William Schabas has noted, sentencing in international criminal law is often little more than an "afterthought."[47]

Bearing these difficulties in mind, what can be gleaned from the actual sentencing practices of the tribunals in our effort to determine the relative gravity of different international crimes?

Sentencing practice at the international criminal tribunals

The principle of proportionality shapes punishment as much in international law as it does in domestic law, and in both contexts it is the gravity of the crime that is the most significant criterion for sentencing. ICTY and ICTR judgments have consistently held that "the overriding obligation in determining sentence is that of fitting the penalty to the gravity of the criminal conduct."[48] ICTY–ICTR jurisprudence recognizes that

although there is no pre-established hierarchy between crimes within the jurisdiction of the Tribunal, and international criminal law does not formally identify categories of offences, it is obvious that, in concrete terms, some criminal behaviours are more serious than others ... [T]he effective gravity of the offences committed is the deciding factor in the determination of the sentence: the principle of gradation or hierarchy in sentencing requires that the longest sentences be reserved for the most serious offences.[49]

A comprehensive 2003 study found that the average sentence meted out at the ICTY for genocide was forty-six years; for crimes against humanity, sixteen years; and for war crimes, eleven years.[50] In a 2010 judgment against seven individuals accused of participating in the

[47] William A. Schabas, "International Sentencing: From Leipzig (1923) to Arusha (1996)," in M. C. Bassiouni, ed., *International Criminal Law*, 2nd edn. (New York: Transnational, 1999), 171.

[48] Banović, Sentencing Judgement (ICTY, 28 October 2003), para. 36; see also Ćesić, Sentencing Judgement (ICTY, 11 March 2004), para. 31; Kamuhanda, Trial Judgement (ICTR, 22 January 2004), para. 765 ("the penalty must first and foremost be commensurate to the gravity of the offense"); Kajelijeli, Trial Judgement (ICTR, 1 December 2003), para. 963 (same).

[49] Nahimana, Appeals Judgement (ICTR, 28 November 2007), para. 1060.

[50] Meernik and King, "The Sentencing Determinants of the International Criminal Tribunal for the Former Yugoslavia: An Empirical and Doctrinal Analysis," 736. As of the time that the study was conducted, however, there had been only one conviction for genocide (Krstić).

Srebrenica massacre, two men found guilty of genocide were sentenced to life imprisonment; one man found guilty of aiding and abetting genocide was sentenced to thirty-five years; three men found guilty of crimes against humanity (including murder) were given sentences ranging from thirteen to nineteen years; and the man found guilty of crimes against humanity (not including murder) was sentenced to only five years.[51]

The rough hierarchy that emerges from ICTY sentencing practice contradicts the assertion in the tribunal's jurisprudence that there is no such ranking of crimes.[52] While in theory judges have rejected graduated sentencing based on the gravity of differing crimes, that is exactly how they have determined the appropriate punishment, notwithstanding the complexities in sentencing discussed above.

If, in practice, there is differential treatment of these crimes in sentencing, can it be explained by reference to the comparative gravity of the respective crimes?

War crimes vs. crimes against humanity

The Erdemović Appeals Judgement

As discussed above, it was the *Erdemović* case that first addressed the existence of a hierarchy among international crimes. The majority of the Appeals Chamber held that *"all things being equal,* a punishable offence, if charged and proven as a crime against humanity, is more serious and should ordinarily entail a heavier penalty than if it were proceeded upon on the basis that it were a war crime."[53] In other words, even if one crime is not categorically more serious than the other, a crime against humanity is more serious and should result in a higher sentence if there is a conviction for both crimes based on the exact same facts.

---

[51] Popović, Trial Judgement (ICTY, 12 June 2010), 832–38.

[52] See, for example, Kunarac, Appeals Judgement (ICTY, 12 June 2002), para. 171.

[53] Erdemović, Appeals Judgement, Joint Separate Opinion of Judge McDonald and Judge Vohrah (ICTY, 7 October 1999), para. 20. This analysis, presented in paragraphs 20 to 27 of the separate opinion, is adopted in paragraph 20 of the Appeals Chamber's judgment:

> [T]he Appeals Chamber, for the reasons set out in the Joint Separate Opinion of Judge McDonald and Judge Vohrah, finds that the guilty plea of the Appellant was not informed and accordingly remits the case to a Trial Chamber other than the one which sentenced the Appellant in order that he be given an opportunity to replead.

In support of this proposition, the Appeals Chamber first examined the elements of each crime, noting that, whereas war crimes "address the criminal conduct of a perpetrator toward an immediate protected object," crimes against humanity "address the perpetrator's conduct not only toward the immediate victim but also toward the whole of humankind."[54] The chamber further remarked:

Crimes against humanity are especially odious forms of misbehavior and in addition form part of a widespread and systematic practice or policy. Because of their heinousness and magnitude they constitute egregious attacks on human dignity, on the very notion of humaneness. They consequently affect, or should affect, each and every member of mankind, whatever his or her nationality, ethnic group and location.[55]

Beyond this nebulous concept of "heinousness and magnitude," the Appeals Chamber explained how the specific elements of crimes against humanity justify its greater moral blameworthiness in comparison to war crimes. In particular, the tribunal reasoned that, unlike war crimes, crimes against humanity require the following additional elements:

[C]rime[s] against humanity: (a) must have been committed as part of the widespread or systematic perpetration of such acts, not necessarily by the accused himself; but certainly (b) in the knowledge that the acts are being or have been committed in pursuance of an organized policy or as part of a widespread or systematic practice against a certain civilian group.[56]

The Appeals Chamber thus concluded that, in terms of proportionality,

[t]he gravity of crimes against humanity when compared with that of war crimes is enhanced by these facets. They indicate that crimes against humanity are not isolated and random acts but acts which will, and which the perpetrator knows will, have far graver consequences because of their additional contribution to a broader scheme of violence against a particular systematically targeted civilian group.[57]

It bears emphasizing that this question was considered in view of Erdemović having been charged with two crimes for the *same* underlying act (that is, the mass murder at Srebrenica). Because crimes against humanity require that the prosecutor prove additional elements – namely, that the massacre was part of a widespread or systematic attack, and that the accused was aware of that context – the Appeals Chamber concluded that it was an inherently more serious crime.

---

[54] *Ibid.*, para. 21.   [55] *Ibid.*
[56] *Ibid.*   [57] *Ibid.*, para. 22.

Since the Appeals Chamber attributed a lower gravity to war crimes, it remitted the case to a new Trial Chamber. Erdemović entered a new guilty plea only for war crimes, and his initial sentence of ten years' imprisonment was reduced to five years'.

The Tadić Sentencing Appeal

The *Tadić* case, the second appeals proceeding at the ICTY, reversed *Erdemović* by rejecting a hierarchy on which war crimes and crimes against humanity were positioned. *Tadić* remains the controlling opinion in ICTY jurisprudence on this matter.[58] Its application of the principle of proportionality in the context of international criminal law, however, gives rise to misgivings.

Dusko Tadić was convicted of multiple counts of war crimes and crimes against humanity for his involvement in the infamous detention camps set up in the Prijedor region of northern Bosnia. The Trial Chamber imposed a higher sentence for his convictions for crimes against humanity than for war crimes, relying upon the *Erdemović* precedent, in addition to authorities in ICTR jurisprudence.[59]

In the appeal on sentencing, Tadić argued that "the sentence imposed on a defendant should reflect the seriousness of the actual acts committed and the defendant's level of culpability for them, and that he should not be exposed to a higher sentence for the same acts simply because of the legal description attached to them."[60] The Appeals Chamber agreed, ruling that

> there is in law no distinction between the seriousness of a crime against humanity and that of a war crime. The Appeals Chamber finds no basis for such a distinction in the Statute or the Rules of the International Tribunal construed in accordance with customary international law; the authorized penalties are also the same, the level in any particular case being fixed by reference to the circumstances of the case.[61]

The separate opinion of Judge Mohamed Shahabuddeen elaborated on the reasoning underlying the majority opinion's ruling in three respects.[62] First, Judge Shahabuddeen drew a distinction "at the level

---

[58] See Popović, Trial Judgement (ICTY, 10 June 2010), para. 2134 (citing Kunarac, Appeals Judgement [ICTY, 12 June 2002], para. 171; Tadić, Judgement in Sentencing Appeals [ICTY, 26 January 2000], para. 69); see also Stakić, Appeals Judgement (ICTY, 22 March 2006), para. 375.

[59] Tadić, Sentencing Judgement (ICTY, 11 November 1999), para. 28.

[60] Tadić, Judgement in Sentencing Appeals (ICTY, 26 January 2000), paras. 65–66.

[61] *Ibid.*, para. 69.

[62] *Ibid.*, Separate Opinion of Judge Shahabuddeen.

of principle" between the "material seriousness" and the "juridical seriousness" of a crime. Second, he claimed that crimes against humanity were originally conceptualized not to create a more serious crime,
but rather simply to fill a lacuna in international criminal law with
respect to victims of atrocities not covered by war crimes. Third, he
observed that the relevant legal sources provide no support for a hierarchy between war crimes and crimes against humanity.

Regarding the first point concerning material and judicial seriousness, Judge Shahabuddeen set forth an explanation that recalls the
earlier discussion in Chapter 2 regarding the relative gravity of murder
and rape:[63]

> As to material seriousness, looking at the character of the acts proscribed by a
> crime, it is generally possible to say that one crime is more serious than another.
> But that does not always translate into the proposition that the former is legally
> more serious than the latter. It may be that in some systems the penalty for
> murder is the same as that for rape; if so, there could be difficulty in saying that
> one offence is legally more serious than the other, even though there could be a
> view (varying from society to society) that, from a material standpoint, there is
> a difference in seriousness. *Unless some other method of juridical ranking is prescribed,*
> *what is significant is the scale of penalties provided. A crime against humanity may be*
> *viewed as the most heinous of all crimes; but, as between it and a war crime, the law of the*
> *Tribunal stipulates no ranking and provides for a common penalty.*[64]

In other words, Judge Shahabuddeen argued that it is possible for one
crime to be more serious than another in the abstract, but to nevertheless result in the same penalty. He thus drew a distinction between
stigma and sentencing, suggesting that greater moral opprobrium does
not necessarily require greater punishment.

Regarding the second point and the lacuna in international criminal
law, Judge Shahabuddeen distinguished between the "use of specified
grounds to criminalize an act not otherwise within the pale of criminality" and the "use of the grounds of criminalization to define the seriousness of the newly created crime in relation to other crimes."[65] He
contended that crimes against humanity first emerged in order to fill
in a normative gap in international criminal law rather than to create a
category of offenses more serious than war crimes. It was because war
crimes did not apply where perpetrators and victims were nationals

[63] See 17–22.
[64] Tadić, Judgement in Sentencing Appeals, Separate Opinion of Judge Shahabuddeen
(ICTY, 26 January 2000), 37–38 (emphasis added).
[65] *Ibid.*, 38.

of the same or of allied states that the Charter of the International Military Tribunal required a new category to prosecute certain atrocities. Thus "the concept of crimes against humanity went to the criminalization of the act on the international plane; it did not go to establish that the crime, once created, was *ipso facto* more serious than a war crime in relation to the same act."[66] For Judge Shahabuddeen, even the requirement of a widespread or systematic attack did not make crimes against humanity

intrinsically more serious than a war crime: what follows from there being no proof that the act was committed in pursuance of such an organized policy or as part of such a widespread or systematic practice is that there is simply no crime cognisable at international law unless the act happens to be a war crime.[67]

Finally, regarding the legal foundation for a hierarchy of international crimes, Judge Shahabuddeen noted that "no suggestion appears in the penal regime of the Tribunal that, as compared with a war crime, a crime against humanity is intrinsically meritorious of severer punishment."[68] He pointed out that neither the ICTY Statute nor the general practice regarding prison sentences in the courts of the former Yugoslavia lends support to the idea that crimes against humanity should be punished more severely.[69]

Upon closer examination, the foregoing arguments are not entirely convincing. With respect to the last argument, the mere fact that there is no sentencing tariff or other formal hierarchy of crimes does not lead to a conclusion that one crime is not more serious than the other, given that such a distinction may be recognized by the exercise of judicial discretion in sentencing. As noted in Judge Cassese's separate opinion in the *Tadić* Sentencing Appeal, the majority mistakenly assumed that the principle of *nulla poena sine praevia lege poenali* – "no crime [can be committed], no punishment [can be imposed], without a previous penal law" – applies in international criminal law in the same way that it does in domestic systems. Judge Cassese pointed out that in "international criminal law the determination of penalties has for long been left to the courts. Only recently have international instruments provided some broad guidelines (but no sentencing tariff)."[70] Thus, the *nulla poena sine praevia* principle is not only "inapplicable in

---

[66] *Ibid.*, 38–40.   [67] *Ibid.*, 42.
[68] *Ibid.*, 46–47.   [69] *Ibid.*, 47.
[70] Tadić, Judgement in Sentencing Appeals, Separate Opinion of Judge Cassese (ICTY, 26 January 2000), para. 4.

international criminal law," but it is also an error to infer anything at all from the silence of the law on this matter.[71] In taking the absence of an explicit sentencing tariff as implying that no alternative method of judicial ranking is available, the majority was, in Cassese's view, engaged in excessive formalism.

With respect to the Appeals Chamber's view that the ICC Statute does not consider war crimes as less serious than other crimes,[72] Article 8(1) of the ICC Statute does indicate that war crimes are less grave than crimes against humanity; it provides that the "Court shall have jurisdiction in respect of war crimes in particular when committed as a part of a plan or policy or as part of a large-scale commission of such crimes." As previously discussed, plan, policy, and scale "are not elements of war crimes."[73] Nonetheless, this provision clearly suggests "that individual war crimes which are not committed as part of a plan or policy shall be prosecuted *only if they are of such a gravity as to indeed be of concern to the international community as a whole.*"[74] In other

---

[71] *Ibid.*

[72] See Tadić, Judgement in Sentencing Appeals, Separate Opinion of Judge Shahabuddeen (ICTY, 26 January 2000), 41:

> Nor does any difference in seriousness appear in the Statute of the International Criminal Court. Article 8(1) of the Statute states that the "Court shall have jurisdiction in respect of war crimes in particular when committed as part of a plan or policy or as part of a large-scale commission of such crimes." ... [T]hat does not say that a war crime cannot be committed in other circumstances; nor does it require proof of the specified circumstances as a necessary ingredient of a war crime. It does however show that a war crime can in fact be committed in the same circumstances as a crime against humanity. The provision does not bear on the relative position of war crimes as a class on any scale of criminality relating to breaches of international humanitarian law generally.

[73] See William J. Fenrick, "Article 8, War Crimes, Paragraph 1," in Otto Triffterer, ed., *Commentary on the Rome Statute of the International Criminal Court* (Baden-Baden, Germany: Nomos, 1999), 181.

[74] See Andreas Zimmermann, "Article 5, Crimes Within the Jurisdiction of the Court," in Otto Triffterer, ed., *Commentary on the Rome Statute of the International Criminal Court*, 2nd edn. (Oxford, UK: Beck/Hart, 2008), 129, 133 (emphasis added) (referring to Article 1 of the ICC Statute, which restricts the Court's jurisdiction to "the most serious crimes of concern to the international community as a whole"). By way of example, situations of such exceptional gravity could include prosecution of an isolated, but especially serious case involving use of poisonous weapons – primarily in order to deter others from committing similar acts – even if the scale and gravity do not amount to a crime against humanity. The undeterred use of such weapons, even if it is not part of a plan or policy and even if it does not actually result in human casualties, could be "of concern to the international community as a whole" because of the implications of a precedent of impunity on future prevention. The same considerations may not necessarily apply to more "routine" war crimes such

words, although war crimes are international crimes falling within the ICC's jurisdiction, as a general rule they are deemed worthy of international prosecution *only if* there is a further element of scale or gravity accompanying their commission. As Judge Cassese wrote in the *Tadić* Sentencing Appeal:

> The drafters of the Statute intended to spell out the notion that in principle the ICC should concentrate on the most egregious instances of war crimes, while lesser categories of such crimes should be prosecuted and tried by national courts to the greatest extent possible. This appeared to them to be warranted by the need for the ICC not to be inundated with war crimes cases that could be easily tried by national courts.[75]

Apparently, the same considerations do not apply to crimes against humanity, presumably because, absent the requirement of a nexus with armed conflict, what distinguishes these crimes from ordinary domestic crimes such as murder or rape is their intrinsic gravity. In other words, crimes against humanity are considered to be so serious that the qualification used for war crimes is not required.[76]

With respect to the normative function of crimes against humanity, Judge Shahabuddeen correctly observed that this new offense was reluctantly incorporated into the Nuremberg Charter in order to avoid jurisdictional lacunae in relation to atrocities that did not fall within the ambit of war crimes. The US Military Tribunal noted in the *Justice* case that "the prohibitions on crimes against humanity [in Control Council Law No. 10] are not surplusage, but are intended to supplement the preceding sections on war crimes by including acts absent from the preceding sections."[77] Beyond this function of supplementing

as isolated murder or rape, when not committed as part of a large-scale attack against a civilian population.

[75] Tadić, Judgement in Sentencing Appeals, Separate Opinion of Judge Cassese (ICTY, 26 January 2000), para. 13.

[76] See Richard May and Marieke Wierda, "Is There a Hierarchy of Crimes in International Law?," in Lal Chand Vohrah, Fausto Pocar, Yvonne Featherstone, Olivier Fourmy, Christine Graham, John Hocking, and Nicholas Robson, eds., *Man's Inhumanity to Man: Essays on International Law in Honour of Antonio Cassese* (The Hague: Kluwer Law International, 2003), 511, 522 ("[T]his requirement ... reflects the fact that all crimes tried by international courts have to meet a minimum jurisdictional threshold of seriousness to qualify as international crimes").

[77] *United States v. Josef Altstoetter (Justice case), Trials of War Criminals Before the Nuremberg Military Tribunals Under Control Council Law No. 10*, vol. III (1949), 972. It should be noted that, unlike the International Military Tribunal, the US Military Tribunal was not applying the Nuremberg Charter as such. Rather, it was "an international tribunal established by the International Control Council, the high legislative

war crimes, however, the relationship between the two crimes was ambiguous. In its *Kupreškić* judgment the ICTY Trial Chamber noted that

at that time the class of "crimes against humanity" had just emerged and there were concerns about whether by convicting defendants of such crimes the courts would be applying *ex post facto* law ... [A]s a consequence, the relevant criminal provisions at the time did not draw a clear-cut distinction between the two classes of crimes.[78]

Based on this historical matrix, the ICTY Appeals Chamber in *Tadić* came to the conclusion that, instead of a hierarchical relationship, the two crimes simply protect different interests. That is, the view was that crimes against humanity were intended as an "alternative" to war crimes when the latter were inapplicable. In this context Bing Bing Jia writes that, although crimes against humanity are

offences which may be committed in armed conflict or time of peace[,] ... [w]hat makes them a distinct type of international crime is, first of all, the fact that they are committed for non-military purposes, in the sense that the aims are not closely related to a military campaign or battle and that they are not part of a military operation plan.[79]

As noted earlier, war crimes and crimes against humanity share the core interest of protecting human dignity. In addition, the underlying acts for both crimes (that is, murder, rape, and so on) relate to fundamental violations of physical integrity. Furthermore, both the ICTY and the ICTR have interpreted the term *civilian population* as a core element of crimes against humanity in light of humanitarian law: "To the extent that the alleged crimes against humanity were committed in the course of an armed conflict, the laws of war provide

branch of the four Allied Powers ... controlling Germany (Control Council Law No. 10, 20 Dec. 1945)" (see *Trial of Frederick Flick and Five Others (Flick case)*, *Trials of War Criminals Before the Nuremberg Military Tribunals Under Control Council Law No. 10*, vol. VI [1949], 1188). Its provisions with respect to war crimes and crimes against humanity, however, were virtually identical to those contained in the Nuremberg Charter.

[78] Kupreškić, Trial Judgement (ICTY, 14 January 2000), para. 676.
[79] See Bing Bing Jia, "The Differing Concepts of War Crimes and Crimes Against Humanity in International Criminal Law," in Guy S. Goodwin-Gill and Stefan Tahuon, eds., *The Reality of International Law: Essays in Honour of Ian Brownlie* (Oxford, UK: Oxford University Press, 1999), 27. This article is quoted because it seems to have influenced the ICTY judges. See, for example, Tadić, Judgement in Sentencing Appeals, Separate Opinion of Judge Shahabuddeen (ICTY, 26 January 2000), 36 note 7.

a benchmark against which the Chamber may assess the nature of the attack and the legality of the acts committed in its midst."[80] In substance, therefore, war crimes committed on a widespread or systematic scale amount to crimes against humanity. Although a war crime is not formally a "lesser included offence,"[81] it is reasonable to conclude that, in situations of armed conflict involving fundamental violations of the physical integrity of civilians, the widespread or systematic occurrence of war crimes is subsumed by crimes against humanity.[82] The implication is that the category of crimes against humanity was not intended merely to fill a gap in international law or to supplement war crimes, but also to create a new, broader, and more serious "umbrella" crime.

Finally, notwithstanding Judge Shahabuddeen's argument that "material seriousness" can be distinguished from "juridical seriousness," the legal elements of crimes against humanity suggest that, all things being equal, it is the more serious offense juridically. It may be true that, either *in abstracto* or if a war crime and crime against humanity charge are totally factually unrelated, a comparison of relative gravity may be a difficult task. For example, the use of poison gas to kill thousands of soldiers in combat qualifies only as a war crime because there is no attack against a civilian population, but it may be more serious than a single opportunistic killing that qualifies as

---

[80] Kunarac, Appeals Judgement (ICTY, 12 June 2002), para. 91; see also Martić, Appeals Judgement (ICTY, 8 October 2008), paras. 299, 302 ("the Appeals Chamber finds that the definition of civilian contained in Article 50 of Additional Protocol I reflects the definition of civilian for the purpose of applying Article 5 of the Statute and that the Trial Chamber did not err in finding that the term civilian in that context did not include persons *hors de combat*"). The ICTR has also sought to define *civilian* by reference to the laws of war, but unlike the ICTY (which excludes soldiers *hors de combat* from the notion of *civilian*), *civilian* is defined in the controlling *Akayesu* judgment as "people who are not taking any active part in the hostilities, including members of the armed forces who laid down their arms and those persons placed hors de combat by sickness, wounds, detention or any other cause." The *Akayesu* Trial Chamber noted that "this definition assimilates the definition of 'civilian' to the categories of person protected by Common Article 3 of the Geneva Conventions; an assimilation which would not appear to be problematic": Akayesu, Trial Judgement (ICTR, 2 September 1998), para. 582 note 146; see also Bisengimana, Trial Judgement (ICTR, 13 April 2006), para. 48 (noting that the *Akayesu* definition has been consistently followed in the jurisprudence).

[81] Kunarac, Appeals Judgement (ICTY, 12 June 2002), paras. 171–72; Jelisić, Appeals Judgement (ICTY, 5 July 2001), para. 82; see also Akayesu, Trial Judgement (ICTR, 2 September 1998), para. 470.

[82] See, for example, Kupreškić, Trial Judgement (ICTY, 14 January 2000), paras. 698–704.

a crime against humanity because it is linked to widespread or systematic persecutory violence against an ethnic group. However, if we are to move beyond the formalism embraced by the ICTY Appeals Chamber in *Tadić*, the relative gravity of the respective crimes may be assessed based on a substantive comparison of their elements. Indeed, the general principles of criminal law relating to proportionality may require such an analysis. Even if sentencing is disregarded, the mere stigma attached to particular types of conduct is itself part of the punishment and thus implicates normative ranking or "juridical seriousness." At the very least, it may be concluded based even on Judge Shahabuddeen's analysis that, if the facts are identical with respect to a charge of war crimes and crimes against humanity, the latter is the more serious offense.

In comparing the two categories, it may be contended that, insofar as crimes against humanity apply outside the context of armed conflict, war crimes should be considered more serious because the "code of chivalry" among combatants[83] requires of them a higher degree of valor than is required of civilians.[84] In the *Corfu Channel* case, however, the International Court of Justice referred to "certain general and well recognized principles, namely: elementary considerations of humanity, *even more exacting in peace than in war.*"[85] Indeed, excesses committed in the intrinsically inhumane context of war may be regarded as less reprehensible than those committed in peacetime, with its greater possibilities for deliberation and self-restraint. What is most important, however, is the mental element distinguishing these two categories.

The view that war crimes and crimes against humanity are objectively different, but not different in terms of gravity, overlooks the basic assumptions underlying the principle of proportionality in criminal law. The degree of blameworthiness that retributive theory attaches to each of the two categories hinges primarily on the subjective or mental element of crimes. As discussed in Chapter 2, the retributive theory

---

[83] See generally, Robert C. Stacey, "The Age of Chivalry," in Michael Howard, George J. Andropoulos, and Mark R. Shulman, eds., *The Laws of War: Constraints of Warfare in the Western World* (New Haven: Yale University Press, 1994), 27.

[84] See, for example, Erdemović, Appeals Judgement, Joint Separate Opinion of Judge McDonald and Judge Vohrah (ICTY, 7 October 1997), para. 84 (expressing the view that "soldiers or combatants are expected to exercise fortitude and a greater degree of resistance to a threat than civilians ... Soldiers, by the very nature of their occupation, must have envisaged the possibility of violent death in pursuance of the cause for which they fight").

[85] 1949 ICJ Rep. 4, 22 (emphasis added).

of punishment posits that, in exercising free moral choice, those who willingly make evil choices are "blameworthy" and "deserve" punishment, and that punishment should be proportionate to the degree of blameworthiness, or moral turpitude, attached to particular conduct. In comparing two crimes, if one contains an additional element of *mens rea* or requires proof that the accused intended a greater harm, it follows that a greater degree of blameworthiness is attached to that crime.

Deterrence, in turn, posits that the prospective criminal is a rational calculator exercising choice, such that the prospective punishment deters the potential criminal by counterbalancing and outweighing the benefits of the criminal act in question. In terms of "wrongdoing" under the deterrence principle, punishment is apportioned according to the importance of the social interest that is threatened, in order to differentiate the incentives for avoiding particular categories of crime. If the punishment and stigma attached to two crimes are identical, even though one of the crimes requires an additional element of *mens rea* or a further dimension of dangerous criminality, the capacity to deter the greater harm is undermined because there is no incentive not to commit the more serious offense.

The importance of the mental element in determining the gravity of an offense cannot be overemphasized. Stephen Schulhofer points out that an emphasis on actual harm, rather than intention to cause harm, is contrary to the purposes of punishment, such as deterrence and retribution:

If, for example, a person attacks his wife and tries to kill her, he will be guilty of assault and attempted murder even if she escapes unharmed. He will also commit a battery if she is injured, mayhem if the injury is of certain especially serious types, and murder if she dies. The applicable penalties generally increase accordingly.[86]

He points out, however, that

both the defendant's state of mind and his actions may have been identical in all four of the cases supposed. The precise location of a knife or gunshot wound, the speed of intervention by neighbors or the police, these and many other factors wholly outside the knowledge or control of the defendant may determine the ultimate result. Accordingly, the differences in legal treatment

[86] Stephen J. Schulhofer, "Harm and Punishment: A Critique of Emphasis on the Results of Conduct in the Criminal Law," *University of Pennsylvania Law Review* 122 (1974): 1498.

would seem at first blush inconsistent with such purposes of the criminal law as deterrence, rehabilitation, isolation of the dangerous, and even retribution – in the sense of punishment in accordance with moral blame.[87]

Schulhofer thus maintains that the unsuccessful or partial execution of a crime should be treated exactly the same as its successful or complete execution:

[S]anctions are assumed to influence people at the point at which they embark on a given course of anti-social conduct, with certain perceptions as to its potential consequences ... [T]here is ... some reason at least to begin with the assumption that where conduct and the actor's perceptions as to its consequences are the same, the penalty should be the same, regardless of the actual outcome.[88]

Although Schulhofer's position is powerfully presented and persuasive up to a point, it needs to be noted that there are cogent arguments for treating inchoate or attempted crimes as less serious; for example, if the penalty will be the same anyway, then the attempted murderer might be tempted to "finish off" his victim. The aim of the present discussion, however, is not to provide a comprehensive analysis of inchoate crimes, but rather to emphasize the primacy of intention, as opposed to actual harm, in modern theories of criminal law.

Indeed, an intention- rather than a results-oriented approach to punishment appears consistent with the overall evolution of the contemporary criminal law. It is increasingly apparent that the focus of social protection should be the mind of the actor, and not the act itself. As George Fletcher notes in relation to criminal attempts:

In [the twentieth] century, a subtle shift has occurred in the danger perceived in criminal attempts. For many who favor earlier stages of liability, the question is not whether the act is dangerous to a specific potential victim, but whether the *actor* is dangerous to society as a whole. *As those who worked on the [US] Model Penal Code expressed their philosophy of criminalization: "The basic premise here is that the actor's mind is the best proving ground of his dangerousness."* The shift from act to mind, then, coincides with a shift from focusing on the threats posed by dangerous actions to the danger posed by dangerous people.[89]

When viewed from the perspective of retribution, the perpetrator's degree of blameworthiness should be based on the intention behind

---

[87] *Ibid.*, 1498.   [88] *Ibid.*, 1602.
[89] George P. Fletcher, *Basic Concepts of Criminal Law* (Oxford, UK: Oxford University Press, 1998), 177 (emphasis added).

the conduct rather than its actual result. As Schulhofer observes, "Moral culpability may turn on the nature of the acts committed, the offender's motives and intent, extenuating circumstances, and so on, but the occurrence of harm has no apparent bearing on the degree of moral blameworthiness."[90]

It would seem, then, that, as a general principle, it is the mental element that determines the degrees of blameworthiness or gravity of a crime. For example, a perpetrator may bring about the material or objective element of killing through the infliction of grievous bodily harm resulting in the death of a victim, but various mental or subject-ive states, including premeditation, intention, or recklessness, result in different legal classifications of the crime. In each case, the objective or material element is identical – namely, the death of the victim through the infliction of grievous bodily harm. But the gravity of the conduct depends primarily on the mental element required for each particular category of crime.[91] Similarly, even if the material element of murder-ing a civilian is identical, the category of war crimes requires a lesser mental element than that pertaining to crimes against humanity.

This difference in the mental element explains why crimes against humanity may not be more serious than war crimes *in abstracto*, but more serious when applied to the same material facts. In his separ-ate opinion in the *Tadić* Appeals Judgement, Judge Cassese recognized that

some categories of crimes which, in theory, might be considered as less serious than other categories, may in practice instead prove inherently much graver: suffice it to mention war crimes such as the bombardment of an undefended town or the killing of hundreds of enemy combatants through the use of pro-hibited weapons. It goes without saying that these instances of war crimes may in practice turn out to be more inhumane and devastating than some instances of crimes against humanity such as the deportation or imprisonment of civil-ians ... [O]ne cannot say that a certain class of international crimes encom-passes facts that are more serious than those prohibited under a different criminal provision. *In abstracto* all international crimes are serious offences and no hierarchy of gravity may *a priori* be established between them.[92]

But that is not to say that there is no hierarchy whatsoever among the core international crimes. Judge Cassese noted that, in assessing

[90] *Ibid.* [91] *Ibid.*, 76.
[92] Tadić, Judgement in Sentencing Appeals, Separate Opinion of Judge Cassese (ICTY, 26 January 2000), paras. 6–7.

the degree of wrongdoing, it must be determined "whether *the very same fact imputed to an accused*, if characterized as a war crime, may be regarded as more or less serious than if it is instead defined as a crime against humanity."[93] In order for murder to be classified as a war crime, "it is sufficient for the *actus reus* to consist of the death of the victim as a result of the acts or omissions of the perpetrator, while the requisite mental element must be the intent to kill or to inflict serious injury in reckless disregard of human life."[94] For murder to be classified as a crime against humanity, however, the act must "be part of a widespread or systematic practice," and "the murderer must have acted in the knowledge that his or her conduct formed part of this overall context."[95] Based on these differing mental elements,

[i]t follows that the murder at issue forms part of a whole pattern of criminality, and may amount to ... "system criminality" (encompassing large-scale crimes perpetrated to advance the war effort, at the request of, or with the encouragement or toleration of government authorities), as opposed to "individual criminality" (embracing crimes committed by combatants on their own initiative and often for reasons known only to themselves). In addition, the requisite intent of the perpetrator is more serious than in murder as a "war crime": the perpetrator must not only intend to cause the death of one or more persons, but must have done so while being aware that this conduct was a common practice.[96]

Judge Cassese thus maintained that, in the case of a crime against humanity, "the murder possesses an objectively greater magnitude and reveals in the perpetrator a subjective frame of mind which may imperil fundamental values of the international community to a greater extent than in the case where that offence should instead be labeled as a war crime." In such circumstances, the "international community and the judicial bodies responsible for ensuring international criminal justice therefore have a strong societal interest in imposing a heavier penalty upon the author of such a crime against humanity, thereby also deterring similar crimes."[97] He concluded:

[93] *Ibid.*, para. 10.   [94] *Ibid.*, para. 12.   [95] *Ibid.*, para. 14.
[96] *Ibid.*, paras. 12, 14. It should be noted that references in this excerpt to "large-scale crimes perpetrated to advance the war effort, at the request of, or with the encouragement or toleration of government authorities" form a contentious definition of an element of crimes against humanity and do not necessarily reflect the current state of ICTY jurisprudence (see 37–39).
[97] Tadić, Judgement in Sentencing Appeals, Separate Opinion of Judge Cassese (ICTY, 26 January 2000), para. 15.

If the above considerations are accepted, it follows that whenever an offence committed by an accused is deemed to be a "crime against humanity," it must be regarded as inherently of greater gravity, all else being equal (ceteris paribus), than if it is instead characterised as a "war crime." Consequently, it must entail a heavier penalty (of course, the possible impact of extenuating or aggravating circumstances is a different matter which may in practice nevertheless have a significant bearing upon the eventual sentence).[98]

In summary, notwithstanding the absence of sentencing tariffs, the complexities of combining "gravity of crime" with "individual circumstances" and broader social objectives, and the difficulties associated with categorizing crimes against humanity as inherently more serious than war crimes *in abstracto*, the principle of proportionality justifies and indeed requires a hierarchy, at least where such charges have an identical factual basis. Moreover, despite the rejection of a formal hierarchy, the sentencing practices of the ICTY and the ICTR have, in fact, differentiated between war crimes and crimes against humanity. As set forth below, the hierarchical relationship between crimes against humanity and genocide is even more apparent. However, genocide remains far from achieving the exalted status of a "crime of crimes" that is an inherently more serious category of wrongdoing.

Genocide vs. crimes against humanity

In contrast to the comparison between war crimes and crimes against humanity, there is somewhat greater authority suggesting that genocide is more serious than crimes against humanity. This difference reflects the fact that, unlike war crimes, genocide specifically emerged as a particular species of the broader category of crimes against humanity. From its very inception in treaty law, the greater gravity of the crime of genocide was reflected by the resolve of the international community to adopt the Genocide Convention, while leaving crimes against humanity to the less urgent Formulation of the Nuremberg Principles and the Draft Code of Offences Against Peace and Security. As the UN secretary-general noted in the *travaux préparatoires*, in adopting the convention, the "General Assembly wished to give *special treatment* to the crime of genocide because of the *particular gravity* of that crime, which aims at the systematic extermination of

---

[98] *Ibid.*, para. 16.

human groups."[99] In contrasting the general category of crimes against
humanity with genocide, it was pointed out that

the treatment of certain criminal acts falling within the same category as distinct offences is not innovation. Examples exist in state penal systems. Thus
homicide which is the denial of an individual human being's right to live
is divided into several different categories: manslaughter, homicide, murder,
and even parricide or regicide.[100]

Thus, although all crimes against humanity "shock the conscience of
humankind," genocide was considered to occupy a more specific niche
as the *ultimate* international crime, thus warranting the prompt adoption of an international treaty. Soon after the adoption of the convention, the privileged status of genocide was confirmed in jurisprudence,
including the *Justice* case, in which the US Military Tribunal held that
genocide was "the prime illustration of a crime against humanity."[101]
Similarly, in the *Eichmann* case, the District Court of Jerusalem affirmed
that genocide was "the gravest type of 'crime against humanity.'"[102]

   The particular gravity of genocide was also reflected in the deliberations leading to the adoption of the ICC Statute. In particular, the
initial Draft Statute for an International Criminal Court submitted by
the International Law Commission to the General Assembly in 1994[103]
proposed "inherent jurisdiction" solely over the crime of genocide,
whereas states parties could opt in or out of other crimes. In supporting this proposal, the commission was of the view that

the prohibition of genocide is of such fundamental significance, and the occasions for legitimate doubt or dispute over whether a given situation amounts to
genocide are so limited, that the Court ought, exceptionally, to have inherent
jurisdiction over it by virtue solely of States participating in the draft Statute,
without any further requirement of consent or acceptance by any particular
State.[104]

---

[99] Ad Hoc Committee on Genocide, Relations Between the Convention on Genocide
on the One Hand and the Formulation of the Nuremberg Principles and the
Preparation of a Draft Code of Offences Against Peace and Security on the Other,
UN Doc. E/AC.25/3 (1948), 6 (emphasis added).
[100] *Ibid.*
[101] *United States v. Josef Altstoetter (Justice case), Trials of War Criminals Before the Nuremberg
Military Tribunals Under Control Council Law No. 10*, vol. III (1949), 983.
[102] Attorney General of Israel v. Eichmann, 36 I.L.R. 18, 41 (District Court of Jerusalem,
1961).
[103] See *Report of the International Law Commission on the Work of its Forty-sixth Session*, UN
GAOR, 49th Sess., Supp. No. 10, at 29, UN Doc. A/49/10 (1994).
[104] *Ibid.*, 67–68.

In response to the view of some commission members that favored inherent jurisdiction over a broader range of crimes, Christian Tomuschat maintained: "Genocide was undeniably the most horrible and atrocious of crimes under general international law and he found it incomprehensible that anyone could be reproached for placing too much emphasis on it."[105] Similarly, James Crawford pointed out: "Among what were described as the 'crime of crimes,' genocide was the worst of all."[106] Although inherent jurisdiction was eventually applied to all the core international crimes under the ICC Statute, Schabas observed that the International Law Commission's initial proposal "confirmed genocide's position at the apex of the pyramid of international crimes."[107]

As noted at the end of Chapter 3, the jurisprudence of the ICTR has been ambiguous as to the status of genocide and the question of a hierarchy of international crimes. The *Akayesu* and *Kambanda* judgments of 1998 were at odds with one another, with the former rejecting and the latter embracing a hierarchy of crimes. That said, however, the ICTR seems largely to have accepted the *Kambanda* Trial Chamber's position that war crimes are of lesser gravity than crimes against humanity and genocide:

The Chamber has no doubt that despite the gravity of the violations of Article 3 common to the Geneva Conventions and of the Additional Protocol II thereto, they are considered as lesser crimes than genocide or crimes against humanity. On the other hand, it seems more difficult for the Chamber to rank genocide and crimes against humanity in terms of their respective gravity. The Chamber holds that crimes against humanity, already punished by the Nuremberg and Tokyo Tribunals, and genocide, a concept defined later, are crimes which particularly shock the collective conscience. The Chamber notes in this regard that the crimes prosecuted by the Nuremberg Tribunal, namely the holocaust of the Jews or the "Final Solution," were very much constitutive of genocide, but they could not be defined as such because the crime of genocide was not defined until later.[108]

Although the Trial Chamber recognized the difficulty of distinguishing the gravity of crimes against humanity and that of genocide, it went on to note:

---

[105] *Yearbook of the International Law Commission 1994*, vol. I, 214, para. 21.

[106] *Ibid.*, 208, para. 41.

[107] William A. Schabas, *Genocide in International Law* (Cambridge, UK : Cambridge University Press, 2000), 91.

[108] Kambanda, Trial Judgement (ICTR, 4 September 1998), para. 14.

The crime of genocide is unique because of its element of *dolus specialis* (special intent) which requires that the crime be committed with the intent to destroy in whole or in part, "a national, ethnic, racial or religious group as such"; hence the Chamber is of the opinion that genocide constitutes the *crime of crimes*, which must be taken into account when deciding the sentence.[109]

This hierarchy among the core international crimes was followed in subsequent ICTR decisions in which genocide was referred to as "the gravest crime"[110] and systematically resulted in a higher sentence.[111]

Later decisions, however, tended to equivocate on this point, perhaps influenced by the ICTY's jurisprudence that there was no hierarchy of international crimes.[112] In the 1999 *Kayishema* case, the Trial Chamber cited the *Kambanda* dictum that genocide was the "crime of crimes" in determining the accused's sentence for genocide,[113] but upon review the Appeals Chamber held that

there is no hierarchy of crimes under the Statute, and all of the crimes specified therein are "serious violations of international humanitarian law," capable of attracting the same sentence ... The Appeals Chamber finds that the Trial Chamber's description of genocide as the "crime of crimes" was at the level of general appreciation, and did not impact on the sentence it imposed. Furthermore, upon examining the statements of the Trial Chamber, it is evident that the primary thrust of its finding as to the gravity of the offences relates to the fact that genocide in itself is a crime that is extremely grave. Such an observation is correct, and for these reasons, there was no error in its finding on this point.[114]

Although this reasoning has been followed in some later cases,[115] the *crime of crimes* nomenclature has subsequently been used by the

---

[109] *Ibid.*, para. 16 (emphasis added).

[110] Akayesu, Trial Judgement (ICTR, 2 September 1998), para. 470.

[111] See, for example, summary of ICTR jurisprudence on this point in Blaškić, Trial Judgement (ICTY, 3 March 2000), para. 800 (noting that convictions for genocide at the ICTR all resulted in life imprisonment, with one exception).

[112] It may be observed that at least one judge from the *Tadić* Judgement in Sentencing Appeals (which, as discussed above, denied a hierarchy of crimes), Mohamed Shahabuddeen, became a member of the ICTR Appeals Chamber and sat on the *Kayishema* Appeals Chamber. Generally, several other Appeals Chamber judges from the ICTY also came to sit on the ICTR Appeals Chamber, which may explain the subsequent confluence of jurisprudence on this point.

[113] Kayishema, Trial Judgement, Sentence (ICTR, 21 May 1999), para. 9.

[114] Kayishema, Appeals Judgement (ICTR, 1 June 2001), para. 367.

[115] Rutganda, Appeals Judgement (ICTR, 26 May 2003), para. 590; Seromba, Trial Judgement (ICTR, 13 December 2006), para. 381; Nahimana, Appeals Judgement (ICTR, 28 November 2007), para. 1060.

Appeals Chamber,[116] and it seems, as the *Kayishema* Appeals Judgement itself states, that in practice – at the "level of general appreciation" – genocide is considered to be the most serious crime.[117] This assessment apparently relates to the additional stigma of this particular crime rather than to a requirement of higher sentencing.

As in the case of comparing war crimes to crimes against humanity, the mental element of genocide merits further consideration. As discussed earlier, genocide requires an additional mental element, a further dimension of moral turpitude, compared to the crime against humanity of persecution.[118] A perpetrator of persecution chooses his victim because of that individual's membership in a particular group; the *génocidaire* does the same but goes a step further in intending to destroy the group as such. In other words, the category of persecution seeks to protect a group from discriminatory acts, whereas that of genocide seeks to protect the group's very physical existence. As the ICTY recognized in the *Kupreškić* Trial Judgement:

> From the viewpoint of *mens rea*, genocide is an extreme and most inhuman form of persecution. To put it differently, when persecution escalates to the extreme form of wilful and deliberate acts designed to destroy a group or part of a group, it can be held that such persecution amounts to genocide.[119]

A complicating factor in asserting that genocide is categorically more serious than crimes against humanity is the exclusion of political, social, and other "identifiable" groups from the scope of protection of the Genocide Convention. In effect, the effort to destroy a political or social group qualifies *only* as the crime against humanity of extermination or persecution. It is unclear why mass murder against such groups "as such" is lesser in gravity than similar acts against members of "national, ethnic, racial, or religious" groups.

In defense of the exclusion of certain groups under the Genocide Convention, Schabas maintains:

> Attacks on groups defined on the basis of race, nationality, ethnicity and religion have been elevated, by the Genocide Convention, to the apex of human

---

[116] Niyitegeka, Appeals Judgement (ICTR, 9 July 2004), para. 53.

[117] See also Rutaganda, Appeals Judgement (ICTR, 26 May 2003), para. 590 (similarly holding that there is no hierarchy but declining to overturn a trial judgment that had referred to genocide as the "crime of crimes").

[118] See 42–43.

[119] Kupreškić, Trial Judgement (ICTY, 14 January 2000), para. 636; see also Brdjanin, Trial Judgement (ICTY, 1 September 2004), para. 699.

rights atrocities, and with good reason. The definition is a narrow one, it is true, but recent history has disproven the claim that it was too restrictive to be of any practical application. For society to define a crime so heinous that it will occur only rarely is testimony to the value of such a precise formulation. Diluting the definition, either by formal amendment of its terms or by extravagant interpretation of the existing text, risks trivializing the horror of the real crime when it is committed.[120]

Although Schabas's view has merit, there is no obvious difference between mass murder in Bosnia or Rwanda, for example, and the mass murder of millions in the Stalinist Soviet Union or in Cambodia under the Khmer Rouge, solely because of their belonging to particular political or social groups. It is difficult to see how the inclusion of such groups or the characterization of such events as genocide risks "trivializing the horror" represented by this crime. Indeed, the *travaux préparatoires* of the Genocide Convention indicate that exclusion of such groups was the result of questionable political motives rather than "good reason," as suggested by Schabas. This issue is considered at greater length in Chapter 5. For present purposes, it is sufficient to observe that, notwithstanding the exclusion of certain groups under the definition of genocide, the crime against humanity of extermination or persecution still requires a lower mental element compared to the *dolus specialis* of genocide, whether in terms of degree or scope. Extermination subsumes the elements of murder and merely requires that, in addition, the killings occur on a mass scale.[121] Unlike persecution, it does not require discriminatory intention and, unlike genocide, it does not require an intention to destroy a protected group "as such." In other words, although these crimes against humanity encompass the destruction of political, social, or other groups not falling within the ambit of genocide, they do not require the *dolus specialis* that is the distinguishing element of genocide.

The same mental element that distinguishes genocide, however, raises other questions as to whether it is categorically more serious than crimes against humanity. In particular, as previously discussed, it is sufficient *ex hypothesi* for a conviction of genocide that the perpetrator committed a single killing with the requisite *dolus specialis* to destroy a group, irrespective of the objective existence of a broader

---

[120] William A. Schabas, *Genocide in International Law: The Crime of Crimes*, 2nd edn. (Cambridge: Cambridge University Press, 2009), 133.

[121] Ntakirutimana and Ntakirutimana Appeals Judgement (ICTR, 13 December 2004), paras. 522, 542; Stakić, Appeals Judgement (ICTY, 22 March 2006), para. 260.

context. It may be recalled that, with crimes against humanity, a single killing may be sufficient provided that the perpetrator has knowledge that his or her act is linked to the broader context of a widespread or systematic attack, implying the objective existence of such an attack. A crime against humanity is committed in a context where there will necessarily be a multiplicity of victims, whereas a genocide may, in theory, have only a single victim. This theoretical possibility may lead some to conclude that genocide is not necessarily more serious than crimes against humanity.[122]

From a legal viewpoint, it may be concluded that genocide is the ultimate crime only in a limited and qualified sense. As with the comparison between war crimes and crimes against humanity, genocide is not more serious categorically, but carries a higher stigma and sentence where, all else being equal, the same conduct is charged variously under war crimes, crimes against humanity, and genocide. This result may be a disappointing one insofar as genocide is considered to be the pinnacle of evil. It is paradoxical that the logic of the same international law within which this supernorm first emerged fails to confer on genocide anything but a limited and qualified hierarchical distinction. Where, then, does this word derive its power? The answer is found not in the dispassionate realm of legal reasoning, but rather, as we shall see, in the unspeakable anguish of a man for whom words became expressions of mourning in search of an elusive closure.

---

[122] See, for example, M. Cherif Bassiouni, *Crimes Against Humanity in International Law* (New York: Knopf, 1992), 473–74. In discussing the pre-Rome Statute lacunae in the law of crimes against humanity, he questioned "if it is logical to have a legal scheme whereby the intentional killing of a single person can be genocide and the killing of millions of persons without intent to destroy the protected group in whole or in part is not an international crime."

5 Naming the nameless crime

On 9 December 1948, after a protracted drafting process that lasted nearly two years,[1] the Genocide Convention was adopted by the UN General Assembly, one day before the adoption of the Universal Declaration of Human Rights.[2] The convention was the United Nations' first international human rights instrument, but it was more than just a legal instrument. The Nuremberg Tribunal had initiated a purification process within the international community, and the convention was its endpoint – the final legal ritual in condemning Nazi crimes. The convention's preamble solemnly declared that genocide is "contrary to the spirit and aims of the United Nations and condemned by the civilized world," and expressed the conviction that international cooperation is required "in order to liberate mankind from such an odious scourge." To that end, pursuant to Article I of the convention, "Contracting Parties confirm that genocide, whether committed in time of peace or in time of war, is a crime under international law which they undertake to prevent and to punish."

On that day, in "the grand Palais de Chaillot in Paris where the UN Assembly had been meeting, the excitement was palpable." When the 55–0 vote was announced, a "storm of applause rocked the hall. It came from the delegates and from the gallery filled with observers, lobbyists, and ordinary citizens."[3] Herbert Evatt, the Australian president of the UN General Assembly, triumphantly announced that "the supremacy

---

[1] For a comprehensive overview of the drafting process, which began in early 1947, see William A. Schabas, *Genocide in International Law: The Crime of Crimes*, 2nd edn. (Cambridge: Cambridge University Press, 2009), 59–116.

[2] General Assembly Resolution 260A (III) (9 December 1948).

[3] William Korey, *An Epitaph for Raphael Lemkin* (New York: Jacon Blaustein Institute for the Advancement of Human Rights, 2001), 1.

of international law had been proclaimed and a significant advance had been made in the development of international criminal law."[4] All knew that the historic convention was largely the product of a single man, Polish jurist and philologist Raphaël Lemkin. As John Humphrey noted in his diaries, "Never in the history of the United Nations has one private individual conducted such a lobby."[5] Steven Jacobs explains that Lemkin was

the man primarily responsible for the United Nations' passage of the Genocide Convention by virtue of his own untiring efforts in calling upon UN delegates daily and writing literally hundreds upon hundreds of letters worldwide to the great, near-great, and ordinary in all walks of life to enlist their support for its passage.[6]

As the applause echoed through the General Assembly, President Evatt descended from the podium to congratulate Lemkin. The foreign minister of Pakistan joked that the United Nations' first human rights treaty should be called the "Lemkin Convention."[7]

Seizing on the importance of this unprecedented development in international law, a group of journalists rushed from the hall to file their stories but soon returned to get a quote from the man who had made it all happen. John Hohenberg, a writer for the *New York Post*, recalled:

Through session after session and hearing after hearing, the lonely crusader steered his precious Convention through the intricacies of United Nations procedures. And finally, on December 9, 1948, he sat in the General Assembly session at the Palais de Chaillot in Paris and witnessed the adoption by a unanimous vote of what has come to be known formally as the United Nations Convention on the Prevention and Punishment of the Crime of Genocide.

Now, he was a story in every sense of the word and worthy of a cabled interview. But after we had filed our pieces on the Genocide Convention, we looked everywhere and found not a trace of him. Had he been in character, he should have been strutting proudly in the corridors, proclaiming his own merit and the virtues of the protocol that had been his dream. But in this, his finest hour, he was gone.

---

[4] See UN GAOR, 3rd Sess., 179th plen. mtg., 852, UN Doc. A/PV.179 (1948).
[5] John P. Humphrey, *Human Rights and the United Nations: A Great Adventure* (New York: Transnational, 1984), 54.
[6] Steven L. Jacobs, "Lemkin, Raphael," in Israel W. Charney, ed., *Encyclopedia of Genocide*, vol. II (Santa Barbara, CA: ABC-CL10, 1999), 403–04.
[7] Korey, *An Epitaph for Raphael Lemkin*, 1.

It was A. M. Rosenthal of *The New York Times*, I think, who finally guessed what had happened and led some of us into the darkened Assembly chamber in the Palais de Chaillot. The session had long since adjourned. On the stage where the President of the Assembly had proclaimed the unanimous adoption of the Genocide Convention, a cleaning woman was moving back and forth in the eerie light of a single electric bulb. And below, in the same seat he had occupied that day, was Raphael Lemkin.

When we went to him and said we wanted an interview, he begged off. "Let me stay here alone," he muttered, and the tears rolled down his cheeks. And this was a man we had thought to be a clown, a publicity hound, a self-seeking fanatic.[8]

Ever since he coined the word *genocide* in his book *Axis Rule in Occupied Europe*, published in 1944,[9] Lemkin had worked tirelessly for the day that international law would finally prohibit this heinous crime. But the adoption of the convention was not merely a great accomplishment for a learned jurist and passionate advocate of international law. It was also deeply personal. Lemkin, a Polish Jew, had lost forty-nine members of his family in the Holocaust, including all of his uncles, aunts, and cousins save two. Most crushing of all was the death of his parents, particularly his mother.[10] He had once called the convention "an epitaph on my mother's grave,"[11] and in his autobiography described it as the transformation of his anguish into a "moral striking force."[12] Behind this apparent success was a man deep in mourning, attempting to render the enormity of his suffering manageable within the confines of legal abstractions and treaty drafting. Lemkin's juridical and linguistic accomplishment was extraordinary, a singular contribution to international law that exhausted both his abilities and his resources. He died in 1959, penniless and alone, from a massive heart attack in a shabby one-room apartment in Manhattan.[13]

---

[8] John Hohenberg, "The Crusade That Changed the UN," *Saturday Review*, 9 November 1968.

[9] Raphael Lemkin, *Axis Rule in Occupied Europe: Laws of Occupation, Analysis of Government, Proposals for Redress* (Washington, DC: Carnegie Endowment for International Peace, 1944).

[10] John Cooper, *Raphael Lemkin and the Struggle for the Genocide Convention* (New York: Palgrave Macmillan, 2008), 72.

[11] Mary Harrington, "Save Lives, Cultures, Souls," *New York Post Home News Magazine*, 17 June 1948 (as cited in Korey, *An Epitaph for Raphael Lemkin*, 2).

[12] Raphael Lemkin, *Totally Unofficial: The Autobiography of Dr. Raphael Lemkin*, 3 (unpublished, undated manuscript, in New York Public Library, Manuscript and Archives Division, Raphael Lemkin Papers, Box 2: Bio- and Autobiographical Sketches of Lemkin).

[13] Jacobs, "Lemkin, Raphael," 403.

Raphaël Lemkin: a biographical sketch

Lemkin's story says much about the deeper meaning underlying the word *genocide* – that is, beyond its legal definition. As a young Jewish boy growing up in Poland in the early 1900s, Lemkin had tasted the bitter fruit of anti-Semitism. But in his memoirs, he downplayed the significance of this trauma in provoking his interest in group-based discrimination.[14] He attributed his initial curiosity in the subject to the novel *Quo Vadis* by the Polish writer Henryk Sienkiewicz, which he read in 1912. Sienkiewicz describes a massacre of early Christians by the Romans, with the mob eagerly cheering as lions tore the Christians to pieces. William Korey describes young Lemkin's reaction:

Running to his mother for comfort, the anguished eleven-year-old cried: "They applauded! Why did they not call the police?" Raphael's wise mother, who was largely responsible for the boy's education, was said to have replied: "That is a most important question, but it is more than I can answer. You must study more and think more and find the answer for yourself." The episode pricked a profound concern in the sensitive youngster. He wanted to be certain that the killing of the early Christians "was a bad thing." His mother responded that it was "very bad." On a further exchange, Raphael wanted to know whether killing is nowadays immune from punishment: "When people kill people today, they get put in jail, don't they?" The mother with some hesitation answered: "Yes, they get put in jail."

For Lemkin, *Quo Vadis* and the discussion about its meaning with his mother engendered a life-long concern, and he gave the episode prominence in his autobiography. He told an interviewer: "That was the day I began to crusade [against genocide] because I started looking for the answer."[15]

This search would instill in Lemkin a voracious appetite for historical literature on massacres throughout the ages: the deaths of the Carthaginians at the hands of the Romans, the millions slaughtered by Genghis Khan, the Huguenots murdered in France, the persecution of Catholics in Japan.[16] His research would later form the basis for his planned tome, *History of Genocide*, a monumental work that he was never able to complete.[17]

The Ottoman Turks' massacre of more than a million Armenians in 1915 left an especially strong impression on the young Lemkin. Six years later, after he learned that an Armenian activist named Teilerian had assassinated Talaat Pasha, head of Turkey's police forces, in 1915,

---

[14] Cooper, *Raphael Lemkin and the Struggle*, 12.
[15] Korey, *An Epitaph for Raphael Lemkin*, 5 (citations omitted).
[16] *Ibid.*   [17] See Cooper, *Raphael Lemkin and the Struggle*, 230–42.

Lemkin had a memorable exchange with one of his professors at Lvov University.[18] Korey describes the encounter as follows:

Lemkin asked whether it would have been more appropriate to have the Turk arrested for the massacre [rather than to arrest Teilerian]. The professor's comments stunned him: "There wasn't any law under which he could be arrested." The naïve Lemkin shot back: "Not even though he had had a part in killing so many people?" The response of his teacher set Lemkin back on his heels. "Let us take the case of a man who owns some chickens. He kills them. Why not? It is not our business. If you interfere, it is trespass." Lemkin reacted with irritation: "The Armenians were not chickens."

The professor overlooked Lemkin's sardonic reply. He sought to drive home his argument: "When you interfere with the internal affairs of a country, you infringe upon that country's sovereignty." It was the traditional argument that prevented and precluded action by the international community to restrain regimes guilty of mass murder or those that engage in torture as well as other gross human rights violations. Lemkin offered an angry response rooted in logic, though not in international law: "So it's a crime for Teilerian to strike down one man, but it is not a crime for that man to have struck down one million men." The professor was both condescending and contemptuous: "You are young and excited … If you knew something about international law …" The sentence was not completed. But it posed the core question for Lemkin. Could not an international law be established designed to deal with mass murder? The query quickly led to a shift in Lemkin's academic goal. From philology he moved on to the study of law, specifically international law.[19]

In his early thirties Lemkin presented his first concrete legal proposal on genocide (a word he had yet to coin) to the Fifth International Conference for the Unification of Penal Law, held in Madrid in 1933 under the auspices of the League of Nations. Lemkin's report was accompanied by draft articles "to the effect that actions aiming at the destruction and oppression of populations should be penalized."[20] In particular, he proposed that two new international crimes of *barbarity* and *vandalism* be declared *delicta juris gentium* through conclusion of an international treaty. The "crime of barbarity" was conceived as "oppressive and destructive actions directed against individuals as members of a national, religious, or racial group," and the "crime of vandalism" as "malicious destruction of works of art and culture because they represent the specific creations of the genius of such

[18] In a way that was eerily reminiscent of Lemkin's later proclamation that the Genocide Convention had been "an epitaph on my mother's grave," the assassin had proclaimed "That is for my mother" before quickly giving himself up.

[19] Korey, *An Epitaph for Raphael Lemkin*, 8.

[20] Lemkin, *Axis Rule in Occupied Europe*, 91.

groups."[21] His proposal was ultimately unsuccessful, yet in this early episode it is apparent that the philologist Lemkin was "seeking to break free of the fetters of ordinary language" in order to capture the horrors of what he would later call genocide.[22]

Lemkin's proposal was motivated at least in part by the rise of Adolf Hitler in Germany,[23] and in the coming years Lemkin did actually present some speeches at international conferences on his proposal for the "crime of barbarity."[24] Nevertheless, in this interwar period Lemkin did not give "his original proposals too much attention,"[25] busy as he was "with his own plans for reinvigorating the collective security system of the League of Nations and writing his book on exchange control."[26]

The onset of World War II steered Lemkin back onto the path of his earlier initiative. After a dramatic flight from Warsaw following the German *Blitzkrieg* of September 1939, he found refuge in Sweden.[27] It was there, in 1940–41, that Lemkin appears to have stumbled upon a trove of German occupation laws. He had the idea of undertaking a legal analysis of Nazi occupation decrees throughout Europe, and to that end he persuaded the Swedish Foreign Ministry to instruct its consular officials to send him as much documentation on the subject as possible.[28] This research eventually resulted in his seminal work *Axis Rule in Occupied Europe*, published in 1944. It was in that book that Lemkin coined the word *genocide*. He later told an interviewer that he had been inspired to invent the term after listening to Winston Churchill's 1941 radio broadcast referring to Nazi atrocities as "a crime without a name."[29] In his book Lemkin noted that

genocide does not necessarily mean the immediate destruction of a nation, except when accomplished by mass killings of all members of a nation. It is intended rather to signify a coordinated plan of different actions aiming at the destruction of essential foundations of the life of national groups, with

---

[21] *Ibid.*; see also Raphael Lemkin, *Les actes créant un danger général (interétatique) considérés comme délits de droit des gens* (Paris: A. Pedone, 1933).

[22] Korey, *An Epitaph for Raphael Lemkin*, 9.

[23] Lemkin was remarkably prescient here. He would later heroically claim that he was present at the Madrid conference and that, when he began speaking, the German delegation had walked out of the chamber in protest, implying that his proposals had been directed squarely at them. This "incident" was later revealed to be an exaggeration. Lemkin had, in fact, been forbidden by Warsaw to attend the conference and had sent only his written report. See Korey, *An Epitaph for Raphael Lemkin*, 12.

[24] *Ibid.*   [25] Cooper, *Raphael Lemkin and the Struggle*, 76.

[26] *Ibid.*, 30.   [27] Lemkin's flight is described *ibid.*, 26–39.

[28] *Ibid.*, 30; Korey, *An Epitaph for Raphael Lemkin*, 15.

[29] Korey, *An Epitaph for Raphael Lemkin*, 14.

the aim of annihilating the groups themselves. The objectives of such a plan would be disintegration of the political and social institutions, of culture, language, national feelings, religion, and the economic existence of national groups, and the destruction of the personal security, liberty, health, dignity, and even the lives of the individuals belonging to such groups. Genocide is directed against the national group as an entity, and the actions involved are directed against individuals, not in their individual capacity, but as members of the national group.[30]

In addition to providing a new term and concept to describe the destruction of national groups, Lemkin advocated the conclusion of an international treaty to outlaw genocide. In view of the unprecedented gravity of Nazi crimes, he pointed to the inadequacy of international law in protecting national groups from annihilation:

The [Nazi] techniques of genocide represent an elaborate, almost scientific, system developed to an extent never before achieved by any nation. Hence the significance of genocide and the need to review international law in the light of the German practices of the present war. These practices have surpassed in their unscrupulous character any procedures or methods imagined a few decades ago by the framers of the Hague Regulations. Nobody at that time could conceive that an occupant would resort to the destruction of nations by barbarous practices reminiscent of the darkest pages of history.[31]

In making the case for an international treaty to prohibit genocide, Lemkin referred to the evolution of international law as expressed in the growing "interest in national groups as distinguished from states and individuals."[32] He remarked that such a trend was "quite natural, when we conceive that nations are essential elements of the world community."[33]

[30] Lemkin, *Axis Rule in Occupied Europe*, 79.
[31] *Ibid.*, 90.   [32] *Ibid.*
[33] *Ibid.*, 91. He continues:

> The world represents only so much culture and intellectual vigor as are created by its component national groups. Essentially the idea of a nation signifies constructive cooperation and original contributions, based upon genuine traditions, genuine culture, and a well-developed national psychology. The destruction of a nation, therefore, results in the loss of its future contributions to the world. Moreover, such destruction offends our feelings of morality and justice in much the same way as does the criminal killing of a human being: the crime in the one case as in the other is murder, though on a vastly greater scale. Among the basic features which have marked progress in civilization are the respect for and appreciation of the national characteristics and qualities contributed to world culture by the different nations – characteristics and qualities which, as illustrated in the contributions made by nations weak in defense and poor in economic resources, are not to be measured in terms of national power and wealth.

Lemkin's *Axis Rule* reads as the dispassionate academic work of a jurist – an intriguing contrast to the emotional advocacy that would characterize his later lobbying efforts for adoption of the Genocide Convention. Even though the full scale of the Holocaust was yet to be revealed, *Axis Rule* pointed presciently to the ominous fate of European Jews. Referring to passages from *Mein Kampf*, he warned that "[s]ome groups – such as the Jews – are to be destroyed completely,"[34] and cited the American Jewish Congress's estimation that approximately 1.7 million had already been "killed by organized murder": "The Jews for the most part are liquidated within the ghettos, or in special trains in which they are transported to a so-called 'unknown' destination."[35]

Despite Lemkin's own missing family, *Axis Rule* did not see the Nazi regime as a threat only to Jews. As Cooper notes, "Although he was right when he stated that the aim of the Nazis was the annihilation of the Jews, he did not appreciate the scale on which they had succeeded by the time his book was published at the end of 1944, and for this reason he tended to underplay the uniqueness of the Jewish situation."[36] Instead of emphasizing the situation of the Jews, the chapter entitled "Genocide" analyzes the persecution of the many national groups then under German domination, such as Lemkin's fellow citizens in Poland.[37] In fact, Lemkin's national group is mentioned more than his religious one.[38] Although there is an entire section devoted to the "Legal Status of the Jews," it is mentioned that Jews are only *"one of* the main objects of German genocide policy."[39] *Axis Rule* casts a broad net, grouping under genocide not only physical destruction, but also the political, social, cultural, and economic measures that had been imposed upon virtually all nationalities and minorities under Nazi occupation. Lemkin's chief concern seemed to be with the overarching aim of the Nazi regime – the Germanization of Europe – rather than the plight of any specific group.

After the end of the war, Lemkin's soaring reputation in the burgeoning field of international criminal law secured him a position as

---

[34] *Ibid.*, 81.   [35] *Ibid.*, 89.
[36] Cooper, *Raphael Lemkin and the Struggle*, 58.
[37] See Lemkin, *Axis Rule in Occupied Europe*, 79–95.
[38] William Korey noted that Lemkin "shared the universalistic approach to society and history that characterized the great German philosophers of history of the nineteenth century. Though conscious of his Jewish heritage, Lemkin, like his parents, was indifferent to Orthodox Judaism and was not attracted to Zionism": Korey, *An Epitaph for Raphael Lemkin*, 6.
[39] Lemkin, *Axis Rule in Occupied Europe*, 78 (emphasis added).

advisor, beginning in the summer of 1945, to Justice Robert Jackson at the Nuremberg Trials.[40] This position enabled him to influence the preparation of the indictment and the presentation of arguments before the tribunal. Thus, within the rubric of crimes against humanity under Article 6(c) of the Charter of the International Military Tribunal, the indictment charged the accused with

deliberate and systematic genocide, viz., the extermination of racial and national groups, against the civilian populations of certain occupied territories in order to destroy particular races and classes of people, and national, racial or religious groups, particularly Jews, Poles, and Gypsies.[41]

This became the first reference to the crime of genocide in legal proceedings.[42]

It was only in the summer of 1946 that the tragic fate of Lemkin's family became known to him. Distraught at being unable to locate any family members, and suffering from high blood pressure, Lemkin was hospitalized for a week toward the end of July 1946.[43] Upon his release, he discovered that his brother Elias, sister-in-law, and their two sons were alive and in Berlin, but that forty-nine other family members had perished, including his parents: "They had died in the Warsaw ghetto, in concentration camps, on death marches, and in the gas chambers."[44] In his autobiography Lemkin explained his reaction after learning of the deaths:

[40] Cooper, *Raphael Lemkin and the Struggle*, 63. Cooper also observes that, "[a]ccording to Paul Rassinier, *Axis Rule in Occupied Europe* 'was the most talked-about work in the corridors of the Nuremberg Court in late 1945–early 1946 time'": *ibid.*, 70. Jackson, a justice on the US Supreme Court, was chief US prosecutor at the trials.
[41] *Trial of the Major War Criminals Before the International Military Tribunal, 14 November–1 October 1946* (1947), vol. I, 43–44.
[42] There were also other references, such as the concluding speech of the British prosecutor Hartley Shawcross (*Trial of the Major War Criminals Before the International Military Tribunal, Nuremberg, 14 November 1945–1 October 1946* [1947], vol. XIX, 497–98), where he remarked:
> Genocide was not restricted to extermination of the Jewish people or of the Gypsies. It was applied in different forms to Yugoslavia, to the non-German inhabitants of Alsace-Lorraine, people of the Low countries and of Norway. The techniques varied from nation to nation, from people to people. The long-term aim was the same in all cases ... to achieve genocide. They deliberately decreased the birth rate in the occupied countries by sterilization, castration and abortion, by separating husband from wife and men from women and obstructing marriage.
[43] Cooper, *Raphael Lemkin and the Struggle*, 72.
[44] Korey, *An Epitaph for Raphael Lemkin*, 26.

I felt that the earth was receding from under my feet and the sense of living was disappearing. But soon I transformed my personal disaster into a moral striking force. Was I not under a moral duty to repay my mother for having stimulated in me the interest in Genocide? Was it not the best form of gratitude to make a "Genocide pact" as an epitaph on her symbolic grave and as a common recognition that she and many millions did not die in vain?[45]

As Korey suggests, this "vast personal loss transformed Lemkin. The crusader now became a zealot, a driven personality, determined more than ever to inscribe in international law the crime of genocide and also its punishment."[46]

In September 1946, Lemkin traveled to Paris in an attempt to introduce the concept of criminalizing genocide into the peace treaties then being negotiated. His proposal was unsuccessful, dismissed by delegates as a tangential issue. According to Cooper, "Lemkin became so despondent that on the third day of his stay in Paris, he once again fell ill and was taken to an American military hospital in the French capital."[47] Soon after, on 1 October 1946, the judgment of the Nuremberg Tribunal was delivered. When Lemkin realized that the term *genocide* had not been included, he was devastated, despite the judgment's recognition that the "mass murders and cruelties 'were a part' of a plan to get rid of whole native populations, by expulsion and annihilation, in order that their territory could be used for colonization by Germans."[48] Nevertheless, Lemkin would, remarkably, later call learning of the judgment "the blackest day" of his life.[49] Lemkin could no longer divorce his

---

[45] Lemkin, *Totally Unofficial*, 3.   [46] *Ibid.*

[47] Cooper, *Raphael Lemkin and the Struggle*, 73.

[48] *Judgement of the International Military Tribunal for the Trial of German Major War Criminals* (1950), 52.

[49] Korey, *An Epitaph for Raphael Lemkin*, 25. Lemkin believed that the "evidence produced at the Nuremberg trial gave full support to the concept of genocide": Raphael Lemkin, "Genocide as a Crime in International Law," *American Journal of International Law* 41 (1947): 145, 147. This view was affirmed many years later in the *Kambanda* case (*Prosecutor v. Kambanda*, Judgement and Sentence [ICTR, 4 September 1998], para. 16), in which the ICTR Trial Chamber noted, as quoted earlier, that "the crimes prosecuted by the Nuremberg Tribunal, namely the holocaust of the Jews or the 'Final Solution,' were very much constitutive of genocide, but they could not be defined as such because the crime of genocide was not defined until later." The secondary Nazi trials under Control Council Law No. 10 were more willing to incorporate the crime of genocide in their judgments. See, for example, *United States v. Greifelt et al. (RuSHA Case)*, 13 *Law Reports of Trials of War Criminals* 1, 2 (1948), before the United States Military Tribunal, in which the accused were charged with participating in a "systematic program of genocide, aimed at the destruction of foreign nations and ethnic groups, in part by murderous extermination, and

academic interests from his deeply emotional condition, and it was this fusion that propelled him on his historic campaign for the adoption of the Genocide Convention:

Disillusioned and heart-broken by news of the death of his parents, the lack of response from the delegates at the Paris conference and the judgement of the Nuremberg Tribunal, all following rapidly on each other, Lemkin remained ill. One day while still confined to his bed in the military hospital in Paris Lemkin happened to hear on the radio about the forthcoming meeting of the General Assembly of the United Nations in New York. Lemkin was electrified by the news, believing that here at last was a forum which would listen to him. He spent several days devising his plan and persuaded his doctors to discharge him from the hospital, which they were willing to do provided he travelled back to the United States on a ship and not by aeroplane. Lemkin already possessed a medical report from a Dr. Savage which stated that he was "hypertensive, mildly exhausted, and apprehensive of flight." Through his contacts, Lemkin wangled a passage on a troop transport.[50]

And so began Lemkin's remarkable lobby at the United Nations. His "crusade" came at considerable cost to his health and private life. His manic work schedule and, no doubt, internal psychic turmoil resulted in continuous ailments and occasional hospitalizations. He eschewed any serious romantic attachment and any semblance of a social life.[51] On 28 November 1948, he drafted a letter to Ernest Gross, the American delegate to the Paris Assembly, laying bare his raw motivation: "Genocide has taken the lives of my dear ones; the fight against genocide takes my health. I am ready to give my life for this cause."[52]

in part by elimination and suppression of national characteristics." The tribunal described genocide as a "master scheme ... devised by the top ranking Nazi leaders in pursuance of their racial policy of establishing the German nation as a master race and to this end exterminate or otherwise uproot the population of other nations." The increasing references to genocide were the result of the UN General Assembly's adoption of Resolution 96(I) in 1946, which first declared genocide to be an international crime and expressed the United Nations' intention to adopt a treaty. See, for example, *United States v. Alstötter et al. (Justice Trial)*, (1948) 3 *Trials of War Criminals* 1, 983:

> The General Assembly is not an international legislature, but it is the most authoritative organ in existence for the interpretation of world opinion. Its recognition of genocide as an international crime [in Resolution 96(I)] is persuasive evidence of the fact. We approve and adopt its conclusions ... [and] find no injustice to persons tried for such crimes.

[50] Cooper, *Raphael Lemkin and the Struggle*, 74–75.
[51] Lemkin's personal troubles during this period are described *ibid.*, 111–18.
[52] Cited *ibid.*, 169. Apparently, Lemkin excised this passage from the final draft of the letter that was sent.

Lemkin's crusade did not end with the adoption of the convention on 9 December 1948. The mission to have the convention adopted was soon replaced with one to have it ratified. With the sufficient number of ratifications, the convention entered into force on 12 January 1951 – a day that Lemkin later referred to as one "of triumph for mankind and the most beautiful day of my life." In his autobiography he asked himself, "Is this the moment for which I was hoping and working so many years?" He answered: "My joy was mixed with anxiety and fear."[53] After ratification, the crusade continued: In an attempt to persuade nonsignatory countries to become parties to the convention, he "expend[ed] selfless and almost super-human effort, reaching out to individuals all over the globe."[54] The failure of his adopted country, the United States, to ratify the convention caused him particular anguish. With unflagging energy, he mounted a vigorous lobby in the US Senate in the late 1940s and early 1950s. But Lemkin could not persuade US policymakers to sign his beloved convention. He became pigeonholed as "a 'loner,' a man obsessed with a single idea," and in his frustration began quarreling even with his most loyal supporters.[55] By 1954, Cooper notes, an appointment to the International Court of Justice was potentially available to him if he would have "toned down his vociferous campaigning for the Genocide Convention. But he was unwilling to do this. Cut off from many former friends, Lemkin grew increasingly isolated, despondent and paranoid."[56]

In his last years, Lemkin moved toward a certain "withdrawal from life." Troubled by ill health and diminished energy, he started looking inward and found "expression in poetry as the circle of my friends decreases. I become conscious of aging and try to adjust myself."[57] In March 1957 he penned the following poem:

Oh heart don't stop beating
in a fleeing to end it all
I wish to see my roses
bloom in my garden again
stop this cutting pain
Delay eternity's call.[58]

---

[53] Korey, *An Epitaph for Raphael Lemkin*, 54.
[54] Cooper, *Raphael Lemkin and the Struggle*, 188.
[55] *Ibid.*, 207. Lemkin's struggle with the United States Senate is described at pages 189–208.
[56] *Ibid.*, 268.   [57] *Ibid.*
[58] Tanya Elder, "What You See Before Your Eyes: Documenting Raphael Lemkin's Life by Exploring His Archival Papers, 1900–1959," *Journal of Genocide Research* 7 (2005): 469, 491.

When Lemkin died in 1959, his name had faded from public consciousness, and he remained almost completely unknown to history until scholars began to pay attention to his legacy at the time of the American ratification of the convention in 1988.[59]

Lemkin had once boasted, as World War II raged on, that if his proposals for the "crime of barbarity" had been adopted by the League of Nations at the Madrid conference of 1933 they would "prove useful now by providing an effective instrument for the punishment of war criminals of the present world conflict."[60] He told an audience at the North Carolina Bar Association in May 1942 that the rejection of his proposal was "one of the thousand reasons why I am now here before you and why your boys are fighting and dying in different parts of the world at this very moment."[61] Such was Lemkin's faith in the effectiveness of international law. He realized that "[w]hether a Convention on Genocide will stop the crime [of genocide,] we do not believe that such a question is fair. Does a penal code stop all crime in society? The significance of a penal law lies mostly in its preventative nature."[62] Nevertheless, Lemkin would surely have been surprised and disappointed by how little influence his convention would have on the world stage; witness the genocides of the late twentieth century in Cambodia, Bosnia, and Rwanda.

Lemkin was no doubt a devoted apostle of international law, but it seems more likely that the loss of virtually his entire family in the Holocaust, not to mention the horrors inflicted on the Jewish people and his native country of Poland, were the main influences in his passion for international criminal law.[63] Driving him ever forward, he once said, was "a mixture of blood and tears of millions of innocent

[59] See Korey, *An Epitaph for Raphael Lemkin*, preface.
[60] Lemkin, *Axis Rule in Occupied Europe*, 92.
[61] Korey, *An Epitaph for Raphael Lemkin*, 11.
[62] *Ibid.*, 55 (citing an undated, unpublished paper found in Lemkin's archives).
[63] Cooper, *Raphael Lemkin and the Struggle*, 272, 276. Cooper notes:
> Raphael Lemkin liked to present himself as a universal man, an interpretation which has been followed by most historians. His roots, however, were in the quagmire of ethnic conflict in pre-War Eastern Europe and were authentically Jewish ... As Lemkin's friend the historian Philip Friedman acknowledged, "there can be no doubt that the fundamental stimulus that induced its originator to develop this theory [of genocide] and to fight for its adoption on the international stage for many years in a heroic struggle of one against the many, was the great Jewish tragedy during Nazi rule in Europe."

people throughout the ages and of the last few years. Among them were also the tears of my parents and friends."[64] Evidently, the force propelling his advocacy was, in great part, unbearable grief. Beyond the idealistic pursuit of justice and the intellectual curiosity of the jurist, the adoption of an international treaty against genocide became for him an elaborate tribute to those close relations who had perished in the Holocaust. Equally important was the desire to redeem his overwhelming loss, to work through the violent disintegration of his personal world, and to avoid succumbing to unspeakable anguish. As a result of the Holocaust, Lemkin's relatively abstract commitment to international justice was radically internalized, and his commitment to the conceptualization and prohibition of genocide in international law assumed an added dimension of restoring balance in a traumatized personal universe. Perhaps these factors help to explain the apparently dispassionate and numbing academic analysis reflected in his work, coupled with the intense emotions expressed in his relentless pursuit of an international treaty against genocide. Unfortunately, it seems, the "epitaph" on his mother's grave that Lemkin sought to erect through the Genocide Convention was never quite complete. The rationalist credo of law could not provide the catharsis he so desperately sought.

Lemkin's story highlights the inherent tension in reducing genocide to law. What is at once deeply personal, tragic, and somehow beyond comprehension in the enormity of its evil is sterilized in the confines of legal terminology, construed as universally accessible through a rational exercise of categorizing, naming, and attributing responsibility to specific perpetrators. The desire to bring overwhelming events into orderly control is a prominent theme in the emergence of genocide as a legal concept. His struggle, his work of mourning, reflects a broader narrative of how the world attempted to grapple with evil so radical that it profoundly challenged our assumptions about humankind and historical progress. In the developments that followed, from the Nuremberg Judgment, to the Genocide Convention, to the Eichmann trial, the paradigmatic conception of the Holocaust, its particularity and uniqueness, had to contend with its legal representation and the universality of its meaning.

---

[64] Lemkin, *Totally Unofficial*, 21 (as cited in Cooper, *Raphael Lemkin and the Struggle*, 87).

Confronting the Holocaust through legal ritual

In his concluding speech before the International Military Tribunal at Nuremberg, the French prosecutor Auguste Champetier de Ribes was moved to explain that "the conception of the gigantic plan of world domination and the attempt to realize it by every possible means," including the "scientific and systematic extermination of millions of human beings and more especially of certain national or religious groups whose existence hampered the hegemony of the German race," were crimes "so monstrous, so undreamt of in history throughout the Christian era up to the birth of Hitlerism, that the term 'genocide' has had to be coined to define it."[65]

The devastating gravity and convulsive scale of the Holocaust shook the blind confidence in modernity's promise of progress and the presumed superiority of western civilization. It radically challenged conceptions of human nature, and even the presence of a divine being. The *Endlösung*, conceived by the Nazis as the "Final Solution" to the "contamination of Aryan blood" by racially "inferior" Jews and Gypsies, consumed millions of lives and marked a radical departure from the past through the manifestation of hitherto unimaginable barbarity. Jürgen Habermas captured this *post-histoire* sentiment by observing:

There [in Auschwitz] something happened, that up to now nobody considered as even possible. There one touched on something which represents the deep layer of solidarity among all that wears a human face; notwithstanding all the usual acts of beastliness of human history, the integrity of this common layer had been taken for granted ... Auschwitz has changed the basis for the continuity of the conditions of life within history.[66]

The catastrophic seduction of a universe built on rational certainty, the loss of innocence and total disillusionment with past conceptions, was so pervasive that for Theodor Adorno, "[a]fter Auschwitz, there is no word ... not even a theological one, that has any right unless it underwent a transformation."[67]

But it was precisely the rational process of "naming" and labeling that became the dominant theme in reckoning with the enormity of

[65] *Trial of the Major War Criminals Before the International Military Tribunal, Nuremberg, 14 November 1945–1 October 1946* (1947), vol. XIX, 531.
[66] Jürgen Habermas, *The New Conservatism: Cultural Criticism and the Historians' Debate* (Cambridge, MA: MIT Press, 1989).
[67] Theodor W. Adorno, *Negative Dialectics* (New York: Continuum, 1983), 367 [originally published 1973].

the Holocaust. Despite its ancient origins, genocide first emerged in the modern era, as a paradigmatic crime built on the legacy of the Holocaust. Translating its historical specificity into universally applicable legal concepts and reconciling its ineffability with the requirements of legal certainty raise far-reaching questions about the boundaries between legal and meta-legal discourse. To the extent that adopting the Genocide Convention was part of the "work of mourning" or a reflection upon, and response to, the excesses of modern civilization, it could be considered as part of a progressive transformative process that encourages critical self-examination, awakens empathy, and seeks to improve upon the past. To the extent that adopting the convention was a ritual of closure, it could be seen as an effort to situate the trauma of a shattered self-conception externally, to create the illusion of progress so as to avoid a deeper, more challenging encounter with the unprecedented violence of the modern age.

More generally, the subjection of the Holocaust to the certainty and finality of law – whether through trials, drafting treaties, or discourse shaped by abstractions – inevitably threatens to banalize its enormity. Its reduction to a manageable narrative through the attribution of liability within the confines of legal process may have been necessary to demystify the seemingly insurmountable gravity of Nazi crimes, and it was also a means of reckoning with the past and perhaps even of acting to prevent similar occurrences in the future. Underneath the façade of progress and international law, we may have defined and condemned the "ultimate crime," but to what extent has this legal process facilitated expedient and self-deceptive disengagement?

Martti Koskenniemi has questioned

our need to deal with genocide, nuclear weapons, or massive suffering in terms of a universalising language of human rights, treaty obligation, legal rules and principles. To formalise such experiences in a legal language and "method" involves a banalisation that makes available all the routine defences, excuses and exceptions and triggers a technical debate which may end up by paralysing our ability to act and undermining our intuitive capability to empathise and thus also the condition for entering into a rudimentary communal relation with others.[68]

The interplay between the distancing evinced by reducing the Holocaust to a legal abstraction, on the one hand, and the need to connect

---

[68] Martti Koskenniemi, "International Law in a Post-realist Era," *Australian Yearbook of International Law* 16 (1995): 1, 14.

emotionally with the intimate reality of the suffering it entailed, on the other – the tension between the universal and the particular – was exemplified in the elaborate legal rituals undertaken in the postwar years in order to reckon with the Nazi crimes: namely, the Nuremberg Trials, the adoption of the Genocide Convention, and the Eichmann trial in Israel.

Nuremberg Trials

The inadequacy of legal process and formalism as a response to genocide appears to have been at the forefront of Hannah Arendt's mind in the immediate aftermath of the Nuremberg Trials. In an exchange of letters with her mentor, Karl Jaspers, in 1946, she conveyed serious misgivings as to the representation of the Holocaust's enormity within the strictures of legal process:

The Nazi crimes, it seems to me, explode the limits of the law, and that is precisely what constitutes their monstrousness. For these crimes, no punishment is severe enough. It may be essential to hang Goering, but it is totally inadequate. That is, the guilt, in contrast to all criminal guilt, oversteps and shatters any and all legal systems. That is the reason why the Nazis in Nuremberg are so smug.[69]

She later wrote in *The Origins of Totalitarianism* that the radical dehumanization of "alien races" culminating in the "Final Solution" was such an "outrage to common sense" that it led to the surfacing of a new guilt that could not be vindicated by any conception of moral culpability. The Nazis, she concluded,

have discovered without knowing it that there are crimes which men can neither punish nor forgive. When the impossible was made possible it became the unpunishable, unforgivable absolute evil which could no longer be understood and explained by the evil motives of self-interest, greed, covetousness, resentment, lust for power, and cowardice; and which therefore anger could not revenge, love could not endure, friendship could not forgive. Just as the victims in the death factories or the holes of oblivion are no longer "human" in the eyes of their executioners, so this newest species of criminals is beyond the pale even of solidarity in human sinfulness.[70]

A legal response to Nazi crimes was by no means an inevitable outcome of the postwar political configuration. To the contrary, there had

[69] "Letter to Karl Jaspers," in *Hannah Arendt/Karl Jaspers: Correspondence 1926–1969*, eds. Lotte Kohler and Hans Saner, trans. Robert Kimber and Rita Kimber (New York: Harcourt Brace Jovanovich, 1992), 51, 54.
[70] Hannah Arendt, *The Origins of Totalitarianism* (New York: Harcourt Brace, 1979), 459.

been a "half serious" recommendation by Josef Stalin to dispense justice by simply shooting 50,000 Nazi General Staff officers. Even Winston Churchill could not resist this temptation, as reflected in his insistence that the major Nazi war criminals be summarily executed rather than allowing them to benefit from the propaganda effects of a public trial.[71] The legendary American publisher Joseph Pulitzer went so far as to urge the shooting of 1.5 million Nazis.[72] It was American pressure that eventually resulted in the decision to establish an International Military Tribunal; ironically, though victims' cries for justice were heard worldwide, the Nuremberg Tribunal materialized because of the legal imagination of a handful of influential New York lawyers, all of whom were far removed from the actual horrors of the war.[73] This *noblesse oblige* arose from an impulse to subject the disruptive events of World War II, along with its atrocities, to the disciplined control of law.[74] Henry Stimson, the US secretary of war and the primary proponent of the tribunal, expressed the structuring premises underlying this resort to legal process. In opposing the proposal of the US secretary of treasury, Henry Morgenthau, Jr., for summary execution of Nazi leaders, Stimson emphasized that such trials "afford the most effective way of making a record of the Nazi system of terrorism and of the effort of the Allies to terminate the system and prevent its recurrence."[75] The courtroom thus became a controlled space within which the Allied victory and the triumph of liberal values were consecrated through the cleansing ritual of moral condemnation founded on legal objectivity. What was rectified on the battlefield by force was legitimized in history through a conclusive judgment of Nazi culpability and Allied moral superiority.

Hans Kellner has suggested that Arendt's unease with this ritual of closure was that

no available conclusion to the drama was adequate to the events. The stage of representation offered by the Nuremberg courtroom and its noose was absurdly disproportionate to the acts represented. In wishing to employ the

---

[71] See István Deák, "Misjudgment at Nuremberg," *New York Review of Books*, 7 October 1993, 48.

[72] *Ibid.*

[73] See Telford Taylor, *The Anatomy of the Nuremberg Trials* (New York: Knopf, 1992), 41.

[74] See, for example, Kenneth Anderson, "Nuremberg Sensibility: Telford Taylor's Memoir of the Nuremberg Trials," *Harvard Human Rights Journal* 7 (1994): 281, 290.

[75] Henry L. Stimson, "Memorandum Opposing the Morgenthau Plan, 9 September 1944," in US Department of State, *Foreign Relations of the United States: The Conference at Quebec, 1944* (Washington, DC: Government Printing Office, 1972), 125.

events of the Holocaust as beyond emplotment, she dreamed of an imaginary mode of representation that would place the characters and their deeds in a proper relation to reality.[76]

The response of Jaspers in a letter to his former student Arendt is as instructive as it is intriguing. Aware that no mode of representation was entirely sufficient, and proceeding with a "prudent wisdom [that considered Arendt's concern] within the bounds and psychological necessities of audience expectations,"[77] Jaspers drew her attention to the perils and pitfalls of imbuing the "Final Solution" with the inscrutable quality of a transcendent evil. Reducing it to the mundane confines of legal process, he argued, may be the best response to the megalomaniac self-depiction of the Nazi leadership as possessing evil "genius." Such a response would, in effect, deny them the stature that they coveted:

[A] guilt that goes beyond all criminal guilt inevitably takes on a streak of "greatness" – of satanic greatness – which is, for me, as inappropriate for the Nazis as all the talk about the "demonic" element in Hitler and so forth ... It seems to me that we have to see these things in their total banality, in their prosaic triviality, because that's what truly characterizes them. Bacteria can cause epidemics that wipe out nations, but they remain merely bacteria. I regard any hint of myth and legend with horror.[78]

Jaspers's response sheds light on Arendt's later depiction of the trial of Adolf Eichmann as "the banality of evil."[79] The demystification of Nazi crimes through legal process was achieved, in part, through the depiction of the accused as common criminals. As Hartley Shawcross declared in the British prosecution's opening statement at the Nuremberg Trials: "If murder, raping, and robbery are indictable under the ordinary municipal laws of our countries, shall those who differ from the common criminal only by the extent and systematic nature of their offenses escape accusation?"[80] The imagery of "gangsters" engaged in "an inexhaustible round of triumph and revenge,

[76] Hans Kellner, "'Never Again' Is Now," in Keith Jenkins, ed., *The Postmodern History Reader* (London: Routledge, 1997), 397, 398.

[77] *Ibid.*

[78] *Hannah Arendt/Karl Jaspers*, eds. Kohler and Saner (as cited in Gordon A. Craig, "Letters on Dark Times," *New York Review of Books*, 13 May 1993, 12).

[79] See Hannah Arendt, *Eichmann in Jerusalem: A Report on the Banality of Evil* (New York: Viking, 1964).

[80] *Trial of the Major War Criminals Before the International Military Tribunal* (1947), vol. III, 92.

defeat and resentment," was invoked.[81] The major war criminals were reduced to psychopaths at the helm of a modem state, to a mere "array of Mafia chieftains."[82] This denigration was combined with the pedantry of rules and procedures – described by an observer of the trial as "a citadel of boredom"[83] – to complete the banalization process. But this reductive process was as much about the culpability of the perpetrators as it was about distancing the triumphant values of "rational modernity" from the "irrational barbarity" that had arisen in its midst. The narrative constructed an image of Nazis as an aberration, as a radical deviation from modernity and western liberal values, thus displacing their crimes in an external and alien dimension belonging elsewhere. In an elaborate ritual of exorcism, the grand Nazi conspirators were portrayed as illiberal strangers, barbarian intruders in the otherwise civilized world of those who stood in judgment, as the diabolical "alter" who had to be cast away from the temple of humanity to restore the equilibrium of a radically disturbed moral self-conception.[84]

The banal image of the major Nazi war criminals as mere gangsters still had to be reconciled with the unprecedented historical character of their crimes. A grand narrative was required in order to capture the magnitude of these monstrous crimes. In a report submitted to US president Harry Truman in 1945, Justice Robert H. Jackson wrote that "[w]e must establish incredible events by credible evidence."[85] The case against the Nazi leadership, he claimed, had to be "factually authentic and constitute a well-documented history of what we are convinced was a grand, concerted pattern to incite and commit the aggressions and barbarities which have shocked the world."[86] Nazi crimes had to be recorded "with clarity and precision"; otherwise, "we cannot blame

---

[81] See Albert Camus, *The Rebel*, trans. Anthony Bower (London: Hamish Hamilton, 1954), 150.

[82] Robert Conot, *Justice at Nuremberg* (New York: Harper & Row, 1983), 146.

[83] See Rebecca West, *A Train of Powder* (New York: Viking, 1955), 3. In chronicling the trial, her account is replete with expressions of frustration at the monotony of the proceedings. The trial, she insisted, "was boredom on a huge historic scale" (p. 7), and even painful: "All these people wanted to leave Nuremberg as urgently as a dental patient enduring the drill wants to up and leave the chair" (p. 11). She described her work as "the water-torture, boredom falling drop by drop on the same spot on the soul" (p. 17).

[84] See, for example, Anderson, "Nuremberg Sensibility," 281, 288–89.

[85] Robert H. Jackson, *The Nürnberg Case* (New York: Cooper Square, 1971), 10.

[86] *Report of Robert H. Jackson, United States Representative to the International Conference on Military Trials, London 1945* (Washington, DC: Government Printing Office, 1949), 48, avalon.law.yale.edu/subject_menus/jackson.asp.

the future if in days of peace it finds incredible the accusatory generalities uttered during the war."[87] Without doubt, this impulse was meritorious and made the task of denial or revisionism more difficult. Primo Levi, for instance, recalls how guards at the concentration camps would taunt inmates by saying that, even if they survived, their stories of Nazi monstrosities would never be believed.[88] In this respect the trials served an important role in what one might call the psychological reconstruction of Germany following the war.

What emerged from the trials was not merely a factual record, but an official, interpretive narrative, or meta-narrative, of the Nazi war effort – including, but not limited to, the Holocaust. The tribunal held that aggressive war was the "supreme international crime, differing only from other war crimes in that it contains within itself the accumulated evil of the whole."[89] This view was driven by a prosecution strategy that focused on a theory of a Nazi grand conspiracy in which belligerent militarism figured most prominently. The Holocaust was represented "essentially as the horrific consequence of a war of aggression."[90] As discussed in Chapter 3, this approach was partially shaped by the reluctance to rely too heavily on the disputed concept of crimes against humanity. But the construction of a narrative centered on aggressive war – in addition to reflecting the political interest of the Allied powers in reasserting the inviolable sovereignty of states in the postwar international order – meant that the narrative would inescapably fail to reflect the particular character and purpose of the Nazi persecution of Jews.

Largely because the evidentiary base for the prosecution at Nuremberg drew so heavily upon German documents captured at the conclusion of the war, the first generation of Holocaust historians subscribed to what Christopher Browning has called the "Nuremberg view" that the Holocaust was the product of "criminal minds, infected with racism and antisemitism, carrying out criminal policies through criminal organizations."[91] Despite the limited perspective of this

[87] Ibid.
[88] See Primo Levi, *The Drowned and the Saved*, trans. Raymond Rosenthal (New York: Vintage, 1989), 11–12 (referring to Simon Wiesenthal, Joseph Wechsberg, ed., *The Murderers Among Us* [New York: McGraw Hill, 1967]).
[89] *Trial of the Major War Criminals Before the International Military Tribunal, Nuremberg, 14 November 1945–1 October 1946* (1947), vol. I, 186.
[90] Lawrence Douglas, "The Memory of Judgment: The Law, the Holocaust, and Denial," *History and Memory* 7 (1996): 100, 105.
[91] Christopher Browning, "German Memory, Judicial Interrogation, and Historical Reconstruction: Writing Perpetrator History from Postwar Testimony," in Saul

scholarship – developed within the confines of official records and the legal processes at Nuremberg – the resulting elements of detachment and temporal distance created an intellectual space for exploring other dimensions of the Holocaust. The initial scholarly emphasis on "ideological history, focusing on antisemitism and racism among the perpetrators, or institutional history focusing on the implementation of Nazi racial policy"[92] was displaced in 1961 by Raul Hilberg's monumental work *The Destruction of the European Jews*.[93] The "Nuremberg view" was superseded by the representation of the Holocaust as "a vast and complex administrative process carried out by a multitude of often faceless bureaucrats who were infused with an 'elation' or 'hubris' because they were making history."[94] Since that time, successive generations of Holocaust scholarship have each presented a fresh perspective, with some drawing on records of perpetrators, others on those of victims or bystanders. The surfacing of new evidence, consideration of different or broader perspectives, and new questions reflecting the concerns of new generations all work to influence historical scholarship, underscoring that judicial decisions are fixed and immutable, whereas historiography is relentlessly moving in new directions. These evolving viewpoints illustrate why history as captured in legal judgments and their immediate aftermath is final only for legal purposes – and is anything but definitive.[95]

Although Nazi atrocities against Jews were conveyed at the Nuremberg Trials in terms of political control and military strategy, the unprecedented totalizing dimensions of the Holocaust were not altogether lost at the Nuremberg Trials. Jackson recognized the all-encompassing nature of European Jewry's destruction when he declared at trial: "It is my purpose to show a plan and design, to which all Nazis were fanatically committed, to annihilate all Jewish people."[96] He thus conceded the concept of ideological extermination as an end in itself, without invoking the neologism *genocide*. This conception of the Nazi crimes was diluted, however, by the continuing emphasis on the persecution

Friedlander, ed., *Probing the Limits of Representation* (Cambridge, MA: Harvard University Press, 1992), 22, 26.

[92] *Ibid.*

[93] Raul Hilberg, *The Destruction of the European Jews* (London: W. H. Allen, 1961).

[94] Browning, "German Memory, Judicial Interrogation, and Historical Reconstruction," 26.

[95] See, for example, Mark Osiel, "Ever Again: Legal Remembrance of Administrative Massacre," *University of Pennsylvania Law Review* 144 (1995): 463, 631–32.

[96] *Trial of the Major War Criminals Before the International Military Tribunal*, vol. II (1947), 118.

of Jews as a means of eliminating barriers to the greater end of waging aggressive war:

> Nor was [the policy of starvation and extermination] directed against individual Jews for personal bad citizenship or unpopularity. The avowed purpose was the destruction of the Jewish people as a whole, as an end in itself, *as a measure of preparation for war, and as a discipline of conquered peoples.*[97]

The deliberate avoidance of the Holocaust at the center of the trial reflected, in part, the unease with which the new concept of crimes against humanity was perceived, including the requirement of a nexus with crimes against peace or war crimes. But more important for our purposes was the implicit recognition that aggressive war was far more determinate and familiar, and that it did not require that the tribunal, at the outset, understand or cope with the Nazis' unprecedented, ideologically based effort to exterminate an entire race. As Lawrence Douglas has observed:

> By treating crimes against humanity as ancillary to the principal crime of military aggression, Jackson's approach shifted attention away from those atrocities that presented, in Arendt's mind, the greatest challenge to the concept of ordered legality. While criminalizing military belligerence can be dismissed as an exercise in futility, the *acts* that Jackson sought to punish can be seen as less disruptive of jurisprudential assumptions than genocide. Genocide, as Arendt suggests, undermines confidence in all jurisprudential understandings, be they inspired by natural or positive law traditions. The criminalization of aggressive warfare, unusual as this may be, represents no more than the extension of legal principles that control domestic conduct into relations between nations.[98]

The Nuremberg Judgment was a means of reckoning with both the past and the future. In emphasizing the transcendent importance of punishing the major Nazi war criminals, Jackson remarked, "What makes this inquest significant is that these prisoners represent sinister influences that will lurk in the world long after their bodies have returned to dust." His goal as prosecutor was to "show them to be living symbols of racial hatreds, of terrorism and violence, and of the arrogance and cruelty of power. They are symbols of fierce nationalisms and of militarism, of intrigue and war-making which have embroiled Europe generation after generation." In Jackson's view, there could be

---

[97] *Ibid.*, 119 (emphasis added).
[98] Lawrence Douglas, "Film as Witness: Screening Nazi Concentration Camps Before the Nuremberg Tribunal," *Yale Law Journal* 105 (1995): 449, 462.

no compromise with evil forces that "would gain renewed strength if we deal ambiguously or indecisively with the men in whom those forces now precariously survive."[99] The men in the dock at Nuremberg were thus regarded as mere transient repositories of greater currents, ones that had been devastating in the past and that were bound to resurface in the future – absent the preventative effect of international justice. "Successor justice is both retrospective and prospective," Otto Kirchheimer has observed. "In laying bare the roots of iniquity in the previous regime's conduct, it simultaneously seizes the opportunity to convert the trial into a cornerstone of the new order."[100] In delegitimizing the Nazi past, the tribunal contributed to the transformation of postwar German identity and helped to prevent the resurgence of Nazi barbarity. It also served to legitimize the postwar order revolving around the United Nations, founded on the prohibition of war and on the emerging acceptance of universal human rights as a foundation for international peace and security.

The Genocide Convention

Although the Nuremberg Tribunal was oriented, in part, toward the future, it had constructed the narrative of Nazi crimes within the confines of legal precedent and existing concepts that were accessible and adaptable to credible judicial proceedings. Against that background, the crime of genocide emerged in order to fill a perceived void both in the legal idiom and in historical understanding. By the same token, whereas the primary work of the Nuremberg Tribunal was to pass judgment against particular Nazi criminals, the Genocide Convention was conceived more as an abstract conceptualization and universal representation of the Holocaust's paradigmatic crimes. It was an attempt to supersede the specificity of the Nuremberg Tribunal by establishing new legal norms that would not only bind, but also prevent and, if necessary, punish future acts of genocide.

The American delegation had urged that the convention "be adopted as soon as possible, before the memory of the barbarous crimes which had been committed faded from the minds of men."[101] In order to

---

[99] *Trial of the Major War Criminals Before the International Military Tribunal*, vol. II (1947), 99.

[100] Otto Kirchheimer, *Political Justice: The Use of Legal Procedure for Political Ends* (Princeton: Princeton University Press, 1961), 336.

[101] UN GAOR, 3rd Sess., 6th Cmte., 64th mtg., UN Doc. A/C.6/SR.63 at 4–5 (1948); Hirad Abtahi and Philippa Webb, eds., *The Genocide Convention: The Travaux Préparatoires*, vol. II (Leiden and Boston: Martinus Nijhoff, 2008), 1290.

underscore the historical specificity of the crime of genocide, some
delegates sought to amend the preamble to contain an express condemnation of Nazi and fascist racial theories "in order to affirm the
existence of the *organic relationship* between genocide and the nazi-
fascist ideology."[102] The amendment, proposed by the Soviet Union,
would have added a preambular paragraph indicating "that the crime
of genocide is organically bound with Fascism–Nazism and other similar race 'theories' which propagated racial and national hatred, the
domination of the so-called 'higher' and the extermination of the
so-called 'lower' races."[103] Reflecting the tension between the unprecedented character of the Holocaust and its perception as an "ancient"
crime, other delegates countered that "it was wrong to consider genocide as being an exclusive product of fascism–nazism" since "history revealed many previous cases of genocide."[104] Others outside the
European theater were more directly concerned that the Holocaust
should not be privileged in relation to their own plights. The Chinese
delegate, for example, asserted that references to "past events" such as
the Nuremberg trials should be deleted from the preamble, for "otherwise it would be necessary to cite all parallel cases and, in particular, those which involved Japan."[105] In order to avoid reduction of the
convention to a mere denunciation of the Holocaust, other delegates
emphasized that it was "dangerous to create the idea that genocide
should only be punished if it were a product of fascism–nazism" or to
suggest that "the Convention was concerned only with that historical
accident."[106] The deliberations, it was asserted, should consider "only
the legal aspect of the convention" as an abstract norm "and leave aside
everything that might be inspired by a desire for propaganda."[107]

Some delegates hardly masked their skepticism about what they perceived as a thinly veiled attempt to achieve a self-deceptive closure –
and to put in place an effective means of prevention – through the
Genocide Convention. No less of an eminent personage than Hartley

---

[102] See Abtahi and Webb, eds., *The Genocide Convention*, 36 (emphasis added).
[103] See *Report of the Committee and Draft Convention Drawn Up by the Committee*, UN Doc.
E/794, at 10 (1948).
[104] *Ibid.*, 8.
[105] UN GAOR, 3rd Sess., 6th Cmte., 65th mtg., UN Doc. A/C.6/SR.65 (1948); Abtahi and
Webb, eds., *The Genocide Convention*, 1316.
[106] See *Report of the Committee and Draft Convention Drawn Up by the Committee*, UN Doc.
E/794, 8.
[107] UN GAOR, 3rd Sess., 6th Cmte., 66th mtg., UN Doc. A/C.6/SR.66 (1948); Abtahi and
Webb, eds., *The Genocide Convention*, 1331.

Shawcross, the British prosecutor at Nuremberg, noted that he "did not feel particularly enthusiastic about the [convention]." "It was a complete delusion," he stated,

to suppose that the adoption of a convention of the type proposed, even if generally adhered to, would give people a greater sense of security or would diminish existing dangers of persecution on racial, religious, or national grounds ...

Recalling the Nürnberg trials, [he] pointed out that nobody believed that the existence of a convention ... would have deterred the nazis or fascists from committing the atrocious crimes of which they had been guilty. Those crimes were largely the crimes of totalitarian States, which would not change their methods because of the existence of a convention to which a number of nations had adhered.[108]

Contrary to the euphoria of Herbert Evatt that "the supremacy of international law had been proclaimed"[109] by adopting the convention, Shawcross considered the novel crime of genocide superfluous. It was, he claimed, "already generally recognized as a crime punishable by law and was simply a new word to describe a particular form or murder" – an apparent reference to the broader category of crimes against humanity.[110] He explained that genocide "was a crime committed not by individuals but by States. No one believed, however, that a State committing those crimes would be restrained by the existence of a convention, or would surrender itself for trial to an international tribunal."[111] Rejecting a liberal reconstruction of unpleasant realities through the rule of law, he soberly portrayed "victor's justice" as the only effective means of prevention and punishment. He pointed to the "obvious truth" that "individual genocide was already punishable by the laws of all countries, whereas genocide committed by States was punishable only by war."[112] In a final assault on the structuring ritual of international treaty making, he suggested:

While making no significant contribution to international law, the convention might set forth more clearly the detestation with which genocide should be regarded ... [The delegates] should not take measures which might delude

[108] Abtahi and Webb, eds., *The Genocide Convention*, 1306.
[109] UN GAOR, 3rd Sess., 179th plen. mtg., 852, UN Doc. A/PV.179 (1948).
[110] UN GAOR, 3rd Sess., 6th Cmte., 64th mtg., UN Doc. A/C.6/SR.64 (1948); Abtahi and Webb, *The Genocide Convention*, 1307.
[111] Abtahi and Webb, eds., *The Genocide Convention*, 1307.
[112] *Ibid.*

people into thinking that some great step forward had been taken whereas in reality nothing at all had been changed.[113]

Shawcross was not alone in his skepticism of international law's postwar euphoria. Eminent jurists such as Hersch Lauterpacht were also keenly aware that the Nuremberg moment represented a very different enterprise than that contemplated under the Genocide Convention. He remarked in 1955 that, "to a considerable extent, the Convention amounts to a registration of protest against past misdeeds of individual savagery rather than to an effective instrument of their prevention or repression."[114]

It does not take much imagination to see the truth in Lauterpacht's prognosis. Since the adoption of the Genocide Convention, there have been numerous instances of genocide, with correspondingly few instances of prevention or punishment. In the post-Cold War context that witnessed the "end of history" and the supposed triumph of liberal values,[115] David Scheffer went so far as to claim that "genocide has become a growth industry."[116] Far from being an effective instrument for preventing and punishing genocide, and far from representing a genuine resolve to vindicate the legacy of the Holocaust, the postwar record reveals blatant indifference to the convention's objectives, if not outright endorsement of massive atrocities in selective instances.

The emphasis on recourse to national courts,[117] the rejection of universal jurisdiction,[118] interstate enforcement through the International Court of Justice,[119] and the reference to a nonexistent international

---

[113] *Ibid.*

[114] Lassa Oppenheim, *International Law: A Treatise*, vol. I, 8th edn., ed. Hersch Lauterpacht (London: Longman, 1955), 75.

[115] Francis Fukuyama, "The End of History?," *National Interest* (Summer 1989): 3.

[116] David J. Scheffer, "International Judicial Intervention," *Foreign Policy* (Spring 1996): 34.

[117] Article VI of the convention provides, in relevant part, that persons charged with genocide "shall be tried by a competent tribunal of the state in the territory of which the act was committed." However, since the vast scale of genocide makes it unlikely to be committed without the participation of a state, it is unrealistic to assume that the same state will bring the perpetrators to trial. See, for example, Payam Akhavan, "Enforcement of the Genocide Convention: A Challenge to Civilization," *Harvard Human Rights Journal* 8 (1995): 229, 232–33.

[118] See *ibid.*, 233–34.

[119] Article IX of the convention provides: "Disputes between the Contracting Parties relating to the interpretation, application, or fulfillment of the present Convention, including those relating to the responsibility of a State for genocide … shall be submitted to the International Court of Justice at the request of any of the parties to the dispute." See *ibid.*, 246–47.

criminal jurisdiction[120] betrayed, from the outset, a lack of genuine resolve to enforce the Genocide Convention. Indeed, it would be half a century before the first international criminal prosecution for genocide – in the 1998 *Akayesu* case before the ICTR.[121] But what is even more significant in gauging the commitment of the international community is the ongoing, gross failure to prevent genocide and other instances of mass killing, even where ample opportunity existed. The issue here is not whether the scope of the duty to prevent genocide under the convention is sufficiently rigorous, since it is doubtful that even the most stringently worded text would have had much effect on world history since 1948.[122] Rather, the issue is a more probing query as to the relationship between a discourse centered on rational legal concepts and hierarchical abstractions, on the one hand, and the potential to experience empathy for, or to engage with the reality of, those slated for destruction, on the other. Of course, the point is not that there is somehow a mechanical "cause and effect" relationship between legal conceptualization and moral paralysis. Rather, the nature of the discourse surrounding such events can reflect a sensibility as to how evil and suffering are understood and appreciated (and then acted upon, or ignored) – especially among bystanders with the capacity to intervene. This issue will be explored further in Chapter 8.

The Eichmann *trial*

In May 1960 in Buenos Aires, Israeli Mossad agents secretly captured Adolf Eichmann, a former SS *Obersturmbannführer* who had been in charge of managing the logistics of the mass deportation of Jews to extermination camps in eastern Europe. Brought to Jerusalem and put on trial before Israeli courts, Eichmann was eventually found guilty

---

[120] Article VI of the convention includes as a means of enforcement "such international penal tribunal as may have jurisdiction with respect to those Contracting Parties which shall have accepted its jurisdiction." No such tribunal existed at the time, however; it would be many decades before there was such a tribunal, the International Criminal Court.

[121] See Akayesu, Trial Judgement (ICTR, 2 September 1998).

[122] Despite much uncertainty, the duty to prevent genocide where there is a "serious danger" that it will occur and where a state party has the necessary "influence" to avert it has been affirmed by the International Court of Justice. See *Application of the Convention on the Prevention and Punishment of the Crime of Genocide* (Bosnia and Herzegovina v. Serbia and Montenegro) (International Court of Justice, 26 February 2007).

of his crimes and executed by hanging in 1962.[123] The *Eichmann* trial represented a departure from the legal rituals of Nuremberg and the Genocide Convention. This justice – meted out by *victims* and not victors – was an attempt by Israel to appropriate the particularity of the Holocaust rather than surrender it to the normative empire of international jurists.

Indeed, the *Eichmann* trial is one of the most telling examples of how profoundly the appropriation of past injustice shapes and reconstitutes collective identity, while exposing at the same time the tension – legal, moral, experiential – between particularity and universality. As discussed previously, the Nuremberg Trials relegated the Holocaust to a mere consequence of aggressive war, thus belittling its magnitude and distorting its underlying causes. Through the *Eichmann* trial, this misrepresentation of the survivors' experience was rectified by placing the Holocaust at the center of the narrative about Nazi crimes. One important aspect of "ownership" was the actual presence of Eichmann before the courts of the people whom he had sought to eradicate, and another was the empowerment of reappropriating justice after centuries of persecution and helplessness.

Beyond these considerations, the naming of the crime itself was a vital element of constructing a narrative of ownership. The accused was charged with "crimes against the Jewish people" under section 1 of the Nazis and Nazi Collaborators (Punishment) Act of 1950. Although this crime replicated the genocide definition contained in Article II of the Genocide Convention, it substituted the term *Jewish people* for the protected groups and the term *Jews* for "members of the group" under the enumerated acts.[124] In place of the broader term *genocide*,

---

[123] See Neil Bascomb, *Hunting Eichmann: How a Band of Survivors and a Young Spy Agency Chased Down the World's Most Notorious Nazi* (New York: Houghton Mifflin Harcourt, 2009).

[124] See *Prosecutor v. Akayesu*, Case No. ICTR-96-4-T (1998), para. 503 (referring to these "crimes against the Jewish people" as "genocide under another legal definition"). It should be noted, however, that Israel has specific enabling legislation for the purpose of implementing the Genocide Convention (see The Crime of Genocide (Prevention and Punishment) Law of 1950, reprinted in *Laws of the State of Israel*, Vol. IV, 5710–1949/50, 101). Furthermore, the Nazis and Nazi Collaborators (Punishment) Act is broader than the Genocide Convention's Article II definition; the former includes acts of cultural destruction such as "destroying or desecrating Jewish religious cultural assets or values." Section 1(b) of the Israeli act provides, in relevant part, as follows:

    "crime against the Jewish people" means any of the following acts, committed with intent to destroy the Jewish people in whole or in part:

the particularized "crimes against Jewish people" came to symbolize the Jews' reappropriation of the juridical narrative of Nazi crimes. As Pnina Lahav observed in her biography of Justice Simon Agranat, deputy-president of the Israeli Supreme Court during the *Eichmann* trial, labeling the Holocaust as a distinct crime against the Jews was far-reaching in the existential construction of a postsurvival national identity and political consciousness:

> The Law against the Nazis and Nazi Collaborators created a new category of crimes: crimes against the Jewish people ... The crime was specific to Jews and created a category hitherto unknown in any legal system. It was precisely for this reason that the crime formed a coherent part of Zionism ... Zionism portrayed the Holocaust less as the vile fruit of totalitarianism and more as the culmination of two millennia of anti-Semitism. The Jews had been defenseless because they did not possess political power. Even in Nuremberg the Allies refused to recognize that the Jews as a nation were especially targeted by the Nazis. The offense, "crimes against the Jewish people," was designed to correct that myopia and to assert, ex post facto and forever, the Jewish point of view.[125]

This legal categorization was ostensibly intended to empower the Jewish national consciousness and to reinforce the official Zionist historical narrative. But the depiction of the Holocaust as the mere consummation of two millennia of anti-Semitism replaced Nuremberg's myopia with a different kind of distortion. Arendt maintained that exclusive emphasis on "crimes against the Jewish people" failed to capture the unprecedented magnitude and essence of a crime that could be adequately represented only by the term *genocide*. The *Eichmann* trial, she suggested,

> [d]emonstrate[d] how little Israel, like the Jewish people in general, was prepared to recognize, in the crimes that Eichmann was accused of, an unprecedented crime, and precisely how difficult such a recognition must have been for the Jewish people. In the eyes of the Jews, thinking exclusively in terms

> > killing Jews;
> > causing serious bodily or mental harm to Jews;
> > placing Jews in living conditions calculated to bring about their physical destruction;
> > imposing measures intended to prevent births among Jews;
> > forcibly transferring Jewish children to another national or religious group;
> > destroying or desecrating Jewish religious or cultural assets or values;
> > inciting hatred of Jews.

[125] Pnina Lahav, *Judgment in Jerusalem* (Berkeley and Los Angeles: University of California Press, 1997), 150.

of their own history, the catastrophe that had befallen them under Hitler, in which a third of the people perished, appeared not as the most recent of crimes, *the unprecedented crime of genocide*, but, on the contrary, as the oldest crime they knew and remembered. This misunderstanding, almost inevitable if we consider not only the facts of Jewish history but also, and more important, the current Jewish historical self-understanding, is actually at the root of all the failures and shortcomings of the Jerusalem trial. *None of the participants ever arrived at a clear understanding of the actual horror of Auschwitz, which is of a different nature from all the atrocities of the past, because it appeared to prosecution and judges alike as not much more than the most horrible pogrom in Jewish history.* They therefore believed that a direct line existed from the early anti-Semitism of the Nazi Party to the Nuremberg Laws and from there to the expulsion of Jews from the Reich and, finally, to the gas chambers. *Politically and legally, however, these were "crimes" different not only in degree of seriousness but in essence.*[126]

The particularization of genocide in the guise of "crimes against Jewish people" had important consequences on the juridical narrative constructed by the *Eichmann* trial. At issue was reconciling the particularity of the Jewish Holocaust with the transcendent universality that made it assume the dimensions of a crime against "humanity" as a whole. Indeed, if these were merely crimes against discrete national groups, they did not possess a broader historical relevance or transcendent importance. It is in this context that we can understand Arendt's lament that at "no point ... did the Jerusalem trial ever mention even the possibility that exterminating an entire ethnic group" – whether Jews, Poles, or Gypsies, for example – "might be more than a crime against the Jewish or the Polish or the Gypsy people," and that it might, instead, be a crime against "the international order, and mankind in its entirely, [which] might have been grievously hurt and endangered."[127]

The tension between the particular and universal was at the core of the jurisprudence emanating from the *Eichmann* trial. As Lahav noted, Justice Agranat understood the full import of asserting the primacy of Israeli law while maintaining the credibility and relevance deriving from compliance with international norms of justice and fairness.[128] In response to the defense submission that the 1950 Israeli Law against the Nazis and Nazi Collaborators constituted ex post facto law in violation of the *nullum crimen sine lege* principle, the Jerusalem district court had

[126] Arendt, *Eichmann in Jerusalem*, 267 (emphasis added).
[127] *Ibid.*, 275–76.   [128] See Lahav, *Judgment in Jerusalem*, 150.

stressed the superiority of Israeli law in the sovereign state of Israel. The Law against the Nazis and Nazi Collaborators, the district court held, was a part of Israeli positive law and, as such, was binding on the courts of the land. It did hold that the law agreed with international norms, but emphasized the impact of the Holocaust on the evolution of the law of nations. This holding contained a symbolic message: Jewish national pride and self-assertion ruled the day. There was poetic justice in this interpretation. If the Final Solution was about the lawless murder of Jews, the *Eichmann* case was about the subjection of the perpetrators to Jewish justice, conceived and applied by the very heirs of those murdered.[129]

Although Justice Agranat endorsed the district court's analysis, he was ambivalent about its approach and thus, upon appeal from the first instance, steered the jurisprudence of the Supreme Court in a different direction. In particular, his concern was to establish that "the validity of the Law against the Nazis and Nazi Collaborators stemmed not from its superiority to the law of nations but from its compatibility with international law. Jewish justice was thereby not different from or superior to the law of nations; rather, it was a part of it."[130] After reviewing

the four categories of the indictment ... he concluded that they had a common denominator, a "special universal characteristic." About "crimes against the Jewish people" he had this to say: "Thus, the category of 'crimes against the Jewish people' is nothing but ... 'the gravest crime against humanity.' It is true that there are certain differences between them ... but these are not differences material to our case." Therefore, he concluded, in order to determine whether international law recognized Israeli jurisdiction stemming from this ex post facto statute, the Court could simply collapse the entire indictment into "the inclusive category of 'crimes against humanity.'" This "simple" technique enabled Agranat to devote the bulk of his opinion to the universal aspects of the *Eichmann* case.[131]

Invoking this symbolic argumentation, the particularity of "crimes against the Jewish people" was reconciled with international law, bringing the legislation under which Eichmann was prosecuted within the realm of historical legitimacy and transcendent relevance reserved for universal norms. Through rooting the Israeli law in the "gravest type of crimes against humanity," the Holocaust was brought back into mainstream consciousness, and in such a way that Jewish ownership did not

[129] *Ibid.*   [130] *Ibid.*   [131] *Ibid.*

negate the broader "shared meanings, perceptions, and reassurances"[132] that wider public discourse and engagement required.

Taken in its entirety, the *Eichmann* jurisprudence recalls the concomitant universality and particularity of genocide – at its inception – as a paradigmatic crime representing the Holocaust. As with "crimes against the Jewish people," the concept of genocide emerged from the factual matrix of the "Final Solution." This viewpoint was reflected in Lemkin's work, the Nuremberg Trials, and the adoption of the Genocide Convention, but its translation into an abstraction – the crime of *genocide* – imbued the paradigm with a shared meaning and broader relevance. By entering the public domain of legal idiom as a crime that was universally prohibited, the crime of genocide and its historical legacy became capable of appropriation by others.

[132] Murray Edelman, *Politics as Symbolic Action* (Chicago: Markham, 1971), 65.

6   Who owns "genocide"?

On 24 October 1997, in the city of Vancouver, Irene Starr told her life story to Reverend Kevin Annett, an Aboriginal rights advocate and former minister of the United Church of Canada:

I was born in Bella Bella [in British Columbia, Canada] in 1945, and lived there until the Indian Agent told my mother "If your children don't go to the residential school, they'll all be put up for adoption." So they scared her into sending me away when I was seven or eight. My heart was broken. It ruined my entire way of thinking and living.

The Alberni school was a terrible, awful place. I wet my bed constantly, I was so lonely and afraid. Whenever I wet my sheets, the staff made me stomp on the sheets in a tub of cold water, up to my waist. I stood in ice water for an hour often, and three women on staff laughed at me as I froze. They'd bang me with a mop whenever I stopped, and tell me to hurry up. Then, I'd have to go to school, frozen, ice cold. I had permanent bladder problems because of that.

I was just a little girl of seven, and I wanted to kill myself. What makes a child want to commit suicide? I was so mistreated. All I heard from the teachers was "You dumb Indian," "You'll never amount to anything." They were constantly smacking me on the head. So I grew up thinking I was ugly and stupid. I was ashamed of myself, and my people, and I wished I was white.

I was always freezing. All I had each night was one little blanket over my cot. I was never warm. All of us were hungry. The food was rotten, the oatmeal and milk was bad. Kids were always getting sick from the food, and many of them refused to eat it. They starved. That's why I thought of killing myself, I was starving there.

A lot of girls got pregnant after they got to the Alberni school. The fathers were the men who worked there. We never knew what happened to the babies. The pregnant girls would be taken to the Alberni Hospital and then come back without their babies. I'd hear them crying all the time: "Where's my baby? What have they done with my baby?"

The staff at the school probably killed most of those babies because they were the fathers. They were not only sadists but murderers. And they got paid to be so.

I've been a loner ever since that school. It still hurts so bad to think of that place. Like the big lady in black, who was always beating me and my sister Donna with a wooden brush, and dragging Donna into a closet to sexually abuse her.

I was hit either with a wooden scrubbing brush or a mop, always on the head. I also got strapped with a leather strap in class, whenever I dozed off, from staying awake all night taking care of the babies. The strap was two inches thick. I had welts on my arms, up to my shoulders.

So many of our people are dying, every day, because of the residential schools. I only got to grade eight. Eventually, beer calmed my nerves. I became an alcoholic, and eventually, a heroin addict.

The church spokesmen, the officials, they don't mean what they say when they speak. I can't understand how those people in the school learned to be so cruel.[1]

This is but one of the many tragic tales to emerge over the past few decades from the public scrutiny of the Canadian Indian residential school system (1879–1986). The Canadian government established the schools, in cooperation with various church institutions across the country; after forcibly removing Canadian Aboriginal children from their families, the goal was to "civilize" them by eradicating their native identity. The brutal treatment in the schools is said to have resulted in the deaths of some 50,000 native children, with countless others becoming victims of serious physical and sexual abuse.[2] Some children were also subjected to medical and scientific experiments, like Jasper Joseph, now a 69-year-old man from Port Hardy, British Columbia:

I was just eight, and they'd shipped us down from the Anglican residential school in Alert Bay to the Nainamo Indian Hospital, the one run by the United Church. They kept me in a tiny room there for more than three years, like

[1] Kevin Daniel Annett, "Statement of Irene Starr (Nee Wilson), Student at Alberni Residential School, Given to (Rev.) Kevin Annett on October 24, 1997, in Vancouver, BC," in Annett Hidden from History: The Canadian Holocaust. The Untold Story of the Genocide of Aboriginal Peoples by Church and State in Canada (Vancouver: Truth Commission into Genocide in Canada, 2005), 178ff. Many other testimonies can be found in books such as Agnes S. Jack, Behind Closed Doors: Stories from the Kamloops Indian Residential School (Kamloops, British Columbia: Secwepemc Cultural Education Society, 2000).

[2] See, for example, John S. Milloy, A National Crime: The Canadian Government and the Residential School System, 1879 to 1986 (Winnipeg: University of Manitoba Press, 1999).

I was a lab rat, feeding me these pills, giving me shots that made me sick. Two of my cousins made a big fuss, screaming and fighting back all the time, so the nurses gave them shots, and they both died right away. It was done to silence them.[3]

In 2005, a group calling itself the Truth Commission into Genocide in Canada issued a report *Hidden from History: The Canadian Holocaust. The Untold Story of the Genocide of Aboriginal Peoples by Church and State in Canada*.[4] The report alleges a "planned and deliberate genocide," its "primary vehicle" being the "Indian Residential School System."[5] The report argues that the various crimes perpetrated in the schools – including murder, torture, rape, the forcible transfer of children, and forced abortion and sterilization – fall under Articles II(a)–(e) of the Genocide Convention.[6] These crimes were intended to "systematic[ally] eradicat[e] … all indigenous populations that would not leave their lands and resources, abolish their own cultures and languages, and become Christians."[7]

Whatever the merits of these legal claims, the evident aim of the report's authors was to situate the stories of those like Irene Starr and Jasper Joseph not within a particular, localized narrative of suffering and oppression, but within the broader history of the Holocaust – the recounted experiences being, apparently, the stuff of genocide. The rhetoric began with the report's title, "the Canadian Holocaust," and was followed by an explicit effort to compare it to the Nazi genocide: "The architect of this massacre, which claimed millions of lives, was that two-headed hydra of Church and State that operated out of a genocidal philosophy of racial superiority indistinguishable from Nazism."[8] It even appropriated the Holocaust's distinctive terminology: "The expression 'Final Solution' was not coined by the Nazis, but by Indian Affairs Superintendent Duncan Campbell Scott in April 1910, when he referred to how he envisioned the so-called 'Indian Problem' in Canada being resolved."[9] Such language recalls the gas chambers of Auschwitz and claims for the Aboriginal victims the same significance and recognition extended to history's "ultimate crime."

---

[3] Annett, *Hidden from History*, 12.   [4] *Ibid.*
[5] *Ibid.*, 128. A similar argument is made in Ward Churchill, *Kill the Indian, Save the Man: The Genocidal Impact of American Indian Residential Schools* (San Francisco: City Light, 2004).
[6] Annett, *Hidden from History*, 43–140.
[7] *Ibid.*, 44.   [8] *Ibid.*, 10.   [9] *Ibid.*, 15.

Some would vigorously dispute this equivalence and claim that "the Nazi attack on the Jews was the only true genocide in history"[10] and brush aside any effort at comparison. Reflecting on the significance of the Holocaust and the importance of remembrance, Charles Maier observes that, between Germans and Jews, "[n]o matter what material or other public debts are paid, confessional memory is demanded as the only valid reparation. And as a claim upon official memory, the victim's anguish comes to be seen as a valuable possession." But he also points to the obvious fact that "[o]ther people also want the [valuable] status of victimhood." The sordid contest over the singularity of the Holocaust and the appropriation of the "genocide" label must be understood as the product of a political culture of recognition in which ownership of anguish is not merely a means of working through trauma or an intermediate step in the sharing of transcendent suffering, but also a means of achieving a form of celebrity. Maier describes the climate of proliferating and contending claims for recognition in contemporary American politics as "a competition for enshrining grievances. Every group claims its share of public honor and public funds by pressing disabilities and injustices."[11]

In this context, the "ultimate crime" has become a much-coveted trophy in a consumer culture of grievance and suffering, alleged or real. In this bazaar of slogans, the utilitarian appeal of privileged labels and emotional self-indulgence is an expedient substitute for the more laborious work of nurturing empathy with the "other." The appropriation of genocide is thus regarded by some as a depreciation of a valuable currency and by others as the supreme sign that public recognition is both deserved and owed. These seemingly opposed, but interrelated, deflationary and inflationary pressures in the "language game"[12] of suffering are manifested both in the claim of the Holocaust's uniqueness and implicit moral superiority and in the abusive or inflammatory application of genocide to manifold grievances, however trivial.

The "uniqueness" of the Holocaust?

To understand the contest over appropriating the label of *genocide*, we must begin with the emotionally charged debate over the "uniqueness"

---

[10] Steven Katz, *The Holocaust in Historical Context*, vol. I, *The Holocaust and Mass Death Before the Modern Age* (New York: Oxford University Press, 1994).

[11] Charles Maier, "A Surfeit of Memory? Reflections on History, Melancholy and Denial," *History and Memory* 5 (1993): 136, 147.

[12] See Ludwig Wittgenstein, *Philosophical Investigations* (Malden, MA: Blackwell 1953).

of the Holocaust. The problems of attributing to the Holocaust such distinction and radical incomprehensibility are manifested in the implicit denial of recognition to others that a discourse of uniqueness arguably entails. Although the proponents of uniqueness are quick to claim that such distinction should not be taken as an indication of moral superiority, they go on to emphasize the Holocaust's "radical" factual differences from other historical events, such as the historical plight of indigenous peoples in the Americas.[13] This effort to factually distinguish the Holocaust is regarded by some as an attempt to establish, under the guise of objective "description," the Holocaust's moral ascendancy. It is contended that the suffering of others is thereby disparaged or denied, which contributes to the continued marginalization of the groups in question.[14] The Romani Holocaust, or *Porrajmos*, is a relevant example. The case is made that Gypsies, likewise slated by the Nazis for total destruction,[15] have been grossly neglected in accounts of Jewish uniqueness: They have been reduced to a mere historical footnote, with far-reaching consequences for the contemporary plight of this persecuted people.[16]

Given the intimate association between genocide and the paradigm of the (Jewish) Holocaust, claims of uniqueness invariably lead to assertions that only the Nazi extermination of Jews qualifies as the "ultimate

[13] See, for example, Steven T. Katz, "The Uniqueness of the Holocaust: The Historical Dimension," in Alan S. Rosenbaum, ed., *Is the Holocaust Unique?* (Boulder: Westview, 1996), 19–20. Katz posits that, in "arguing for the uniqueness of the Holocaust, I am *not* making a *moral* claim, in other words, that the Holocaust was more evil than other events ... I know of no method or technique that would allow one to weigh up, to quantify and compare, such massive evil and suffering." Katz therefore decides to "avoid altogether this sort of counterproductive argument about what one might describe as comparative suffering." Yet Katz also argues that, although "Native American people(s) have been the subject of exploitation, despoliation, rape, violence, and murder since the arrival of Columbus," and however much this "centuries-long record of subjugation and abuse is incontrovertible and tragic," it "differs radically from that represented by the Holocaust for several fundamental reasons, the most basic of which is the role that disease has played in this history" of Native Americans.

[14] See, for example, David E. Stannard, "Uniqueness as Denial: The Politics of Genocide Scholarship," in Rosenbaum, ed., *Is the Holocaust Unique?*, 163, 198–99.

[15] See, for example, Emil Fackenheim, *To Mend the World* (New York: Schocken, 1982), 12 ("With the possible exception of the Gypsies, Jews were the only people killed for the 'crime' of existing").

[16] See, for example, Erika Thurner, *Nazi Policy Against the Gypsies*, presentation to US Holocaust Memorial Council conference, "The Other Victims," Washington, DC, 22–25 February, 1987, 7 (as cited in Ian Hancock, "Responses to the Porrajmos: The Romani Holocaust," in Rosenbaum, ed., *Is the Holocaust Unique?*, 58).

crime." Steven Katz, for one, bluntly claims that "the Nazi attack on the Jews was the only true genocide in history."[17] Yehuda Bauer emphasizes that "it is essential to differentiate between different types of evil," and places genocide and the Holocaust at different points in a "continuum of mass brutalization," with the Holocaust being the "extreme case" or the "farthest point of the continuum."[18] Nonetheless, he concedes that, other than the destruction of European Jewry, the Holocaust should be "a generic name of an ideologically motivated planned total murder of a whole people"; he includes the 1915 massacres of Armenians under the category of "Holocaust-related events."[19]

Leaving aside considerations of historical interpretation, what is the underlying significance of "uniqueness"? Or, as Peter Haidu queries, "is uniqueness a unique quality?"[20] The underlying premise of historiography, he notes, is that all events are unique – a claim that can be fully appreciated only in a comparative context.[21] But uniqueness does not assume superiority, and comparison does not necessarily imply hierarchy. There is a subtle, but profound, difference between comparative analysis based on intersubjective understanding and that based on an objectifying discourse of moral dominance that alienates and subordinates the "other." Israel Charny notes that assertions of "uniqueness" (in relation to genocide) reflect

[p]ressures to define genocide so that a given event of mass murder emerges as more "important" than another, including especially pressures to claim for a given genocide the crown of "ultimate importance." A closely related argument has to do with the assignment of relative degrees of evil to different events of mass murder, so that a given event is taken to represent the greater, incarnate evil in comparison to other events of genocide, which are treated somewhat as more usual events of massacre and slaughter in human history.[22]

Charny acknowledges that a people's privileged conception of its own suffering is understandable: He "never fault[s] or argue[s] with a

[17] Katz, The Holocaust in Historical Context.
[18] Yehuda Bauer, A History of the Holocaust (New York: Franklin Watts, 1982), 332.
[19] Ibid.
[20] Peter Haidu, "The Dialectics of Unspeakability: Language, Silence, and the Narratives of Desubjectification," in Saul Friedlander, ed., Probing the Limits of Representation: Nazism and the "Final Solution" (Cambridge, MA: Harvard University Press, 1992), 277, 295.
[21] See ibid., 295–96.
[22] Israel W. Charny, "Toward a Generic Definition of Genocide," in George J. Andreopoulous, ed., Genocide: Conceptual and Historical Dimensions (Philadelphia: University of Pennsylvania Press, 1994), 64, 68.

THE "UNIQUENESS" OF THE HOLOCAUST?   127

survivor's claim that a given genocide was the ultimate evil of all," and also finds no "fault with collective expressions of such demands for uniqueness of a given genocide when they spring from the same natural folk-outpouring of grief, disbelief, horror, and rage at the tragedy and infamy done to one's people."[23] But beyond such rituals of remembrance, he strongly rejects assigning "objective credence" to "efforts to name the genocide of any one people as the single, ultimate event, or as the most important event against which all other tragedies of genocidal mass deaths are to be tested and found wanting," including what he refers to as "the Holocaust of my people."[24] Charny points out that creating an order of importance between events consigns some victims to historical oblivion:

For me, the passion to exclude this or that mass killing from the universe of genocide, as well as the intense competition to establish the exclusive "superiority" or unique form of any one genocide, ends up creating a fetishistic atmosphere in which the masses of bodies that are not to be qualified for the definition of genocide are dumped into a conceptual black hole, where they are forgotten.[25]

Charny sees this tendency as an objectifying "definitionalism." This "damaging style of intellectual inquiry" represents "a perverse, fetishistic involvement with definitions" in which "the reality of the subject under discussion is 'lost'" – by which he means that the subject is "no longer experienced emotionally by the scholars conducting the inquiry, to the point that the real enormity of the subject no longer guides or impacts on the deliberations."[26]

Abstract assertions of moral superiority not only alienate and deny the "other," but also undermine the moral standing of those making such claims. Moreover, by suggesting that the Holocaust can be conclusively ranked and measured as the "ultimate crime," the enormity of the Holocaust itself is banalized. One is reminded of sterile, statistical debates over the exact number of Holocaust victims, as if such quantification can adequately convey the Holocaust's heinousness.[27]

---

[23] Ibid., 72.   [24] Ibid.   [25] Ibid., 91–92.   [26] Ibid., 91.

[27] See, for example, Eric Hobsbawm, The Age of Extremes (New York: Vintage, 1994), 43: In any case, what does statistical exactitude mean, where the orders of magnitude are so astronomic? Would the horror of the Holocaust be any less if historians concluded that it exterminated not six million (the rough and almost certainly exaggerated estimate) but five or even four? ... Indeed, can we really grasp figures beyond the reality open to physical intuition?

Reducing genocide to a rare commodity in a market of competitive suffering does little to promote the intersubjective understanding and empathy with the "other" that ultimately result in genuine appreciation of historical "lessons" and the transformation of self-conceptions, whether among victims, perpetrators, or bystanders. Fetishistic calls to remembrance and empty incantations of "never again" may actually undermine an authentic emotional connection by reifying a falsely righteous self-conception, thus distracting attention away from a reality of cynical indifference or simple cowardice. There is evidently a disconnection between the "lessons" of the Holocaust and contemporary events. The imperative recognition of the "other" through dialogical mediation of truth and transcendence of artificial boundaries is abandoned in the objectifying discourse of genocide's exclusivity. The ethic of recognition, Haidu maintains, is not intended "to argue a moral condemnation addressed to the past ... that at the same time disregards the present visage of the other." An ethic that functions only to "satisf[y] moral superiority vis-à-vis the monsters of the past, without accepting concrete responsibility for the other who is present at our doorstep," lacks both genuine concern and humanity.[28]

The critique of objectifying discourses is equally, if not more, forcefully applicable to those at the inflationary end of the spectrum, who indiscriminately appropriate genocide and Holocaust imagery to focus attention on their cause. On the positive side, this effort requires the translation of particularized experience into the idiom of shared meanings, thereby making possible both public recognition and wider engagement. But there is also the potential for abuse. Elizabeth Spelman notes that,

once rendered intelligible through its articulation in language or its representability in art, suffering becomes ready for use and thus also for possible abuse by others. The expression of our pain or suffering that makes it available to others opens up the possibility that they will understand what it means to us, but also the possibility that others will mangle our account, especially if they stretch, tuck, or hem our experience in an attempt to tailor it to make sense of their own.[29]

This process is quintessentially characterized by what Lucy Dawidowicz describes as "the glib equation of the destruction of the

[28] Haidu, "The Dialectics of Unspeakability," 283.
[29] Elizabeth V. Spelman, *Fruits of Sorrow: Framing Our Attention to Suffering* (Boston: Beacon, 1997), 4.

European Jews with any disaster or atrocity, with any state of affairs one abhors or even merely dislikes."[30] Spelman points out that invoking the powerful symbolism of the Holocaust

appears to offer at least partial redemption for that suffering: what I or what we went through might turn out to be of help to others; if so, my experiences are not anomalous or at the margins of human existence, but representative of or paradigmatic for the rest of humankind. To the degree that those inflicting suffering try to justify their acts on the grounds that the sufferers are not fully human, the honor apparently paid to such suffering by its being treated as exemplary may signal an important acknowledgement of shared human status.[31]

Thus, the conception of genocide as a "paradigmatic" crime built on the legacy of the Holocaust transforms the particularity or uniqueness of the Jewish or Gypsy experience into the relevance reserved for universal norms, into a mainstream historical event, a recognition of its profound hortatory value for all of humankind. Spelman also cautions, however, that

the very articulation of this [comparative] possibility invites close scrutiny: what if the borrowers are in fact more like scavengers, interested in the suffering of others not as a way of marking deep and pervasive similarities among suffering humanity, and making a case for mutual care, but mainly as a way of trying to garner concern simply for themselves? When are they honoring the suffering of others, when simply compounding it by expropriating yet another product of the horrific labors of the sufferers – their now "exemplary" experiences of suffering?[32]

Appropriation of genocide as a form of moral scavenging unfortunately is an all-too-familiar occurrence. As Michael Ignatieff points out, in the meta-legal discourse of suffering:

"[g]enocide" is a worn and debased term, casually hurled at every outrage, every violence, even applied to events where no death, only shame or abuse, occurs. But it is a word that does mean something: the project to exterminate a people for no other reason than because they are that people. Before the experience of genocide, they may believe it a matter of personal choice whether they belong or believe. After genocide, it becomes their fate.[33]

[30] Lucy S. Dawidowicz, "Thinking About the Six Million: Facts, Figures, Perspectives," in John K. Roth and Michael Berenbaum, eds., *Holocaust: Religious and Philosophical Implications* (St. Paul, MN: Paragon House, 1989), 51, 63.
[31] Spelman, *Fruits of Sorrow*, 9–10.   [32] *Ibid.*, 10.
[33] Michael Ignatieff, *Blood and Belonging: Journeys into the New Nationalism* (London: BBC, 1993), 194–95.

There is, after all, a certain historical reality to the crime of genocide, in addition to a legacy and assumption of extreme suffering, or at least a descriptive typology of a particular evil. The call for intersubjective understanding and inclusive recognition does not somehow collapse all distinctions and boundaries. Rather, it questions the weight and significance attached to such descriptions and to the associated, hierarchical conceptualization of ineffable human experience. There are obvious differences between killing someone solely because of their belonging to an ethnic or racial group and killing a prisoner-of-war to avenge the death of fallen comrades; between the permanent and irredeemable loss of death and the more transient loss caused by deportation of hapless civilians from their homes; and between suffering arising from human agency and that from natural causes, even if famine and disease can often be traced to oppression or other human acts. In the realm of law and social consensus, it may actually be necessary to attribute particular moral value to, or to engage in an invidious ranking of, these different forms of conduct, generating, in turn, a hierarchical ranking of crimes and punishments. But it is an entirely different matter to suggest that such definition and ranking should determine the anguish of the victim and the deeper meaning attributed to intense suffering. What perverse sort of language game would tell a child who has lost his mother to AIDS that his loss is morally inferior to that of the concentration camp victim, and that she is therefore less worthy of empathy and recognition? But why should we even seek to compare or equate the suffering of the AIDS patient and that of the concentration camp victim? The pain and agony of each stand on their own. And how could a scheme of comparisons lead to anything but contentious discourse in which the meaning of pain is lost in decontextualized definitions and hierarchical abstractions?

The view that unrestrained appropriation of symbols is an effective strategy for communicating moral legitimacy and political urgency leads to the same desolation that assertions of uniqueness often represent. Jack Porter, for instance, observes that genocide has been applied to "'race-mixing' (integration of blacks and nonblacks); drug distribution; methadone programs; and the practice of birth control and abortions among Third World people; sterilization and 'Mississippi appendectomies' (tubal ligations and hysterectomies); medical treatment of Catholics; and the closing of synagogues in the Soviet Union."[34]

---

[34] Jack Nusan Porter, "Introduction," in Jack Nusan Porter, ed., *Genocide and Human Rights: A Global Anthology* (Lanham, MD: University Press of America, 1982), 2, 9–10.

Helen Fein similarly notes that "[s]ince genocide is widely conceived of as the most reprehensible of crimes, many people use genocide-labeling both to vent outrage and to describe situations in which they perceive themselves as threatened, regardless of how these situations have come about, the source of threat, the truth of accusation against the putative perpetrator, and so on."[35] She points to a "wave of misuse and rhetorical abuse" of genocide, noting that at times "such labeling verges on the paranoid and incendiary, as when Westerners or Jews are accused of genocide by giving Africans or African-Americans AIDS."[36] In this light, how does the manifestly incongruent and abusive appropriation of the term to these otherwise worthy causes and legitimate concerns communicate the reality of the subject or allow for a closer emotional connection with the plight of the oppressed?

Although they might appear to be diametrically opposed, assertions of uniqueness and indiscriminate, unfounded efforts to appropriate genocide and the historical imagery of the Holocaust both reflect a similar banalization of suffering. What also may result is a competition between the two viewpoints, where claims and counterclaims escalate into rhetorical and ideological assertions about the grievances and suffering of each group, so exaggerated that all empathy is lost.

In faulting such claims, however, we must not lose sight of their actual context. Leo Kuper observes that "disadvantaged groups [have] sought to gain a sympathetic hearing by dramatic denunciation" because of "[e]xperiencing the indifference of the outside world to their suffering."[37] The case of Rwanda demonstrates that the unambiguous horrors of wholesale extermination – open for the world to witness live on television – were largely greeted with indifference, as if the victims were objects in a mindless entertainment spectacle depicting graphic violence. Under such circumstances of alienation and emotional numbness, can desperate resort to the most effective weapons in the rhetorical arsenal of public discourse be blamed? It is true, as Kuper points out, that abusive invocation of genocide has "proved counterproductive in the United Nations, which [has] turned a deaf ear to these extravagant charges." He notes that "the avoidance of extreme charges and rhetoric might contribute to a favorable response"[38] in

---

[35] Helen Fein, "Genocide, Terror, Life Integrity, and War Crimes: The Case for Discrimination," in Andreopoulos, ed., *Genocide: Conceptual and Historical Dimensions*, 95.
[36] *Ibid.*
[37] Leo Kuper, "Theoretical Issues Relating to Genocide: Uses and Abuses," in Andreopoulos, ed., *Genocide: Conceptual and Historical Dimensions*, 31, 35.
[38] *Ibid.*, 36.

some situations. Thus, for instance, "the representatives of the Baha'is, threatened with the violent eradication of their religion in Iran and subjected to systematic discrimination reminiscent of the persecution of Jews by the Nazis in the 1930s, were advised to avoid the charge of genocide, a strategy they successfully followed,"[39] notwithstanding a UN report that described the killings as genocide.[40] But, as he concedes, set against the cynical deference to power and entrenchment of the status quo, resistance "to charges of genocide [in the UN system] is not simply a reaction to the trivializing abuse of the concept."[41]

Invoking genocide

It is instructive to consider some significant instances in which genocide has been invoked in popular discourse to draw attention to a cause. These examples help illustrate the interrelationship between legal definition and meta-legal meaning. They also demonstrate the contrast between the emotional experiencing of such events and their description through distant labels and abstractions.

Vietnam

The "Russell Tribunal," also known as the International War Crimes Tribunal, was established in 1966 at the prompting of British philosopher Bertrand Russell to "pass serious and impartial judgment" on the Vietnam war.[42] In holding that American policy in Vietnam constituted genocide,[43] the tribunal unanimously adopted the written opinion prepared by its president, the French philosopher and playwright Jean-Paul Sartre.[44] The symbolic power of the term *genocide* was not lost on Sartre, who drew parallels between the Holocaust and the American "imperialist genocide"[45] against the Vietnamese. The "truth of the Vietnam war," he contended, was that "it meets all of Hitler's specifications. Hitler killed the Jews because they were Jews. The armed forces of the United States torture and kill men, women and children in Vietnam merely *because they are Vietnamese*."[46] Thus, in the

---

[39] Ibid.
[40] Benjamin Whitaker, Revised and Updated Report on the Question of the Prevention and Punishment of the Crime of Genocide, UN Doc. E/CN.4/Sub.2/1985/6 (1985), para. 24.
[41] Kuper, "Theoretical Issues Relating to Genocide," 31, 36.
[42] Jean-Paul Sartre, On Genocide (Boston: Beacon, 1968), 3.
[43] Ibid., 50–53.   [44] Ibid., 53, 57–85.   [45] Ibid., 85.
[46] Ibid., 82. In support of this conclusion, Sartre refers, inter alia, to the example of an American general who "boasted of hunting 'VCs' from his helicopter and gunning

tribunal's polemic against the Vietnam war, genocide and the echoes of the Holocaust figured prominently. Only by situating American atrocities against the Vietnamese within the domain of genocide could the war's "reality" be reliably described or the tribunal's abhorrence of the war be fully expressed.

Independent of the merits concerning this charge of genocide, the tribunal obviously took the view that the horrors of saturation bombing and the associated, indiscriminate killing of civilians could be conveyed by invoking the moral *gravitas* of the "ultimate crime."

Cambodia

During the short reign of Pol Pot's Khmer Rouge from 1975 to 1979, up to two million of a total population of eight million were executed, tortured, or starved to death in the infamous "killing fields" and death camps of Cambodia.[47] The crimes of the Khmer Rouge, committed in the pursuit of an agrarian, classless utopia, were at the time called "the most serious that had occurred anywhere in the world since Nazism."[48] This horrendous mass murder was understood to be the "ultimate crime" and enshrined in popular discourse as "the Cambodian genocide."

Yet scholarly dispute persists as to whether the majority of the killings legally constitute genocide. Although the Khmer Rouge's effort to exterminate the Buddhist, Vietnamese, and Cham Muslim minorities may qualify as genocide, the vast majority of victims - the intellectuals, bourgeoisie, and other political or social class "enemies" of the Khmer Rouge - belonged to the Khmer majority groups. A UN rapporteur maintained at the time that this amounted to an "auto-genocide" of the Cambodian national group (since Khmers killed other Khmers).[49] But such an argument is juridically untenable. It reflects a creative and

---

them down in the rice paddies. Obviously, the victims were not National Liberation Front soldiers who knew how to defend themselves; they were peasants tending their rice. Sartre adds (at p. 81) that in the

confused minds of the American soldiers "Vietcong" and "Vietnamese" tend increasingly to blend into one another. They often say themselves, "The only good Vietnamese is a dead Vietnamese," or what amounts to the same thing, "A dead Vietnamese is a Vietcong." From the "neo colonialists'" [point of view] in a people's war, civilians are the only visible enemies.

[47] See Ben Kiernan, *The Pol Pot Regime: Race, Power, and Genocide in Cambodia Under the Khmer Rouge, 1975–1979* (New Haven: Yale University Press, 1996), for extensive discussion of the death toll and nature of the genocide.
[48] UN Doc. E/C.4/SR.1510, at 7 (1979).   [49] *Ibid.*

seemingly desperate attempt to invoke the term *genocide* to convey the enormity of the crimes, as if any other categorization would trivialize their magnitude. As Steven Ratner and Jason Abrams observe, the Khmer Rouge "did not target their non-minority victims as members of the Khmer nation"; instead, they either were targeted as "economic, social or political elements whom the Khmer Rouge sought to eradicate" or were "victims of arbitrary violence and harsh conditions that the government imposed on virtually the entire country."[50] A Group of Experts commissioned by the UN General Assembly concluded that the "evidence suggests the need for prosecutors to investigate the commission of genocide against the Cham, Vietnamese, and other minority groups, and the Buddhist monkhood." With regard to the "atrocities committed against the general Cambodian population," the group did not "take a position" on whether the Khmer people "constitute[d] a national group within the meaning of the [Genocide] Convention," though the group did note that "any tribunal will have to address the question should Khmer Rouge officials be charged with genocide against the Khmer national group."[51]

The indictments recently proposed by the prosecutor for the Extraordinary Chambers in the Courts of Cambodia have now answered that question. Four codefendants – Nuon Chea, Ieng Sary, Ieng Thirith, and Khieu Samphan – have all been charged with genocide, crimes against humanity, and war crimes, but the genocide charge relates only to the attempted extermination of the Cham Muslim and Vietnamese minorities. The prosecutor appears to have concluded that the majority of the Khmer Rouge crimes did not qualify as genocide on account of the exclusion of political and social groups from the legal definition.[52]

If the gravity of the Cambodian crimes were determined by reference to hierarchical abstractions and comparative suffering, one of modern history's worst abominations would be relegated to the "second-best" category of crimes against humanity. Yet the monstrous scale of victimization and suffering renders such a conclusion, some would say, manifestly absurd. Beyond the narrow confines of judicial proceedings,

[50] Steven Ratner and Jason Abrams, *Accountability for Human Rights Atrocities in International Law: Beyond the Nuremberg Legacy* (New York: Oxford University Press, 1997), 246.
[51] *Report of the Group of Experts for Cambodia Pursuant to General Assembly Resolution 52/135*, UN Doc. A/53/850, paras. 64–65 (1999).
[52] See www.eccc.gov.kh/english/news.view.aspx?doc_id=364.

the post hoc application of legal labels to such events and experiences is hardly constitutive of their meaning.

Darfur

The ongoing debate over whether atrocities committed by the Sudanese government in Sudan constitute genocide offers a similar example. As noted in Chapter 1, in late 2004, the United Nations sent a high-level panel to Darfur in order to determine whether criminal charges should be referred to the ICC.[53] The commission's crucial finding on this score was as follows:

Generally speaking the policy of attacking, killing and forcibly displacing members of some tribes does not evince a specific intent to annihilate, in whole or in part, a group distinguished on racial, ethnic, national or religious grounds. Rather, it would seem that those who planned and organized attacks on villages pursued the intent to drive the victims from their homes, primarily for purposes of counter-insurgency warfare.[54]

Some legal scholars praised the commission's judicial restraint – notably William Schabas, who even took the occasion to criticize the Krstić judgment of the ICTY for not reaching the same conclusion as the commission despite similar facts in Srebrenica. In particular, Schabas accused the Krstić Trial Chamber of engaging in "patronizing speculation" because it considered that targeting and killing only men of military age was tantamount to genocide.[55] Others, however, echoed the mainstream media's shock, with Nsongura Udombana attacking the commission's "convoluted and contrived" report, accusing it of facilitating the "criminal ambivalence" of the international community. In addition to "hid[ing] the political motive underpinning its Report," the commission's legal reasoning "reflect[ed] the mindset of an international community that, hitherto, has been reluctant to characterize genocide in situations similar to Darfur, to avoid triggering obligations entailed under the Genocide Convention – the obligation to prevent, suppress, and punish genocide."[56] NGOs, among others, also voiced

[53] See p. 4.
[54] *Report of the International Commission of Inquiry on Darfur to the United Nations Secretary-General Pursuant to Security Council Resolution 1564 of 18 September 2004*, para. 640 (25 January 2005), www.un.org/news/dh/sudan/com_inq_darfur.pdf.
[55] William A. Schabas, "Darfur and the 'Odious Scourge': The Commission of Inquiry's Findings on Genocide," *Leiden Journal of International Law* 18 (2005): 871, 881.
[56] Nsongura J. Udombana, "An Escape from Reason: Genocide and the International Commission of Inquiry on Darfur," *International Lawyer* 40 (2006): 41–42.

frustration. For example, Salih Booker, executive director of Africa Action, declared: "Where we disagree [with the commission] is that this is a genocide and it has been going on for two years now. We're just dismayed that this commission could not discover the government's intent."[57] Schabas recounts how,

[a]t a recent conference in New York City to commemorate the Nuremberg judgment, I was given the impression that some consider the Darfur Commission's rejection of the term "genocide" as tantamount to Holocaust denial. How quickly people forget that the term "crimes against humanity" was itself coined to describe the massacres of the Armenians, in May 1915, and was subsequently codified as international law's nomenclature for the perverse acts of the Nazi regime.[58]

The controversy deepened when a pretrial chamber of the ICC subsequently refused to issue an arrest warrant for genocide against Sudanese president Omar Al-Bashir.[59] The ICC Appeals Chamber, however, forced reconsideration of that decision because, in its view, the pretrial chamber had applied an erroneously stringent standard of proof.[60] Soon thereafter, the pretrial chamber confirmed an arrest warrant for Al-Bashir on three counts of genocide.[61]

It is astonishing to consider the amount of attention devoted to this prolonged judicial wrangling. Changing the category of the crimes (or adding another category of crime) would change virtually none of the salient facts: An arrest warrant for exceptionally serious international crimes would still have been issued against Al-Bashir, and the "nightmare of violence" endured by the inhabitants of Darfur would remain no less haunting.

---

[57] *Newshour with Jim Lehrer: Darfur Report* (PBS television broadcast, 2 February 2005), www.pbs.org/newshour/bb/africa/jan-june05/sudan_2–02.html.

[58] Schabas, "Darfur and the 'Odious Scourge,'" 883 (footnotes omitted).

[59] *Prosecutor v. Omar Hassan Ahmad Al Bashir*, Decision on the Prosecution's Application for a Warrant of Arrest Against Omar Hassan Ahmad Al Bashir (Pre-trial Chamber I, International Criminal Court, 4 March 2009).

[60] *Prosecutor v. Omar Hassan Ahmad Al Bashir*, Judgement on the Appeal of the Prosecutor Against the "Decision on the Prosecution's Application for a Warrant of Arrest Against Omar Hassan Ahmad Al Bashir" (Appeals Chamber, International Criminal Court, 3 February 2010).

[61] *Prosecutor v. Omar Hassan Ahmad Al Bashir*, Second Decision on the Prosecution's Application for a Warrant of Arrest (Pre-trial Chamber I, International Criminal Court, 12 July 2010).

Bosnia

In 2007, the International Court of Justice issued a historic decision in the case of *Bosnia v. Serbia*. For the first time, a state was found to be in violation of the Genocide Convention.[62] The court ruled that Serbia had not, in fact, *committed* genocide but had failed in its duty to *prevent* genocide in Srebrenica. In other words, the official state organs of Serbia were found not to be complicit in perpetrating the massacre itself, but to have failed to exercise their influence over Bosnian Serb forces in neighboring eastern Bosnia to prevent the genocide from taking place.

Disappointed reaction from victims was swift. Hedija Krdžić, a 34-year-old woman who had lost her husband, father, and grandfather at Srebrenica, said, "A ruling that Serbia committed genocide in Bosnia means everything to me ... Without such a ruling I fear that one day the massacre will be forgotten."[63] Fatija Šuljić, who lost her husband and three sons at Srebrenica, was dismayed: "This makes me cry. This is no verdict, no solution. This is disaster for our people."[64] Bosnian leaders echoed the victims, with Haris Silajdžić, the Bosnian Presidency's Muslim member, expressing "deep disappointment" and Željko Komšić, its Croatian member, also condemning the judgment: "We who were in Bosnia know what happened here right from the beginning of the war and I know what I will teach my kids."[65]

The terminological debate spilled over into the Serbian Parliament's deliberations on passing a resolution to condemn the Srebrenica massacre – an effort spearheaded by the Serbian president Boris Tadić. In March 2010, the Parliament approved the symbolic resolution but stopped short of calling it genocide – although it condemned "the crime as it is described" in a 2009 European parliamentary resolution, which does actually use the term *genocide*. Janja Beć, a human rights activist, insisted that the failure to use the word *genocide* in the resolution was "so insulting that it could badly influence the relations in

---

[62] *Application of the Convention on the Prevention and Punishment of the Crime of Genocide* (Bosnia and Herzegovina v. Serbia and Montenegro) (International Court of Justice, 26 February 2007).

[63] "We Know What Happened, Serbians," *Sydney Morning Herald*, 27 February 2007.

[64] David Byers, "Court Clears Serbia of Srebrenica Genocide," *Sunday Times* (UK), 26 February 2007.

[65] *Ibid.*

the region … Not only now, but for the next several generations. A crime like this deserves the recognition that it really took place."[66]

Evidently, the court's analysis of the legal subtleties concerning Serbia's state responsibility were lost on the victims. For them, Serbia had committed genocide, and only this characterization of events could adequately capture the heinousness of the crimes that the Bosnians had suffered.

Rwanda

Rwanda did not escape this terminological debate either; western diplomats, seeking to avoid intervention in the ongoing massacres, engaged in a policy of obfuscation and denial. The US government went so far as to instruct its representatives "not to describe the deaths [in Rwanda] as genocide, even though some senior officials believe that is exactly what they represent."[67] Rather, deploying subtle linguistic nuances, the officials were instructed to merely admit that "acts of genocide may have occurred"; the concern was that a label as stark as *genocide* would "inflame public calls for action the Administration is unwilling to take."[68] Philip Gourevitch characterized the surreal, evasive language game of US State Department spokesperson Christine Shelly – described in Chapter 1[69] – as a "semantic squirm."[70]

Of course, this evasive tactic was not without precedent, as the administration had earlier engaged in similar "semantics to avoid taking difficult or unpopular military action" against "ethnic cleansing" in Bosnia-Herzegovina.[71] Nor was the United States by any means alone in this policy of evasion. To give but one example, when the UN Security Council was considering whether to use *genocide* in a resolution about Rwanda, the British ambassador to the United Nations, David Hannay, suggested that the use of the term would potentially turn the council into a "laughing stock."[72] The twisted, all too cynical logic was that the

---

[66] Ron Synovitz, "Serbian Lawmakers Condemn Srebrenica Massacre," *Radio Free Europe/Radio Liberty*, 30 March 2010, www.rferl.org/content/Serbian_Parliament_Begins_Debate_On_Srebrenica_Apology/1997497.html.

[67] Dougal Jehl, "Officials Told to Avoid Calling Rwanda Killings Genocide," *New York Times*, 10 June 1994.

[68] *Ibid.*   [69] See p. 3.

[70] Philip Gourevitch, *We Wish to Inform You That Tomorrow We Will Be Killed with Our Families: Stories from Rwanda* (New York: Picador, 1998), 152.

[71] "US Sidesteps 'Genocide' in Rwanda; Clinton Qualifies Term, but UN General Says 'Horror Show Continues,'" *Star Tribune* (Minneapolis), 11 June 1994.

[72] See Linda Melvern, *A People Betrayed: The Role of the West in Rwanda's Genocide* (London: Zed, 2000), 180.

council would lose face if it labeled the massacres as genocide and then did not intervene (which seemed the likely outcome). The proponents of intervention, such as human rights NGOs, unwittingly engaged in the same discourse of hierarchical abstractions, countering that the events in Rwanda did constitute genocide, thereby triggering an obligation to act under the Genocide Convention.[73] Both opponents and proponents of intervention, however, shared a mistaken assumption that distorted the debate and also obfuscated the true substantive – and not linguistic – question: Should we intervene? In particular, both sides mistakenly assumed that the duty to "prevent and punish" under Article I of the Genocide Convention created a legal obligation for states to intervene in any and all genocidal situations and that the crucial, threshold question was whether the situation was one of genocide.[74] Warren Christopher, President Clinton's secretary of state, ended up deflating this rhetorical debate by simply declaring: "If there's any particular magic in calling it a genocide, I have no hesitancy in saying that."[75] This remark, coming toward the very end of the killings, was much too little, much too late. And it took another four years for President Clinton, during his visit to Kigali in March 1998, to express official contrition to the people of Rwanda – albeit with the by now familiar, and obviously ineffective, incantation of "never again."[76]

It is striking that both proponents and opponents of intervention continually focused the debate on whether the events in Rwanda amounted to "genocide." This emphasis gave such a privileged place to hierarchical abstractions and formal reasoning that the horrors unfolding before the eyes of the world were overshadowed. René Caravielhe, a staff member of Médecins sans frontières, describes in simple terms what he witnessed in those unspeakably dark days:

Jean de Dieu, eleven, was curled up, a ball of flesh and blood, the look in his eyes was a glance from nowhere … without vision; Marie-Ange, aged nine, was propped up against a tree trunk her legs apart, and she was covered in

---

[73] *Ibid.*, 169.
[74] This viewpoint was especially prevalent among members of the press. See, for example, Thomas W. Lippman, "Administration Sidesteps Genocide Label in Rwanda," *Washington Post*, 11 June 1994: "The Clinton administration said yesterday that 'acts of genocide' have occurred in Rwanda but deliberately stopped short of saying the tribal slaughter there is itself genocide – *a declaration that would require US and other foreign intervention under a 1948 international convention*" (emphasis added).
[75] Gourevitch, *We Wish to Inform You*, 153.
[76] See speech of President Clinton, cited in Melvern, *A People Betrayed*, 230.

excrement, sperm and blood, ... in her mouth was a penis, cut with a machete, that of her father ... [nearby] in a ditch with stinking water were four bodies, cut up, piled up, their parents and older brothers.

As Caravielhe then notes, one day "another word will have to be coined more terrible than the word horror, in order to describe this sort of thing."[77]

These scenes from hell were lost as they became entangled in an obfuscating and sterile discourse of legal labeling. The rituals of formal legal reasoning and the strictures of institutional procedure brought the overwhelming enormity of Rwanda's horrors under orderly control. And any pangs of bystander guilt after the fact were dealt with through formal expressions of regret. This surreal moral landscape of evasion and indifference masked in the language of concern illustrates just how removed this self-contained universe of the powerful was from the reality of the subjects. It calls to mind Roland Barthes's *The Eiffel Tower and Other Mythologies*, which contains an especially useful metaphor for the disconnect between the rarified world of international diplomacy, gazing upon the world from great heights of power and privilege, and the horrors transpiring "elsewhere" – in the arena of suffering:

[B]y affording its visitor a whole polyphony of pleasures, from technological wonder to haute cuisine, including the panorama, the Tower ultimately reunites with the essential function of all major human sites: autarchy; the Tower can live on itself: one can dream there, eat there, observe there, understand there, marvel there, shop there; as on an ocean liner (another mythic object that sets children dreaming), *one can feel oneself cut off from the world and yet the owner of a world.*[78]

---

[77] As quoted *ibid.*, 186.
[78] Roland Barthes, *The Eiffel Tower and Other Mythologies*, trans. Richard Howard (Berkeley and Los Angeles: University of California Press, 1997), 17 (emphasis added).

7   Contesting "genocide" in jurisprudence

On 6 June 1939, Chief Justice John Latham delivered the judgment of the High Court of Australia in *Chester v. Waverley Municipal Council.*[1] The plaintiff Chester was the mother of a seven-year-old boy, Maxie. On a Saturday afternoon in August 1937, Maxie had gone to play on a public street with other children after eating his lunch. They played beside a seven-foot-deep open trench excavated by the municipal council that was not properly fenced off. The trench was filled with water, and the irresistible combination of water and the excavated sand brought the neighborhood children to play at the edge of the pool. Maxie accidentally fell in and drowned. When he did not return home after some time, his distressed mother searched for him, but to no avail. Several hours later, she watched as Maxie's lifeless body was found in the trench. As the court's judgment stated, "There was evidence that [Mrs. Chester] thereupon received a severe nervous shock – more than a fright – more than temporary mental disturbance and distress. She sued the council for damages for negligence."[2] The trial judge dismissed the case, and a motion for a new trial was also rejected. The plaintiff then appealed to the High Court.

Justice Latham concluded that the Municipal Council "was guilty of actionable negligence in relation to the child in leaving the trench in the condition in which in fact it was left. If so, the child, if he had been injured and not drowned, would have had a right of action for damages."[3] But, since the mother was the plaintiff, he held that she needed to "establish a duty owed by the defendant to herself and a breach of that duty," which the court then described as "a duty not to

---

[1] *Chester v Waverley Municipal Council*, [1939] HCA 25, (1939) 62 CLR 1 (6 June 1939).
[2] *Ibid.*, 2.   [3] *Ibid.*, 3.

injure her child so as to cause her a nervous shock when she saw, not the happening of the injury, but the result of the injury, namely, the dead body of the child."[4] The court thus considered whether such damage (that is, nervous shock) was "within the reasonable anticipation of the defendant." The majority concluded that it was not:

"A reasonable person would not foresee" that the negligence of the defendant towards the child would "so affect" a mother ... Death is not an infrequent event, and even violent and distressing deaths are not uncommon. It is, however, not a common experience of mankind that the spectacle, even of the sudden and distressing death of a child, produces any consequence of more than a temporary nature in the case of bystanders or even of close relatives who see the body after death has taken place.[5]

The appeal was dismissed.

Justice Herbert Evatt wrote the sole dissenting opinion. This brilliant jurist, whose minority opinions would be adopted by the High Court decades later, took exception to the majority's callous disregard of the plaintiff's emotional state:

It is abundantly clear that until the recovery of the body she did *not* know that her child had been drowned in the trench. Like most mothers placed in a similar situation, she was tortured between the fear that he had been drowned and the hope that either he was not in the trench at all, or that, if he was, a quick recovery of his body and the immediate application of artificial respiration might still save him from death. In this agonized and distracted state of mind and body she remained for about half an hour, when the police arrived and the child's body was discovered and removed.[6]

In a passage demonstrating remarkable empathy, he wrote that:

During this crucial period the plaintiff's condition of mind and nerve can be completely understood only by parents who have been placed in a similar agony of hope and fear with hope gradually decreasing. In the present case the half hour of waiting was the culmination of a long and almost frantic searching which had already reduced her to a state of nerve exhaustion. Even after the finding of the body, an attempt at artificial respiration was made and abandoned only after expert lifesavers had worked on the child's body for some time.[7]

His audacity in challenging the sterile rationalism of the majority went further, as his dissent wandered into the realm of literature:

---

[4] Ibid., 3–4.   [5] Ibid., 6–7.   [6] Ibid., 15.   [7] Ibid.

The Australian novelist, Tom Collins, in *Such Is Life*, has also described the agony of fearfulness caused by the search for a lost child: –
Longest night I ever passed, though it was one of the shortest in the year. Eyes burning for want of sleep, and couldn't bear to lie down for a minute. Wandering about for miles; listening; hearing something in the scrub, and finding it was only one of the other chaps, or some sheep. Thunder and lightning, on and off, all night; even two or three drops of rain, towards morning. Once I heard the howl of a dingo, and I thought of the little girl; lying worn-out, half-asleep and half-fainting – far more helpless than a sheep.

At a later point, in the same novel: –
There was a pause, broken by Stevenson, in a voice which brought constraint on us all. Bad enough to lose a youngster for a day or two, and find him alive and well; worse, beyond comparison, when he's found dead; but the most fearful thing of all is for a youngster to be lost in the bush, and never found, alive or dead.[8]

The sharp contrast between the rationalism of Justice Latham and the poetic plea of Justice Evatt displays a perennial question about human emotion and the boundaries of legal reasoning. How can the rationalist credo of the law be reconciled with intense emotion? And if the judge's display of emotion in this instance arises from a mother's grief for a child lost in a tragic accident, what are the emotions of a judge presiding over a genocide trial? Perhaps it is not a mere coincidence that Justice Evatt was the same Herbert Evatt who, a decade later (as mentioned in Chapter 1), became president of the UN General Assembly and, upon adoption of the Genocide Convention in 1948, celebrated that "the supremacy of international law had been proclaimed."[9]

The gravity of genocide can easily overwhelm our capacity for dispassionate legal reasoning. As much as transgressions such as the Holocaust "defy the ordering of common sense" and seem "extra-territorial to analytic debate,"[10] reducing genocide to law calls for exactly such an ordering and analysis. Indeed, with the establishment of the international criminal tribunals, one might be tempted to think that meta-legal closure through appropriation of genocide has been rendered irrelevant; on this view, the methodological rigors and objective discipline of jurisprudence enable courts to determine conclusively

[8] *Ibid.*, 16.
[9] UN GAOR, 3rd Sess., 19th plen. mtg., 852, UN Doc. A/PV.179 (1948).
[10] George Steiner, *No Passion Spent: Essays 1978–1995* (New Haven: Yale University Press, 1996), 346–47.

whether the "ethnic cleansing" in Bosnia-Herzegovina, extermination in Rwanda, or other such situations amount to genocide – independent of the wider, contested meanings of that term. But as important aspects of the ICTY and ICTR jurisprudence demonstrate, the situation is not so simple. As the tribunals confront the facts of certain cases and attempt to determine how those facts fit into the available legal categories, the tribunals display a discernible angst that their juridical conclusions – was it genocide, or not? – either will provide the victims with meaningful recognition of their suffering or will be interpreted as trivializing the magnitude of the crime and its historical legacy. Thus, notwithstanding that "positive" law's rationality and objectivity may be contrived, such judicial ambitions inflate the law's narrow role – attribution of liability for specific crimes – to that of determining conclusive meaning and closure. This burden is, alas, one that the law cannot bear.

Rwanda and the *Akayesu* case

Even proponents of the Holocaust's uniqueness find it hard not to acknowledge the distinctiveness of the 1994 mass murder that took place in Rwanda[11] – a high-speed, yet low-tech, annihilation of 800,000 Tutsis, with a death rate that was approximately five times that of the Nazis' "Final Solution."[12] Mass murder on such an unimaginable scale naturally attracts the typology of *genocide* in popular discourse. Indeed, in the context of appropriating genocide as a form of meta-legal recognition, it would be difficult to argue that this extermination of the Tutsi minority did not constitute the "ultimate crime." But here, again, the situation is not as simple as it would appear on the surface. Rigorous legal analysis casts doubt on whether the juridical categorization of the events in Rwanda in 1994 as genocide is as straightforward as it may appear at first glance; the central question raised in this context is whether the Tutsis can be considered an "ethnic" group protected by the Genocide Convention. But, on occasion, the jurisprudence of the ICTR glosses over such difficulties in favor of a seemingly teleological

[11] See, for example, Alain Destexhe, "The Third Genocide," *Foreign Policy* (Winter 1995): 3, 4 (arguing that "only three instances of mass slaughter this century can correctly be called genocide": the slaughter of Armenians in 1915–16, the Holocaust, and the Rwandan massacres of 1994).

[12] Linda Melvern, *A People Betrayed: The Role of the West in Rwanda's Genocide* (London: Zed, 2000), 4.

approach in which finer points of legal interpretation are cast aside in an uncompromising effort to apply the *genocide* label.

By way of background, a brief summary of the controversy regarding the scope of the protected groups under the Genocide Convention is necessary. The definition of genocide is restricted to the destruction of "national, ethnical, racial or religious" groups. There is no mention of other types of groups. This listing is exhaustive: The definition is straightforward and nonillustrative,[13] requiring a strict construction, and the *ejusdem generis* rule does not apply, with the consequence that such crimes cannot be expanded or interpreted by analogy.[14] Furthermore, the crime's legislative history indicates a deliberate intention not to include any groups beyond those expressly enumerated. Initial drafts of the convention included a wider range of protected groups, although there was considerable opposition to such a broad scope of protection.[15] In particular, during the final deliberations of the General Assembly's Sixth (Legal) Committee, several delegates – primarily from the Soviet bloc – argued that inclusion of "political" groups was inconsistent with the "scientific" or "objective" meaning of genocide.[16] Others argued for exclusion on the grounds that only "permanent" or "stable" groups could be defined with sufficient accuracy for legal purposes[17] and that the destruction of groups whose members have no choice but to belong to them, versus political groups where membership may be voluntary, represented greater moral turpitude, with the consequence that special protection was justified.[18] Some even pointed out that the inclusion of political groups would curtail the power of states to repress subversive elements engaged in violent political struggle.[19] Those in favor of inclusion countered that genocide was not an immutable concept with a definite etymological meaning,[20] that political groups could be adequately defined in legal terms,[21] that "national" or "religious" groups were no more permanent or stable than political groups,[22] that destruction of political groups with "voluntary" rather than "unavoidable" membership was equally

---

[13] For instance, an illustrative definition would have used terms such as "including" or "not limited to" as an indication that other groups may also be covered even if they are not expressly listed.

[14] See, for example, Article 22(2) of the ICC Statute.

[15] See generally William A. Schabas, *Genocide in International Law: The Crime of Crimes*, 2nd edn. (Cambridge: Cambridge University Press, 2009), 117ff.

[16] UN GAOR, 3rd Sess., 6th Cmte., 74th mtg., UN Doc. A/C.6/SR.74.

[17] *Ibid.*, 61.   [18] *Ibid.*, 111.   [19] *Ibid.*, 58.

[20] *Ibid.*, 107–08, 114.   [21] *Ibid.*, 102.   [22] *Ibid.*, 99.

reprehensible,[23] and that legitimate suppression of revolt against state authority could not be equated with the mass killing of political opponents.[24] The eventual exclusion of political groups reflected a desire to remove a potential impediment to the widespread ratification of the convention.[25] The decision was therefore primarily a practical one and not necessarily based on theoretical or moral imperatives. It also does not take much imagination to see why the Soviets were so insistent on excluding political and social groups from the definition of genocide.

Jurists and social scientists have extensively criticized this normative gap in the definition of genocide, with many arguing that a consistent concept of genocide should protect any group slated for destruction based on an "integral element of human identity."[26] This approach seems to be reflected in the definition of the crime against humanity of "persecution" under Article 7(1)(h) of the ICC Statute, which applies to attacks against "any identifiable group or collectivity" on any ground that is "universally recognized as impermissible under international law." Nevertheless, some scholars have argued that the existing definition of genocide should be retained, despite its shortcomings, in order to maintain normative stability,[27] and others have even argued that the exclusion of political and other groups is morally desirable because broadening the scope of genocide would trivialize its magnitude.[28] The international lawmaking process also favors retention of the existing definition, as is apparent from the rejection of efforts to amend the definition – to include "political" and "social" groups – under the ICC Statute.[29] The availability of crimes against humanity as an acceptable

---

[23] *Ibid.*, 60.   [24] *Ibid.*, 101.

[25] The impasse between the Soviet bloc and western states had become a serious issue; see, for example, the records of the 75th and 128th meetings of the Sixth Committee in Hirad Abtahi and Philippa Webb, eds., *The Genocide Convention: The Travaux Préparatoires*, vol. II (Leiden and Boston: Martinus Nijhoff, 2008), 1405, 1864.

[26] See, for example, Steven R. Ratner and Jason S. Abrams, *Accountability for Human Rights Atrocities in International Law: Beyond the Nuremberg Legacy* (New York: Oxford University Press, 1997), 43: "only when the legal definition of genocide expands to encompass the mass destruction of any human collective based on any integral element of human identity will it fully address the most heinous international offense."

[27] See, for example, Leo Kuper, "Theoretical Issues Relating to Genocide: Uses and Abuses," in George J. Andreopoulos, ed., *Genocide: Conceptual and Historical Dimensions* (Philadelphia: University of Pennsylvania Press, 1994), 31.

[28] See, for example, Schabas, *Genocide in International Law*, 2nd edn., 114.

[29] The drafting process of the ICC Statute provided a unique opportunity to amend the definition of genocide in order to compensate for its perceived deficiencies and

"fall-back" option appears to have undercut the view that changing the definition was a matter of normative urgency.[30]

For present purposes, the question is not whether the definition of genocide should or should not be expanded to include more groups beyond those enumerated. Rather, the significance of this terminological query concerns its potential impact on those who seek to achieve meta-legal closure through appropriations of genocide, and how far the law can be stretched to accommodate such demands without a complete departure from the strictures of legal interpretation and reasoning. Given that the law's exclusion of certain identifiable groups raises questions of moral or descriptive consistency, there is an obvious temptation to use expansive or activist interpretations at least in ambiguous situations that fall near the boundaries of existing jurisprudence.[31]

Since the ICC Statute has incorporated a broad definition of crimes against humanity, and since offenders can also be prosecuted for war crimes, some have suggested that efforts to expand the reach of current genocide law represent a "passing phase" in international criminal law.[32] But this suggestion misses a crucial point. As previously noted, efforts to appropriate genocide are actuated not just by legal substance, as it were, but also by a desire to obtain meta-legal recognition, including enlistment of its moral potency for the purpose of publicity or even propaganda. Despite the availability of alternative norms for imposing either individual or state responsibility, the lingering perception (by some, at least) is that crimes against humanity or other violations of international law are merely "second best" to the "ultimate crime" in the construction of narratives.[33] International criminal law jurisprudence continues to be influenced by the hierarchical abstraction of genocide as the "ultimate crime."

incongruities; see, for example, *Report of the Ad Hoc Committee on the Establishment of an International Criminal Court*, UN GAOR, 50th Sess., Supp. No. 22, UN Doc. A/50/22 (1995). There was tremendous resistance (see para. 60) to tampering with this "authoritative definition … which was widely accepted by States and had been characterized as reflecting customary law by the International Court of Justice."

[30] *Ibid.*, paras. 61, 87.

[31] See, for example, Beth Van Schaack, "The Crime of Political Genocide: Repairing the Genocide Convention's Blind Spot," *Yale Law Journal* 106 (1997): 2259, 2261–62, arguing that the exclusion of political groups from the Genocide Convention is a "blind spot" that "[n]o legal principle can justify."

[32] Schabas, *Genocide in International Law*, 2nd edn., 103–04.

[33] See, for example, *ibid.*, 10 (referring to "crimes against humanity" as the "second tier of the pyramid [of international crimes]").

A salient case in point is the questionable methodology adopted by the ICTR in defining the Tutsis as a protected group in the *Akayesu* case, the celebrated first genocide judgment by an international criminal tribunal.[34] The concern here is not whether classifying the Tutsis as an "ethnic" or other protected group under the Genocide Convention was legally correct or not. Instead, the question is whether the relevant jurisprudence reveals a determination to label the killings in Rwanda as genocide no matter what – that is, even if it does not comport with the minimal strictures of legal reasoning – and whether this determination can be interpreted as actuated by the view that it is somehow vitally important to categorize those events as the "ultimate crime." What makes the actual legal issue so difficult is that the enormous gravity of the Rwandese cataclysm is combined with the intractable question of whether the Tutsi victims belong to a group protected under the definition of genocide.

Gérard Prunier observes that the Hutus and Tutsis have "often and inappropriately been called the 'tribes' of Rwanda. They had none of the characteristics of tribes, which are micronations. They shared the same Bantu language, lived side by side with each other without any 'Hutuland' or 'Tutsiland' and often intermarried."[35] There were physical differences between the two groups, however, and the Tutsis dominated the Hutus in social terms through institutions of the monarchy. Because of the colonial period's obsession with racial differences and civilizational superiority, these distinctions assumed grossly exaggerated proportions. There emerged pseudoscientific theories about racially superior "pastoral invaders" from Ethiopia "bringing with them the kingship institution." The invaders were, of course, the Tutsis, "who had skillfully subjugated the 'inferior' Hutu peasant masses."[36] Thus, in the minds of the European colonizers, the socially heterogeneous – but otherwise racially mixed and ethnically homogeneous – Rwandese kingdom was divided into a Tutsi–Hutu dichotomy, based on an invidious stratification. In this way, myth and reality became blurred and helped generate the alienation and profound animosity that eventually exploded into the 1994 extermination of the Tutsis.[37]

---

[34] Akayesu, Trial Judgement (ICTR, 2 September 1998).

[35] Gérard Prunier, *The Rwanda Crisis: History of a Genocide* (New York: Columbia University Press, 1995), 5.

[36] *Ibid.*, 11.   [37] See generally *ibid.*, 5–11.

In its narrative of the historical context within which the events of 1994 transpired, the *Akayesu* case emphatically recognized the dubious and illusory construction of the Tutsi "ethnic" identity. Affirming the social, rather than ethnic, origins of the Hutu–Tutsi dichotomy, the Trial Chamber noted that "[p]rior to and during colonial rule ... Rwanda was a complex and an advanced monarchy ... that ruled the country through ... official representatives drawn from the *Tutsi nobility*."[38] Rwanda was composed of some "eighteen clans defined primarily along lines of kinship," and the terms *Hutu* and *Tutsi* "referred to individuals rather than to groups. In those days, the distinction between the Hutu and Tutsi *was based on lineage rather than ethnicity. Indeed, the demarcation line was blurred: one could move from one status to another, as one became rich or poor, or even through marriage*."[39] The Trial Chamber went on to explain how the privileged social status of the Tutsi nobility became transformed to an "ethnic" identity. Both the German (between 1897 and 1917) and Belgian colonial authorities (between 1917 and 1962)

relied on an elite essentially composed of people who referred to themselves as Tutsi, a choice which ... was born of racial or even racist considerations. In the minds of the colonizers, the Tutsi looked more like them, because of their height and colour, and were, therefore, more intelligent and better equipped to govern.[40]

It was only in the 1930s that Belgian authorities "introduced a *permanent distinction* by dividing the population into ... groups which they called ethnic groups. In line with this division, it became mandatory for every Rwandan to carry an identity card mentioning his or her ethnicity."[41] Such reference to "ethnic" affiliation on identity cards "was maintained, even after Rwanda's independence and was, at last, abolished only after the tragic events the country experienced in 1994."[42]

Based on this historical account, the Trial Chamber appeared to conclude that the Tutsis do not properly fall within the scope of the groups expressly enumerated in the definition of genocide. But it arrived at the conclusion that it did by departing, it seems, from the confines of reasonable legal interpretation. In determining whether the 1994 massacres satisfied the *dolus specialis* requirement insofar as being targeted

---

[38] Akayesu, Trial Judgement (ICTR, 2 September 1998), para. 80 (emphasis added).
[39] *Ibid.*, para. 81 (emphasis added).   [40] *Ibid.*, para. 82.
[41] *Ibid.*, para. 83 (emphasis added).   [42] *Ibid.*

"against a particular group as such," the chamber referred to the Tutsis as an "ethnic group," but with the following qualifications:

The term *ethnic group* is, in general, used to refer to a group whose members speak the same language and/or have the same culture. Therefore, one can hardly talk of ethnic groups as regards Hutu and Tutsi, given that they share the same language and culture. However, in the context of the [present case], they were, in consonance with a distinction made by the colonizers, considered both by the authorities and themselves as belonging to two distinct ethnic groups; as such, their identity cards mentioned each holder's ethnic group.[43]

At first sight, this statement suggests that the chamber found the Tutsis to be an "ethnic" group and that this finding is based on the colonizers' arbitrary imposition of that identity upon certain segments of the people living in Rwanda – a distinction subsequently consolidated in the embracing of this myth by the Tutsis and Hutus themselves. This conclusion would comport, for instance, with the approach of the Trial Chamber in *Kayishema*, where an ethnic group was defined as "one whose members share a common language and culture; *or, a group which distinguishes itself as such (self identification); or, a group identified as such by others, including perpetrators of the crimes (identification by others)*."[44] It should be noted that this reasoning is unpersuasive. Although the term *ethnic* was included in the convention to "extend protection to doubtful cases,"[45] ethnic groups cannot be identified exclusively on the basis of subjective elements; according to current established case law of both the ICTY and the ICTR, some sort of corresponding objective element is also required.[46]

Upon closer examination, however, it is apparent that, unlike *Kayishema*, the *Akayesu* case did not find that the Tutsis were an "ethnic" group. Rather, in overcoming the problem of situating them within the definition of genocide, the Trial Chamber simply expanded the range

---

[43] *Ibid.*, para. 122 note 56.

[44] Kayishema, Trial Judgement (ICTR, 21 May 1999), para. 98 (emphasis added).

[45] UN GAOR, 3rd Sess., 6th Cmte., 75th mtg., UN Doc. A/C.6/SR.75; Abtahi and Webb, *The Genocide Convention*, 1412.

[46] See, for example, Stakić, Appeals Judgement (ICTY, 22 March 2006), para. 25; Brdjanin, Trial Judgement (ICTY, 1 September 2004), para. 684; Semanza, Trial Judgment (ICTR, 15 May 2003), para. 317; Kajelijeli, Trial Judgement (ICTR, 1 December 2003), para. 811; see generally Schabas, *Genocide in International Law*, 2nd edn., 125–29. Schabas notes (p. 28) that "[i]n practice, however, the subjective approach seems to function effectively virtually all the time. Trying to find an objective basis for racist crimes suggests that the perpetrators act rationally, and this is more credit than they deserve."

of protected groups through an audacious application of the *ejusdem generis* principle that it justified by an unsupported reference to the Genocide Convention's legislative history, or *travaux préparatoires*. In its findings on law, the reasoning began with recognition of the obvious fact that the relevant provision (Article 2) of the ICTR Statute, like the Genocide Convention, "stipulates four types of victim groups, namely national, ethnical, racial or religious groups."[47] The chamber then suggested that these groups share the common characteristic of "stability" and "permanence" as distinct from "the more 'mobile' groups which one joins through individual voluntary commitment, such as political and economic groups."[48] The judgment then leaped to the conclusion that "it is particularly important to respect the intention of the drafters of the Genocide Convention – which, according to the *travaux préparatoires*, was to ensure the protection of any stable or permanent group."[49] As such, the chamber found that "at the time of the alleged events, the Tutsi did indeed constitute a *stable and permanent group* and were identified as such by all."[50]

In invoking the legislative history of the convention to justify the extension of the protected groups by analogy, the Trial Chamber made no reference whatsoever to specific statements in the *travaux préparatoires*. Nor did it address the considerable controversy and disagreement – both in the *travaux préparatoires* and contemporary discourse – concerning the concept of groups with "immutable" versus ephemeral characteristics. By any standard, the Trial Chamber's legal methodology in *Akayesu* was highly problematic. First, its reasoning blatantly violated the *nullum crimen sine lege* principle (requiring strict interpretation of crimes), both because the chamber failed to adopt a "strict construction" of the crime that resolved ambiguities in favor of the accused and because it applied the *ejusdem generis* principle (expanding crimes by analogy) to define an essential element of the crime, contrary to the dictates of international criminal law. Furthermore, the chamber resorted to the *travaux préparatoires* of the Genocide Convention as "supplementary means of interpretation" without first establishing that the "ordinary meaning" of the terms under the "general rule of interpretation" gave rise to an "ambiguous or obscure" meaning or led "to a result which is manifestly absurd or unreasonable."[51] In any event,

[47] Akayesu, Trial Judgement (ICTR, 2 September 1998), para. 510.
[48] *Ibid.*, para. 511.   [49] *Ibid.*, para. 516.   [50] *Ibid.*, para. 702.
[51] See Articles 31(1) and 32 of the Vienna Convention on the Law of Treaties.

the suggestion that the list of protected groups is illustrative and not exhaustive, or that it includes only permanent or stable groups, indicates at best a highly selective or erroneous reading of the convention, and at worst a deliberate disregard or distortion of its legislative history. Indeed, as noted above, despite the chamber's explicit reliance on the *travaux préparatoires* to justify its position, it made no reference to any statements made by delegates during the drafting process of the convention. Also noteworthy is that the situation was not one in which a passionate teleological interpretation was embraced to "progressively develop" the ambiguous content and ambit of humanitarian law, unless such interpretation is taken to mean disregard even for the pretension of legal reasoning. Nor was there a jurisdictional imperative for such expansive interpretation (given the availability of crimes against humanity and war crimes under the ICTR Statute) or, based on the Trial Chamber's own finding that the Tutsis did not constitute an "ethnic" group within the definition of genocide, a reasonable ambiguity as to whether the Tutsis were a protected group.

The question then arises: What was the underlying intention of the judges in this rather unusual ruling? It is not unreasonable to infer that the judges' main concern was to ensure that the Tutsis fell within the definition of genocide, even at the cost of disregarding the minimal strictures of legal reasoning. After all, it may have been inconceivable for them not to categorize this horrendous mass murder as the pinnacle of evil. In the competitive marketplace of comparative suffering, such hierarchical abstractions and invidious stratification are indispensable forms of recognition. In ascribing the crown of ultimate importance to the Tutsi victims, the bystanders register their outrage and empathy, and bring the overwhelming dimensions of this monstrosity to closure. Of course, for the Trial Chamber in *Akayesu* or other cases, it did not help matters much that, in establishing the ICTR, a repentant Security Council had apparently overcompensated for its earlier denial by adopting a resolution that expressly recognized that genocide had occurred in Rwanda.[52] Thus, through incorporating genocide into the council's resolution, the extreme evil and our complicity therein were surmounted and cast away, and the burden of contemplating our actions and self-conception in the wake of the Rwandan cataclysm was replaced by facile abstractions and self-congratulatory platitudes.

---

[52] Security Council Resolution 955 (8 November 1994).

The issue here is not whether the mass killing of Rwandan Tutsis constituted genocide or not, but how far the tribunal was willing to go in order to arrive at the conclusion that it did. In the face of public pressures to label the horrors as the ultimate crime, it would have been catastrophic for the judgment to hold that, because the Tutsis were not an "ethnic group," the definition of genocide did not apply. Unlike the Trial Chamber in *Akayesu*, later ICTR cases, in arriving at the conclusion that genocide was applicable, actually found ways to reach that conclusion within the reasonable bounds of legal interpretation.

Ultimately, the question is whether, without the label of genocide, the horrors would somehow fail to speak for themselves. Are the voices of the survivors not sufficient to reflect the immense gravity of what transpired? Does it matter so much if the Rwandese cataclysm was "merely" a crime against humanity and not genocide?

Bosnia and the *Jelisić* case

In contrast to the *Akayesu* case at the ICTR, the *Jelisić* case at the ICTY is an example of judges departing from the strictures of the law in order to *avoid* applying the *genocide* label – so that the crown of ultimate importance would not be awarded to a deranged, small-time homicidal thug, Goran Jelisić. In that case, the legal element subject to teleological manipulation was the *mens rea* or *dolus specialis* to destroy a group in whole or in part, which is another significant limiting element in the definition of genocide. The pliability and often misunderstood nature of this concept[53] make it susceptible to judicial maneuvering – for example, in responding to inflationary or deflationary pressures concerning the labeling of crimes.

As the *Jelisić* case points out, "It is in fact the *mens rea* which gives genocide its speciality and distinguishes it from an ordinary crime and other crimes against international humanitarian law."[54] Without this special intent, an act of mass killing or other destruction of a group, no matter how extreme and odious, does not qualify as genocide. The two elements of this intent requirement are "that the victims belonged to an identified group" and "that the alleged perpetrator must have committed his crimes as part of a wider plan to destroy the group as

---

[53] See discussion of *dolus specialis* in Chapter 3.
[54] Jelisić, Trial Judgement (ICTY, 14 December 1999), para. 66.

such."[55] Thus, the victims are selected *because* of their membership in a national, ethnic, racial, or religious group[56] *and* "for the realisation of an *ulterior motive*, which is to destroy, in whole or in part, the group of which the individual is just one element."[57] Although motive is irrelevant in attributing liability,[58] the "degree" of intent required by the *dolus specialis* standard is that, beyond mere "knowledge," the perpetrator must consciously desire to destroy, or "shares the goal" of destroying, the target group.[59]

In the *Jelisić* case, this *dolus specialis* requirement plays out against two background questions: Do low-ranking perpetrators have the capacity to commit genocide and, if so, should they be prosecuted for it? As the International Law Commission observed, crimes such as genocide "are of such magnitude that they often require some type of involvement on the part of high level government officials or military commanders as well as their subordinates."[60] Nevertheless, it is clear that individual criminal liability attaches equally to all perpetrators, irrespective of their status in the relevant chain of command. As the *Eichmann* case observed, "even a small cog, even an insignificant operator, is under [the] criminal law liable to be regarded as an accomplice in the commission of an offence."[61]

Questions of liability aside, there may be sound reasons for focusing limited investigative and prosecutorial resources (especially before international criminal tribunals) on the high-ranking political leaders and military commanders who are invariably implicated in creating

---

[55] *Ibid.*   [56] See, for example, *ibid.*, para. 67.
[57] Akayesu, Trial Judgement (ICTR, 2 September 1998), para. 522 (emphasis added); as discussed below, the term *ulterior motive* should not be taken to refer to the *reasons* underlying the acts of the perpetrator as distinct from the special intent to achieve a particular result.
[58] The *motive of a crime* is usually understood as referring to the *reasons* underlying the perpetrator's actions, as distinct from his or her intent. Thus, for example, a person may *intend* to murder another person, but that killing may be done for various different motives including vengeance, pecuniary gain, and so on. On the distinction between intent and motive generally, see George Fletcher, *Rethinking Criminal Law* (Boston and Toronto: Little, Brown, 1978), 452. With respect to international criminal law, see Tadić, Sentencing Judgement (ICTY, 11 November 1999), para. 269; Schabas, *Genocide in International Law*, 2nd edn., 294–306.
[59] See previous discussion on the *mens rea* of genocide in Chapter 3 on this point.
[60] *Report of the International Law Commission on the Work of Its Forty-eighth Session*, GAOR, 51st Sess., Supp. No. 10, UN Doc. A/51/10, at 90 (1996).
[61] *Attorney General of Israel v. Eichmann*, 36 I.L.R. 277, 323 (Supreme Court of Israel, 1962), 323.

the aberrant settings of systematic mass violence within which lower-ranking perpetrators commit atrocities. For instance, the ICC Prosecutor's strategy is to *"focus its investigative and prosecutorial efforts and resources on those who bear the greatest responsibility, such as the leaders of the State or organisation allegedly responsible for those crimes."*[62] Nonetheless, it is also clear that the judicial account of massive atrocities cannot remain wholly oblivious to the multitude of "small fish" – the willing executioners without whose participation the diabolical schemes of the grand conspirators cannot be realized.[63] In terms of constructing engaging narratives of atrocities, the prosecution of low-ranking perpetrators may actually be more likely to "bring home" the intimate reality of otherwise abstract genocidal crimes; such prosecutions provide occasions "for graphically depicting the way in which the genocide unfolded on a daily basis."[64]

Even so, the expenditure of scarce judicial resources on prosecuting "insignificant thugs" at the lowest echelons of state authority may be considered by some as unworthy of what they see as a monumental, systematic crime masterminded by powerful, diabolical architects in the highest echelons of power. The abstract conception of genocide as a unique instrument of totalitarian systems – conditioned by the Holocaust's paradigm – may thus privilege the prosecution and punishment of the elites who have designed and sanctioned genocidal plans, as against their low-level associates whose grim reality it is to do the actual killing. Pressures to exclude such supposedly "trivial" cases from the ambit of genocide may operate to exclude particular prosecutions despite their legal viability. Likewise, judicial efforts to justify such exclusions – that is, to privilege abstract conceptions of the "ultimate crime" rather than the concrete, less sensational deeds of the actual killers – may result in distorted legal reasoning and in confused and confusing precedents.

[62] ICC Office of the Prosecutor, *Paper on Some Policy Issues Before the Office of the Prosecutor* (7 September 2003), www.icc-cpi.int/NR/rdonlyres/1FA7C4C6-DE5F-42B7-8B25-60AA962ED8B6/143594/030905_Policy_Paper.pdf.
[63] See, for example, Payam Akhavan, "Justice in The Hague, Peace in the Former Yugoslavia? A Commentary on the United Nations War Crimes Tribunal," *Human Rights Quarterly* 20 (1998): 737, 779. For an argument that even the *mens rea* of genocide should be redefined in order to more readily encompass low-level perpetrators, see Kai Ambos, "What Does 'Intent to Destroy' in Genocide Mean?," *International Review of the Red Cross* 91 (2009): 833, 876.
[64] See Edward M. Morgan, "Retributory Theater," *American University Journal of International Law and Policy* 3 (1988): 1, 57.

Based on both serious procedural irregularities and manifestly unreasonable factual findings, the foregoing meta-legal considerations appear to have played a central role in the ICTY Trial Chamber's judgment in the *Jelisić* case.[65] The accused, Goran Jelisić – who introduced himself as the "Serbian Adolf" at his initial hearing[66] – had pleaded guilty to charges of war crimes and crimes against humanity for multiple killings, torture, and other inhumane treatment of Bosnian Muslim and Croat detainees at the Luka camp (where he was commander), but he had contested a single count of genocide.[67] Despite the plea of guilty, the prosecutor decided to proceed with a trial on the sole count. Presumably, this course of action was pursued in order to maintain consistency with similar charges in other cases; it also fit into the overall prosecutorial theory of how genocide was committed in the wider "ethnic cleansing" campaign in Bosnia-Herzegovina; and, as a matter of principle, it may have been seen as a way of imposing liability on, and attaching stigma to, the accused for the particular category of crime that most closely corresponded to the extreme gravity of his acts, irrespective of his rank. Having heard the prosecution's case-in-chief, however, the Trial Chamber took the extraordinary step of concluding, *proprio motu*, that, "without even needing to hear the arguments of the Defence, the accused could not be found guilty of the crime of genocide."[68]

Leaving aside the substantive merit of the acquittal, there were serious procedural irregularities that betrayed the Trial Chamber's desire to get rid of the case. Rule 98*bis* of the ICTY Rules of Procedure and Evidence allows for a trial chamber to preempt a full trial through a "judgment of acquittal." This procedure is an exceptional one, however, that should be invoked only if the prosecution's evidence fails to satisfy even the minimum level of proof – for example, the presentation of "a serious *prima facie* case"[69] – without which a prosecution has no chance whatsoever of succeeding. In any event, the evidentiary standard at the "halfway stage" of a trial is lower than that required for conviction ("proof beyond all reasonable doubt") upon conclusion of a trial.[70] Unless the prosecution case has "completely broken down," it is only at the trial's conclusion that the evidence receives final scrutiny

---

[65] Jelisić, Trial Judgement (ICTY, 14 December 1999).
[66] *Ibid.*, para. 102.   [67] *Ibid.*, para. 11.   [68] *Ibid.*, para. 15.
[69] See Blaškić, Decision on the Defence Motion to Dismiss (ICTY, 3 September 1998).
[70] Kordić and Čerkez, Decision on the Defence Motions for Judgement of Acquittal (ICTY, 6 April 2000), para. 11.

as to its reliability and credibility.[71] Such exceptional circumstances, however, did not apply to the *Jelisić* trial.

Near the conclusion of the prosecution's case-in-chief, the Trial Chamber asked the defense whether it planned to submit a motion for a judgment of acquittal pursuant to Rule 98*bis*. Although the defense had indicated that it would not file such a motion,[72] the Trial Chamber – in a blatant demonstration of its eagerness to dispose of the case – subsequently issued a notice that it would render a judgment of acquittal *proprio motu*.[73] In response to this exceptional measure, the prosecutor made an application to be heard[74] prior to the summary termination of the proceedings. But this request was rebuffed on the unexplained ground that the motion to be heard was inextricably connected with the merits of the decision.[75] And, despite promises to the contrary, the prosecution was then denied the opportunity even to make remarks upon delivery of the oral judgment.[76] Not only was the Trial Chamber's judgment of acquittal factually at odds with the case presented by the prosecution, but the Trial Chamber, in its apparent haste to dismiss the case, even applied the wrong test – "proof beyond all reasonable doubt," the standard for actual conviction – in determining whether a Rule 98*bis* judgment of acquittal was justified.[77] What is striking, even alarming, is that this standard of proof (applied at this stage) was manifestly at variance both with all other ICTY jurisprudence[78] and with the standard (namely, presenting a *prima facie* case) that two of the three Trial Chamber judges had applied in an earlier case.[79]

---

[71] See *ibid.*, paras. 25–28.
[72] See telefax from Michael Greaves to Olivier Fourmy dated 1 October 1999, cited in Jelisić, Prosecution's Appeal Brief (Public Redacted Version) (ICTY, 14 July 2000), para. 2.2 note 10.
[73] Jelisić, Notice of a Judgement (ICTY, 10 December 1999).
[74] See Jelisić, Prosecution's Motion to Be Heard (ICTY, 1999).
[75] See Jelisić, Oral Judgement, Transcript (ICTY, 19 October 1999), 2329–30.
[76] See *ibid.*, 2322, where Presiding Judge Claude Jorda indicated that he would hear the prosecution after the Trial Chamber rendered its decision.
[77] See Jelisić, Trial Judgement (ICTY, 14 December 1999), paras. 93, 95, 98, 108, where reference is made to proof "beyond all reasonable doubt."
[78] See, for example, Kunarac *et al.*, Decision on Motion for Acquittal (ICTY, 3 July 2000), paras. 3–4, noting that the Jelisić case is an "exception" to all other ICTY jurisprudence and would not be followed.
[79] See Blaškić, Decision on the Defence Motion to Dismiss (ICTY, 3 September 1998), where Judges Claude Jorda and Fouad Riad – both also in the Jelisić case – applied a much more lenient standard of proof in interpreting Rule 98*bis*.

In addition to these procedural irregularities, the Trial Chamber's interpretation of facts leading to its judgment of acquittal is found seriously wanting, even if the prosecution needed to satisfy the highest standard of proof (beyond a reasonable doubt) in order to proceed with its case. An examination of the prosecution evidence suggests that the judges either seriously misapprehended the facts as presented by the prosecution or that they deliberately dismissed the case prematurely for reasons extraneous to the legal viability of the case against the accused. Even admitting a wide margin of judicial discretion in interpreting evidence, the undisputed facts of the case are sufficient to demonstrate that the Trial Chamber's assessment of the evidence was "unreasonable."[80] In particular, as noted in Chapter 3,[81] in determining whether the evidence is sufficient to support an inference of genocidal intent, such intent can be inferred either from the "words and deeds" of the accused or from a "pattern of purposeful action."[82] In other words, given the difficulty of eliciting direct proof of an accused's mental intent, genocidal *mens rea* may be inferred, at least in part, from a pattern of violent or discriminatory behavior targeting a specific group, such as "the physical targeting of the group or their property; the use of derogatory language towards members of the targeted group; the weapons employed and the extent of bodily injury; [and] the methodical way of planning the systematic manner of killing."[83]

As the following discussion demonstrates, in presenting its case-in-chief, the prosecution persuasively and unambiguously presented an overwhelming factual basis for inferring genocidal intent, with regard to both "words and deeds" and the "pattern of purposeful action." Eager to dismiss the case, however, the Trial Chamber artificially compartmentalized the evidence, with the consequence that the chamber downplayed and dismissed, and arguably distorted or entirely disregarded, the crucial linkages between the words and deeds of the accused in the detention camp and the broader campaign of "ethnic cleansing" in the region.

The Trial Chamber did not dispute that the material element of the crime of genocide had been satisfied. The chamber acknowledged that

---

[80] See Tadić, Appeals Judgement (ICTY, 15 July 1999), para. 64 (establishing the "unreasonableness" standard in reviewing a trial chamber's evaluation of the evidence).

[81] See 44–45.

[82] See Kayishema, Trial Judgement (ICTR, 21 May 1999), para. 93.

[83] *Ibid.*

"hundreds of Muslim and Croat detainees" were killed by the Serbian authorities at the Luka camp[84] and that the accused "regularly executed detainees" there:

According to one witness, Goran Jelisić declared that he had to execute twenty to thirty persons before being able to drink his coffee each morning. The testimony heard by the Trial Chamber revealed that Goran Jelisić frequently informed the detainees of the number of Muslims that he had killed. Thus, on 8 May 1992 he reputedly said to one witness that it was his sixty-eighth victim, on 11 May that he had killed one hundred and fifty persons and finally on 15 May to another witness following an execution that it was his "eighty-third case."[85]

In addition to the killings directly perpetrated by the accused, the Trial Chamber noted – albeit in a mere footnote relating to discriminatory intent – that according to testimony approximately 2,000 to 3,000 of the Muslims in Brčko (that is, the municipality where the Luka camp was situated) disappeared or were killed.[86]

With respect to the *mens rea* or mental element, the Trial Chamber first considered the discriminatory intent of the accused against the Muslim population of Brčko. It found ample evidence that Jelisić acted with such intent:

The testimony heard during the trial shows that the offensive against the civilian population of Brčko, of which the acts of Goran Jelisić formed part, was directed mainly against the Muslim population. A great majority of the persons detained in the collection centres and at Luka camp were Muslim. During interrogations, the Muslims were questioned about their possible involvement in resistance movements or political groups. Most of the victims who were killed during the conflict in Brčko were Muslims.

The words and deeds of the accused demonstrate that he was not only perfectly aware of the discriminatory nature of the operation but also that he fully supported it. It appears from the evidence submitted to the Trial Chamber that a large majority of the persons whom Goran Jelisić admitted having beaten and executed were Muslim. Additionally, many of the elements showed how Goran Jelisić made scornful and discriminatory remarks about the Muslim population. Often, Goran Jelisić insulted the Muslims by calling them "balijas" or "Turks." Of one detainee whom he had just hit, Goran Jelisić allegedly said that he must be [sic] have been mad to dirty his hands with a "balija" before then executing him.[87]

[84] Jelisić, Trial Judgement (ICTY, 14 December 1999), para. 64.
[85] *Ibid.*, para. 103.   [86] *Ibid.*, para. 74 note 101.
[87] *Ibid.*, paras. 74–75.

It is with respect to the crucial "intent to destroy, in whole or in part, the group as such" that the Trial Chamber found the evidence insufficient even for sustaining a *prima facie* case. In arriving at this conclusion, the chamber considered both the intent of the accused to aid and abet a broader, "all-inclusive" crime of genocide in Brčko municipality and his intent to commit genocide in Luka camp in isolation from events transpiring elsewhere. In assessing Jelisić's status as an accomplice to a broader plan to commit genocide, the chamber recognized that the "operation launched by the Serbian forces against the Muslim population of Brčko was organised."[88] But it queried whether "this organisation [was] meant to destroy in whole or in part the Muslim group."[89] The chamber's judgment referred, *inter alia*, to the testimony of a witness who "during an interrogation at the mosque [was told] that 5% of the Muslims and Croats would be allowed to live."[90] But the evidence of mass killings was overwhelming. Other witnesses declared that "on several occasions during their time at Luka they had carried up to twenty bodies,"[91] and exhumations revealed four mass graves containing approximately sixty-six bodies.[92] Although not mentioned in the judgment itself, an additional mass grave contained 216 bodies, and it seems likely that many more bodies were removed to conceal evidence of the mass killings.[93]

Additional evidence was ignored or distorted in the judgment. For example, the prosecution evidence included execution lists containing names of Muslims in leadership positions;[94] a witness "described how the police detectives who interrogated the detainees at Luka camp appeared to decide which detainees were to be executed upon the basis of a document"; and others similarly claimed that lists were relied upon in the execution of Muslims.[95] The Trial Chamber found that it had not been established "that the accused relied on such a list in carrying out the execution."[96] It therefore held that it was impossible "to conclude beyond all reasonable doubt that the choice of victims arose from a precise logic to destroy the most representative figures of the Muslim community in Brčko to the point of threatening the survival

---

[88] *Ibid.*, para. 88.
[89] *Ibid.*   [90] *Ibid.*, para. 89.
[91] *Ibid.*   [92] *Ibid.*, para. 90.
[93] See, for example, Jelisić, Prosecution's Appeal Brief (Public Redacted Version) (ICTY, 14 July 2000), paras. 4.57–4.58.
[94] Jelisić, Trial Judgement (ICTY, 14 December 1999), para. 91.
[95] *Ibid.*, para. 92.   [96] *Ibid.*, para. 93.

of that community"[97] – an apparent reference to the theory, mentioned earlier in the judgment, that the intent to destroy a group "in part" could take in "either a major part of the group or a *representative fraction thereof such as its leaders.*"[98] In arriving at its conclusion that there was no demonstrable connection between the lists and Jelisić's action, however, the Trial Chamber disregarded the accused's own confession that his superiors had given him an execution list containing the names of prominent Muslims, the testimony of several witnesses that such persons were regularly singled out for execution, and the fact that many victims exhumed from the mass graves had been included on Jelisić's execution list.[99]

In considering the question of whether "a major part" of the group, rather than its leadership, was slated for destruction, the Trial Chamber noted that "eighty to a hundred persons out of a total of six to seven hundred detainees ... had a laissez-passer" and that some detainees were exchanged.[100] Despite the implicit suggestion that such releases were inconsistent with an intent to destroy the group, only a small fraction of detainees were thus spared, and no mention is made of testimony that some prisoners were kept alive for exchange purposes and that, more generally, the decision to spare some prisoners was influenced by concerns about international public opinion after the detention camps were exposed.[101]

The Trial Chamber also distorted the available evidence in finding that, although the accused undoubtedly "exercised a *de facto* authority over the staff and detainees at the camp," the prosecution had failed to establish beyond all reasonable doubt "whether the accused killed at Luka camp under orders."[102] The chamber claimed that "no element establishing the chain of command within which he operated has been presented" and that, in particular, "no information has been provided concerning the authority to which he answered."[103] Furthermore, in view of the significant decrease in cruel treatment and murders after Jelisić's departure from the camp,[104] the Trial Chamber considered it "possible" that the accused "acted beyond the

---

[97] *Ibid.*   [98] *Ibid.*, para. 81 (emphasis added).

[99] See, for example, Jelisić, Prosecution's Appeal Brief (Public Redacted Version) (ICTY, 14 July 2000), paras. 4.59–4.64.

[100] Jelisić, Trial Judgement (ICTY, 14 December 1999), para. 94.

[101] See, for example, Jelisić, Prosecution's Appeal Brief (Public Redacted Version) (ICTY, 14 July 2000), para. 4.67.

[102] Jelisić, Trial Judgement (ICTY, 14 December 1999), para. 95.

[103] *Ibid.*, para. 96.   [104] *Ibid.*

scope of the powers entrusted to him."[105] Thus, the Trial Chamber found that "the Prosecutor has not provided sufficient evidence allowing it to be established beyond all reasonable doubt that there existed a plan to destroy the Muslim group in Brčko or elsewhere within which the murders committed by the accused would allegedly fit."[106] It is remarkable, however, that in making such compartmentalized factual findings that tend to isolate the killings as an aberration, the Trial Chamber disregarded the confession of the accused himself, who provided a detailed account of the command structure both in Luka camp and the Brčko municipality. Nor does the chamber make any mention of corroborating testimony by several witnesses that the execution of Muslim detainees was carried out pursuant to superior orders.[107] Also omitted in the chamber's judgment is any mention of the use of refrigerator trucks to carry off hundreds of bodies from Luka camp – which seems to suggest a systematic, methodical plan, rather than a haphazard effort.[108]

There are yet other shortcomings in the Trial Chamber's assessment of the evidence, especially in relation to the chamber's utter refusal to draw, or even to consider the possibility of drawing, reasonable inferences from the facts before it. It refused to consider the possibility of a link between the killings in Luka camp and the wider campaign of "ethnic cleansing" in Brčko, and it refused to consider the question of whether the destruction of a large proportion (at least 2,000 of 3,000) of the Muslims remaining in Brčko might constitute genocide. This latter refusal is especially puzzling in relation to the question of genocidal intent since a significant number of these killings were in Luka camp itself, where "hundreds" of detainees out of a total camp population of 600 to 700 were killed, with only a small fraction spared and the accused having admitted to have personally killed as many as 150 detainees.

The Trial Chamber's determination to avoid drawing even the most obvious inferences is apparent in its failure to probe the implications of Jelisić's guilty plea to crimes against humanity. In the context of that plea, the chamber had observed that the accused was an "active participant" in the "widespread and systematic [attack]"

---

[105] Ibid., para. 97.   [106] Ibid., para. 98.
[107] See, for example, Jelisić, Prosecution's Appeal Brief (Public Redacted Version) (ICTY, 14 July 2000), paras. 4.65–4.70.
[108] Ibid., para. 4.73.

"by the Serbian forces against the non-Serbian population of Brčko."[109] To be sure, knowledge of an attack against a civilian population cannot be equated with the intent to destroy a group. But the Trial Chamber did not even raise the question of whether, and how, the mass killings in the camp and in the wider municipality related to the overall policy of "ethnic cleansing" against non-Serbs in Brčko.

What is most remarkable about the Trial Chamber's judgment is its explicit treatment of the question of Jelisić's genocidal intent. On the one hand, the chamber recognized that the

murders committed by the accused are sufficient to establish the material element of the crime of genocide and it is *a priori* possible to conceive that the accused harboured the plan to exterminate an entire group without this intent having been supported by any organisation in which other individuals participated ... [T]he drafters of the [Genocide] Convention did not deem the existence of an organisation or a system serving a genocidal objective as a legal ingredient of the crime. In so doing, they did not discount the possibility of a lone individual seeking to destroy a group as such.[110]

On the other hand, however, the Trial Chamber noted that "it will be very difficult in practice to provide proof of the genocidal intent of an individual if the crimes committed are not widespread and if the crime charged is not backed by an organisation or a system."[111] And the chamber then proceeded to sidestep the question of whether there was any such organization or system, and to characterize the killings in Luka camp as having occurred independent of any larger, genocidal plan in Brčko.

In this context, the Trial Chamber painted a picture of Jelisić as a lone, opportunistic psychopath, with absolute power over the detainees at Luka camp: He "presented himself as the 'Serbian Adolf'";[112] claimed to have gone to Brčko "to kill Muslims"; remarked to one witness that "he hated the Muslims and wanted to kill them all, whilst the surviving Muslims could be slaves for cleaning the toilets"; asserted that Muslims "had proliferated too much and that he had to rid the world of them";[113] and bragged about killing 150 persons himself.[114] The chamber quoted, with approval, the testimony of witnesses that

Goran Jelisić seemed to take pleasure from his position, one which gave him a feeling of power, of holding the power of life or death over the detainees and

---

[109] Jelisić, Trial Judgement (ICTY, 14 December 1999), para. 57.
[110] *Ibid.*, para. 100.   [111] *Ibid.*, para. 101.
[112] *Ibid.*, para. 102.   [113] *Ibid.*   [114] *Ibid.*, para. 104.

that he took a certain pride in the number of victims that he had allegedly executed. According to another testimony, Goran Jelisić spoke in a blood-thirsty manner, he treated them like animals or beasts and spittle formed on his lips because of his shouts and the hatred he was expressing. He wanted to terrorise them.[115]

Although Jelisić's words and deeds would appear to present a paradigmatic example of genocidal intent, the Trial Chamber questioned the existence of the requisite *dolus specialis*. It concluded, instead, that he merely had a "disturbed personality":[116]

Goran Jelisić led an ordinary life before the conflict. This personality, which presents borderline, anti-social and narcissistic characteristics and which is marked simultaneously by immaturity, a hunger to fill a "void" and a concern to please superiors, contributed to his finally committing crimes. Goran Jelisić suddenly found himself in an apparent position of authority for which nothing had prepared him. It matters little whether this authority was real. What does matter is that this authority made it even easier for an opportunistic and inconsistent behaviour to express itself.[117]

Picking up this theme of inconsistency, the Trial Chamber noted that Jelisić "performed the executions randomly" and issued "laissez-passer to several detainees at the camp ... on his own initiative and against all logic"[118] – from which the chamber inferred that his acts were "not the physical expression of an affirmed resolve to destroy in whole or in part a group as such."[119] That is, not only were Jelisić's actions the product of pathology rather than well-formed genocidal intent, "the behaviour of the accused appears to indicate that, although he obviously singled out Muslims, he killed arbitrarily rather than with the clear intention to destroy a group."[120]

The Trial Chamber's reasoning as expressed in its judgment is opaque. Neither the defense nor even the chamber itself acting *proprio motu* had suggested at any previous point that Jelisić's "mental incapacity" was at issue. No question had been raised concerning whether the accused was capable of forming genocidal intent or of appreciating the consequences of his conduct. Indeed, it was recognized that despite his "disturbed personality," the accused "led an ordinary life before the conflict."[121] It is also significant that, despite the weight that the Trial Chamber attached to Jelisić's "disturbed personality" in

---

[115] *Ibid.*   [116] *Ibid.*, para. 105.   [117] *Ibid.*
[118] *Ibid.*, para. 106.   [119] *Ibid.*, para. 107.
[120] *Ibid.*, para. 108.   [121] *Ibid.*, para. 105.

acquitting him, the chamber did not even consider it as a mitigating circumstance at the sentencing phase.[122] This inconsistency simply makes no sense.

Equally puzzling is the relevance of Jelisić's psychological status to the question of intent. It is fair to interpret the Trial Chamber's judgment as implying that, despite overwhelming evidence that the "Serbian Adolf" acted to exterminate Muslims, a "disturbed personality" somehow negates genocidal intent. If so, the crime of genocide is effectively eviscerated. The crime would apply only to genocidal killers – whether "big fish," "medium fish," or "small fish" – who are somehow "normal" and mentally balanced, and who are not at some profound level actuated by a pathological lust for arbitrary power. The chamber does not – and arguably cannot – explain how deriving great pleasure from "a feeling of power" through total dehumanization and eradication of a victim group is in any way inconsistent with the conscious desire to destroy that group. Indeed, that is precisely the context in which genocides have occurred.

On the matter of Jelisić's supposed inconsistency and how that affected the characterization of his behavior, it is unclear how his "disturbed personality" would prevent him from acting consciously and consistently against Muslims. And, within the facts of the case, there is no adequate explanation as to how Jelisić's singling out Muslims for extermination – his discriminatory intent, explicitly recognized by the Trial Chamber – can be distinguished from his intention to target a group "as such." Since his discriminatory intent was expressed essentially through mass killings, and since he "was not only perfectly aware of the discriminatory nature of the operation [in Brčko, mainly against the Muslim population] but also ... fully supported it,"[123] it is beyond reckoning how the Trial Chamber could have concluded that Jelisić did not intend to destroy Muslims as a group. Nevertheless, the Trial Chamber seemingly reasons that Jelisić individually killed or oversaw the killing of hundreds of Muslims at Luka camp *simply because* they were Muslims, but, because the killings were "random" and actuated by a desire for power, there was no intent to destroy Muslims as a group, either in whole or in part. Although discriminatory intent and intent to destroy the group are technically distinct, separating them in this factual context amounts to evidentiary

---

[122] *Ibid.*, para. 125.   [123] *Ibid.*, para. 75.

hairsplitting – and makes the acquittal for genocide stand not on the facts, but on the equivalent of semantic metaphysics.

The Trial Chamber's findings might appear at least marginally reasonable if it had been responding to a vigorous case by the defense – consisting of plausible counterarguments that raised a reasonable doubt as to guilt. But that was not the case. In view of the prosecution's strong case-in-chief against Jelisić, preempting a full trial through a judgment of acquittal was manifestly unreasonable in substance, even inscrutable. So how can this judgment be understood? Since Jelisić had already pleaded guilty to war crimes and crimes against humanity, it is fair to assume that the judges may have been irritated by the prosecutor's insistence on going to trial on the single count of genocide. In view of the ICTY's overwhelming court docket, the availability of a limited number of trial chambers and courtrooms, the time-consuming and resource-intensive nature of trials before international criminal tribunals, and the consequent prolonged pretrial detention of accused, the Trial Chamber may have considered it frivolous to go to trial on a single count where a conviction was already secured. This concern may have been especially acute in the *Jelisić* case because the presiding judge was Claude Jorda, the newly elected ICTY president, whose primary platform was "to improve the Tribunal's operation and, in particular, to shorten trial length and time spent in detention."[124]

This consideration appears to have also been on the minds of the judges of the Appeals Chamber, who were later called upon to review the *Jelisić* case, notwithstanding their reversal of the Trial Chamber's ruling. In its judgment, the Appeals Chamber first chastised the Trial Chamber for applying an erroneously stringent standard of proof.[125] It then went on to criticize the Trial Chamber's two principal arguments in dismissing the genocide charge. As to the assertion that Jelisić's "disturbed personality" prevented him from forming the requisite *dolus specialis*, the Appeals Chamber rightly held that

there is no *per se* inconsistency between a diagnosis of the kind of immature, narcissistic, disturbed personality on which the Trial Chamber relied and the ability to form an intent to destroy a particular protected group. Indeed, as the prosecution points out, it is the borderline unbalanced personality who is

---

[124] See, for example, *Report on the Operation of the International Criminal Tribunal for the Former Yugoslavia*, 33 (presented by Judge Claude Jorda, President, on behalf of the judges of the tribunal, The Hague, May 2000).
[125] Jelisić, Appeals Judgement (ICTY, 5 July 2001), para. 68.

more likely to be drawn to extreme racial and ethnical hatred than the more balanced modulated individual without personality defects. The Rules visualise, as a defence, a certain degree of mental incapacity and in any event, no such imbalance was found in this case.[126]

Regarding the apparent randomness of Jelisić's violent compulsions, the Appeals Chamber contended:

A reasonable trier of fact could have discounted the few incidents where he showed mercy as aberrations in an otherwise relentless campaign against the protected group. Similarly, the fact that he took "pleasure" from the killings does not detract in any way from his intent to perform such killings; as has been mentioned above, the Tribunal has declared in the Tadić appeal judgement the irrelevance and "inscrutability of motives in criminal law" insofar as liability is concerned, where an intent – including a specific intent – is clear.[127]

However, despite these apparently glaring flaws by the Trial Chamber, the Appeals Chamber declined to remand the case for retrial on the charge of genocide. The chamber noted that Jelisić had already been sentenced to a forty-year term of imprisonment and that the *"ad hoc* nature of the International Tribunal ...*,* unlike a national legal system, means resources are limited in terms of man-power and the uncertain longevity of the Tribunal." Given these factors, the chamber decided "that it is not in the interests of justice" to retry the accused.[128]

But, even here, it appears that additional, unarticulated considerations are implicated. The explanation would be different, and the case would potentially have been remanded, if the accused had been higher in rank or authority. It may be queried, for instance, whether the same considerations of judicial expedience would have applied if the accused was the former Bosnian Serb president Radovan Karadžić or another comparable "big fish." Would an opportunity to ascertain the occurrence of genocide – with its implications for the judicially rendered historical account of "ethnic cleansing" in Bosnia-Herzegovina – have been so readily declined as an onerous burden on the ICTY's busy docket if the accused had been a "big Adolf" rather than a "little Adolf"? As Judge Patricia M. Wald of the Appeals Chamber acknowledged in her partially dissenting opinion,

the resources of the Tribunal are stretched thin and there may well be reason to prioritise cases involving allegations of State-planned and executed crimes,

---

[126] *Ibid.,* para. 70.   [127] *Ibid.,* para. 71.   [128] *Ibid.,* para. 77.

rather than individualistic or opportunistic crimes. Some learned commentators on genocide stress that the currency of this "crime of all crimes" should not be diminished by use in other than large scale state-sponsored campaigns to destroy minority groups, even if the detailed definition of genocide in our Statute would allow broader coverage. In this case, the erratic pattern of Jelisić's killings and his personality disturbances, make the precedential value of a genocide charge problematic.[129]

Judge Wald's opinion must be praised at least for its transparency – its blunt admission that the prosecution of a mere camp commander may dilute the moral value of genocide. What is significant here is that the legal viability of the charge becomes inapposite. The fundamental question of the criminal liability of the accused, the daily reality of ruthless camp guards doing the "dirty work" of genocide, and the brutal victimization of innocent human beings are all casually dismissed in favor of a more abstract conception of genocide as a state-sponsored crime for which only the highest officials should be punished. Even within the confines of judicial proceedings, the legal definition of *genocide* has thus been supplanted by some larger moral conception of the crime as one requiring a special sort of atrocity, beyond the capacity of mere underlings.

Although Lemkin reduced genocide to the cage of legal terminology, the crime seemingly escapes its taxonomy; the power of the word *genocide* overwhelms legal reasoning. Yet one is left asking whether this disregard of "positive" law is a cause for celebration or a corruption of jurisprudence for purposes that should remain extraneous to the law. Put differently, how does either conferring (as in *Akayesu*) or withholding (as in *Jelisić*) the potent symbolism of genocide make a difference in confronting this evil?

---

[129] Jelisić, Appeals Judgement, Partial Dissenting Opinion of Judge Wald (ICTY, 5 July 2001), paras. 2, 64.

8   Silence, empathy, and the potentialities of jurisprudence

On 13 June 1983, Farkhundih Mahmudnizhad was released from Adelabad prison in the Iranian city of Shiraz. She recounted her conversation with Mona Mahmudnizhad, her still imprisoned 17-year-old daughter, as they said good-bye:

I went along with her. The corridor was so narrow that the two of us could hardly walk side by side. We walked a little way and then she stopped. I stopped beside her, and waited for her to speak. She looked into my eyes and said, "Mama, do you know that they are going to execute me?"

Suddenly my whole being seemed to be on fire. I didn't want to believe her. I said, "No, my dear daughter, they are going to let you go. You will get married and have children. My greatest wish is to see your children. No, don't even think that."[1]

Farkhundih Mahmudnizhad, her daughter Mona, and many others imprisoned in Shiraz and across the country were members of the persecuted Bahá'í religious minority, declared to be a "heresy" by the Islamic Republic of Iran. On the day prior to Farkhundih's release, the prosecutor-general had visited the prisoners to conduct the fourth and final part of a legal procedure known as *Istitabih*: "According to the Iranian Government's interpretation of Islamic law, a prisoner holding heretical beliefs was given four opportunities to recant and repent prior to execution and thus save his or her life."[2] They had been admonished and warned: "You have to pass through four stages of guidance

---

[1] Olya Roohizadegan, *Olya's Story: A Survivor's Dramatic Account of the Persecution of Baha'is in Revolutionary Iran* (Oxford, UK: Oneworld, 1993), 220.

[2] Iran Human Rights Documentation Centre, *Community Under Siege: The Ordeal of the Baha'is of Shiraz* (New Haven: IHRDC, 2007), 37, www.scribd.com/doc/17774491 /-Community-Under-Siege-The-Ordeal-of-the-Bahais-of-Shiraz.

to become Muslims, otherwise you will be executed. From tomorrow, two hours of silence will be announced every day. The prison will become your university, and you all have to study."[3] Despite the stark choice between "Islam or execution" (*Islam ya idam*), they had refused to recant their faith. On the evening of 18 June, Mona and nine other women were loaded into a bus, driven to Chawgan Square in Shiraz, and hanged one by one.

Among those few that were spared, there was a sense of urgency to ensure that the world knew what had come to pass within the confines of the prison. As one of them wrote: "there was a purpose in my going. I had often sworn to them – as they had to me – that if I was ever to get out of Adelabad Prison I would tell the world their story, our story."[4] Telling stories, putting into words emotions that defy rational explanation, are essential to the process of healing. This compulsion exists because "[t]raumas cause victims to question fundamental assumptions about their own merit, and about the orderliness of the world. This upheaval of emotional bedrock leaves victims yearning to regain a sense of stability and meaning about themselves and the world around them."[5] By telling their stories instead of suppressing them, victims temper this disabling bewilderment by "translating the chaotic swirl of traumatic ideation and feelings into coherent language"[6] – they take ownership and "experience themselves as authors, rather than as objects, of past traumas."[7] Indeed, some speak of "narrative therapy" in which, through storytelling, a victim is encouraged to "externalize" the trauma, transforming it into something outside that can be examined and evaluated, rather than leaving it inside, for it to burrow into one's psyche, one's soul.[8] As Elaine Scarry observed in her seminal work *The Body in Pain*, the importance of telling one's story and having it heard is that it allows survivors to become "subjects" again.[9]

---

[3] *Ibid.*, 38.   [4] Roohizadegan, *Olya's Story*, xii.

[5] Kent D. Harber and James W. Pennebaker, "Overcoming Traumatic Memories," in Sven-Ake Christianson, ed., *The Handbook of Emotion and Memory: Research and Theory* (Hillsdale, NJ: Lawrence Erlbaum, 1992), 359.

[6] *Ibid.*, 360.   [7] *Ibid.*, 383.

[8] See generally Michael White and David Epston, *Narrative Means to Therapeutic Ends* (New York: W. W. Norton, 1990); Alice Morgan, *What Is Narrative Therapy? An Easy to Read Introduction* (Adelaide, Australia: Dulwich Centre, 2000).

[9] Elaine Scarry, *The Body in Pain* (Oxford, UK: Oxford University Press, 1985) (as cited in Lyn S. Graybill, *Truth and Reconciliation in South Africa: Miracle or Model?* [Boulder: Lynne Rienner, 2002], 82–83).

A psychologist who worked with Holocaust survivors explains that "[t]elling stories helped release tension, elicit warm support from other members, and reconstruct a more genuine discourse."[10] Similarly, an observer of the South African Truth and Reconciliation Commission remarks on the importance of storytelling as a healing process:

> Previously, victims had been tormented with self-blame, the sense that some- how they had deserved what happened to them, or guilt for the fact that their political activity had caused suffering for their families. It is important that victims be allowed to tell their stories, because survivors often feel misunder- stood and ignored, their sacrifice unacknowledged, their pain unrecognized, and their identity lost. Theologian Robert Shreiter writes that individuals cannot survive without a narrative of identity. Through torture and coercion, oppressors attempt to substitute another narrative so that people will acqui- esce in their subjugation. If the original narrative is suppressed, the lie will be accepted as truth. Victims can only overcome suffering by overcoming the narrative of the lie and embracing a redeeming narrative.[11]

But the telling of stories is not just an experience for the individual victim. It is also central to the catharsis of a *society* reckoning with a history of mass violence. And telling stories is not about legal cat- egorization, historical theories, or other distant abstractions and uni- versalizing narratives. It is, above all, about regaining subjectivity by inspiring healing and empathy – the recognition of another human being's suffering. As three authors of the South African *Truth and Reconciliation Commission Report* observed:

> The reality is that the testimony of a single victim relayed to the country by the media will ultimately have had more of an impact upon the national consciousness than any number of volumes of the report. The enduring mem- ory of the Commission will be the images of pain, grief and regret conveyed relentlessly ... to a public that generally remained spellbound by what it was witnessing.[12]

---

[10] Dan Bar-On, "Attempting to Overcome the Intergenerational Transmission of Trauma," in J. Apfel and B. Simon, eds., *Minefields in Their Hearts: The Mental Health of Children in War and Communal Violence* (New Haven: Yale University Press, 1996), 165, 185.

[11] See, for example, Lyn S. Graybill, "Storytelling," in Graybill, *Truth and Reconciliation in South Africa*, 82 (footnotes omitted).

[12] Janet Cherry, John Daniel, and Madeleine Fullard, "Researching the 'Truth': A View from Inside the Truth and Reconciliation Commission," in Deborah Posel and Graeme Simpson, eds., *Commissioning the Past: Understanding South Africa's Truth and Reconciliation Commission* (Johannesburg: Witwatersrand University Press, 2002), 17, 35.

A groundbreaking study by Paul Slovic illustrates this point force-fully.[13] The article presenting the study borrows its title, "'If I Look at the Mass I Will Never Act': Psychic Numbing and Genocide," from Mother Teresa's confession, "If I look at the mass I will never act. If I look at the one, I will."[14] In one experiment, Slovic and his colleagues asked people to donate $5 to the humanitarian organization Save the Children in order to "alleviate the severe food crisis in Southern Africa and Ethiopia." In one of the experimental scenarios, the donors were given broad statistical information – for example, that three million children in Malawi are affected by food shortages, that eleven million people in Ethiopia need immediate food assistance, and that the crisis has caused four million Angolans to leave their homes. In a second scenario, the subjects were told only the story of "Rokia," a 7-year-old girl from Mali, who is "desperately poor and faces a threat of severe hunger or even starvation." Additional details of Rokia's life were pro-vided, accompanied by a color photograph. Slovic and colleagues found that subjects donated almost twice as much to Rokia as they did when faced with statistics describing the suffering millions.

What is even more illuminating, however, is the response to a third experimental scenario, in which subjects were provided with *both* the story of Rokia and the broad statistical information. Surprisingly, in this scenario donations were not much greater than in response to the statistics alone and were significantly less than the decontextualized story of Rokia alone.[15] Nicholas Kristof writes in a similar vein:

Even the right animal evokes a similar sympathy [to that of an identifiable human victim]. A dog stranded on a ship aroused so much pity that $48,000 in private money was spent trying to rescue it – and that was before the Coast Guard stepped in. And after I began visiting Darfur in 2004, I was flummoxed by the public's passion to save a red-tailed hawk, Pale Male, that had been evicted from his nest on Fifth Avenue in New York City. A single homeless hawk aroused more indignation than two million homeless Sudanese.[16]

As Slovic observes, "[o]ur capacity to feel is limited."[17] Primed to respond to the suffering of identifiable individuals, we become numb to the abstract suffering of millions: "the statistics of mass murder or

---

[13] Paul Slovic, "'If I Look at the Mass I Will Never Act': Psychic Numbing and Genocide," *Judgment and Decision Making* 2 (2007): 79.
[14] *Ibid.*, 80.   [15] *Ibid.*, 88–89.
[16] Nicholas Kristof, "Save the Darfur Puppy," *New York Times*, 10 May 2007.
[17] Slovic, "'If I Look at the Mass I Will Never Act,'" 90.

genocide, no matter how large the numbers, fail to convey the true meaning of such atrocities. The numbers fail to spark emotion or feeling and thus fail to motivate action. Genocide in Darfur is real, but we do not 'feel' that reality."[18] Attempting to wrap our minds around the enormity of a situation leads not to greater empathy, but rather to "psychic numbing" or "compassion fatigue."

The philosopher Richard Rorty, in discussing the idea of "sentimental education,"[19] observed that rhetoric about universal human rights can do little to prevent atrocities since violators "do not think of themselves as violating human rights. For they are not doing these things to fellow human beings … They are not being inhuman, but rather are discriminating between the true humans and the pseudohumans":[20]

To get whites to be nicer to blacks, males to females, Serbs to Muslims, or straights to gays, to help our species link up into what Rabossi calls a "planetary community" dominated by a culture of human rights, it is of no use whatever to say, with Kant: Notice that what you have in common, your humanity, is more important than these trivial differences. For the people we are trying to convince will rejoin that they notice nothing of the sort.[21]

The transformation of society cannot be based on "convergence toward an already existing Truth." Truth is simply a construct of language, and language is created rather than found.[22] Instead, we need to engage in a "sentimental education" whereby we attempt to acquire – for instance, through storytelling, poetry, and the testimony of survivors – "an increasing ability to see the similarities between ourselves and people very unlike us as outweighing the differences." On this view, the "relevant similarities are not a matter of sharing a deep true self which instantiates true humanity, but are such little, superficial, similarities as cherishing our parents and our children – similarities that do not interestingly distinguish us from many nonhuman animals."[23] In other words, moral progress "is a matter of wider and wider sympathy" rather than of "rising above the sentimental to the rational."[24]

---

[18] Ibid., 80.
[19] See also Stephen Ryan, *The Transformation of Violent Intercommunal Conflict* (Aldershot, UK: Ashgate, 2007), 131.
[20] Richard Rorty, "Human Rights, Rationality, and Sentimentality," in Rorty, *Truth and Progress: Philosophical Papers* (New York: Cambridge University Press, 1998), 167.
[21] Ibid., 178.
[22] Richard Rorty, *Contingency, Irony and Solidarity* (New York: Cambridge University Press, 1989), xvi.
[23] Rorty, "Human Rights, Rationality, and Sentimentality," 181.
[24] Richard Rorty, *Philosophy and Social Hope* (New York: Penguin, 1999), 82.

What I have proposed in this book is that, beyond the inescapably narrow, rule-oriented context of determining liability through a judicial process, the preoccupation with, and disputes over, the label of *genocide* inescapably result in a distancing from human experience and emotion. As happens with other efforts to approach experience through rational, hierarchical categories, this process of abstraction draws one away from the world and, in the case of genocide, from the horrible and intimate reality of that crime. The result is psychic numbing and moral paralysis, much like what happens with statistics about mass starvation in contrast to the story of 7-year-old Rokia's starvation. Kristof observes that "human rationality or international law" cannot be a sufficient response to genocide unless there is also a public outcry – and an outcry motivated not by platitudes about the "ultimate crime," but by empathy with victims: "One experiment underscored the limits of rationality. People prepared to donate to the needy were first asked either to talk about babies (to prime the emotions) or to perform math calculations (to prime their rational side). Those who did math donated less." He concludes that "maybe what we need isn't better laws but more troubled consciences."[25] But perhaps better and more effective than *troubled consciences* would be *empathy*, the ability to feel the pain of others, to embrace the oneness of humankind.

Empathy is, above all, an emotional connection, a shared realm of experience. A study about narrative therapy for trauma victims notes that "it is by the forming of connections – between past and present, ideals and reality, self and others – that people achieve serenity in a difficult and disruptive world. For trauma victims, the business of connections seems to be of vital importance."[26] Crimes such as genocide victimize the individual as well as the community. For both, connections must be built, empathy restored. But in attempting to bring the rationalist credo of law to bear, in replacing inner meaning with legal definition, we do little service to this "business" of reconnecting. Abstract labeling, statistics about the dying millions, and grand historical narratives numb us to true suffering. More dangerously, they allow us to proclaim moral triumph, an illusory closure, that actually inhibits transformation rather than inspiring empathy. Perhaps what we need beyond our narrow vocation as jurists, politicians, and activists

---

[25] Kristof, "Save the Darfur Puppy."
[26] Harber and Pennebaker, "Overcoming Traumatic Memories," 383.

is not more explanation, analysis, and rationality, but contemplative silence – the ability to listen to the stories of victims and to *feel* them.

There may be valid reasons to crown genocide as the "crime of crimes" in international law. Beyond the peremptory status and universal enforceability of *jus cogens* as reflecting "the deeper conscience of all nations,"[27] the invidious stratification of evil is an essential and inescapable feature of a coherent and equitable normative scheme for attributing criminal liability. In particular, whether based on retributive or deterrence/utilitarian theories, a hierarchy of moral turpitude corresponding to different types of conduct is a categorical imperative in the apportionment of punishment, however imprecise and ambiguous such ranking may be. While the privileging of particular crimes over others may remain the subject of contention and dispute in the face of changing realities and shifting priorities, the principle of proportionality remains entrenched in our basic conceptions of criminal justice.

The problem with stratifying evil through the medium of legal abstractions arises where it is imbued with exaggerated significance – beyond the limited confines of the law. Within a legal framework, the impartial ascertainment of facts, conclusive determination of guilt or innocence, and assignment of culpability through sentencing all imply certainty, finality, and closure, however contrived and limited it may be. But where legal narratives are portrayed, implicitly or otherwise, as a definitive means of containing ineffable realities, jurisprudence may succumb to a broader "temptation of closure"[28] that creates the illusion of empathy, vindication, and progress while evading the painful work of mourning, contemplation, and transformation in the wake of cataclysm. In this respect, appropriating the crime of genocide is especially enticing because it represents the pinnacle of evil, founded on the paradigm of the Holocaust. Whether a broad or restrictive interpretation of genocide is embraced, the fetishistic invocation of this privileged abstraction reflects an inclination to inflate what is merely a legal concept into something much more – into something that gives suffering a deeper, more symbolic meaning. Despite

---

[27] Ulrich Scheuner, "Conflict of Treaty Provisions with a Peremptory Norm of General International Law and Its Consequences," *Zeitschrift fur auslandisches offentliches Recht und Volkerrecht* 27 (1967): 520, 524.

[28] See Saul Friedlander, "Trauma, Memory, and Transference," in Geoffrey Hartman, ed., *Holocaust Remembrance, the Shapes of Memory* (Oxford, UK, and Cambridge, MA: Blackwell, 1994), 252, 261.

the tremendous contributions that the ICTY and the ICTR have made to the development of international criminal law, the tribunals are not immune from this tendency to see genocide as a symbol, not just a legal category.

Violations of the core international crimes provoke our passions in poignant ways. In the "disenchanted" universe of modernity, bereft of religious belief, these norms represent a desperately needed moral compass, our clinging to the "sacred" amidst the secular ordering rituals of the contemporary world. They situate our normative discourse in the transcendent sphere of "unquestionable doctrines."[29] Our professions of allegiance to these unimpeachable axioms are an essential aspect of our self-definition as progressive, civilized, and compassionate beings wedded to the "cosmopolitan faith"[30] of "globalization, interdependence, democracy and the rule of law."[31]

Despite the positivist legal constructs that are invariably deployed in jurisprudence, the "unthinkability" of crimes such as genocide "brings to the surface the limits of rational argument and the character of normative knowledge."[32] Perhaps more so than any other aspect of the "compelling law" – in the inner sanctum of the *jus cogens* – such crimes compel us to dispense with the supposed objectivity and emotional distance that would ordinarily characterize the process of legal reasoning. Under the guise of a "teleological desire to solidify the humanizing content of ... humanitarian norms," we casually blur the distinction between the *lex lata* and the *lex ferenda*, surreptitiously merging the law as it is with the law as it ought to be.[33] Indeed, the dedicated legal practitioner may even celebrate the "centrality of passion" or "the absence of calculating reason" in such jurisprudence as a

---

[29] See, for example, "Introduction: Secular Ritual: Forms and Meanings," in Sally F. Moore and Barbara G. Myerhoff, eds., *Secular Ritual* (Amsterdam: Van Gorcum, 1977), 3: "An essential quality of the sacred is its unquestionability. Unquestionable tenets exist in secular political ideologies which are as sacred in that sense as the tenets of any religion. Secular ceremonies can present unquestionable doctrines and can dramatize social/moral imperatives without invoking the spirits at all."

[30] See Martti Koskenniemi, "Between Commitment and Cynicism: Outline for a Theory of International Law as Practice," in *Collection of Essays by Legal Advisers of States, Legal Advisers of International Organizations and Practitioners in the Field of International Law* (United Nations Sales No. E/F/S/99.V.13, 1999), 495, 496.

[31] *Ibid.*, 495.

[32] Martti Koskenniemi, "Faith, Identity, and the Killing of the Innocent: International Lawyers and Nuclear Weapons," *Leiden Journal of International Law* 10 (1997): 157.

[33] Theodor Meron, "The Geneva Conventions as Customary Law," *American Journal of International Law* 81 (1987): 348, 361.

sign of *"genuine commitment"*[34] or as a welcome opportunity to reaffirm unqualified adherence to the sacred mores of a liberal identity.

In coming to terms with monstrous atrocities, the jurist should be wary of abandoning conventional legal methodology for a teleological jurisprudence as a means of expressing righteous indignation. The fear is not that an otherwise "neutral" or "objective" legal reasoning will be consumed by what Aristotle depicted as the "wild beast" of desire or that it will be corrupted by erratic passion and unwieldy subjectivity.[35] Rather, the *caveat* is not to stray into a deceptive closure that fails to grasp the profound subtleties of working through traumatic events without suffocating ineffable meaning; the imperative is to respect the capacity of such restraint to inspire genuine reflection, empathy, and transformation. In other words, what is celebrated as "progressive" jurisprudence may also reflect a misguided search for closure, a yearning for a facile catharsis in the emotionally disconnected oblivion of legal abstractions. While overly strict and sterile jurisprudence may reflect callous disregard for the ordeal of victims, moral platitudes may represent a subliminal need to rationalize the irrational, to manage the unmanageable, and to create the semblance of order in the face of disintegration and chaos, without genuine commitment or empathy. Such attempts at closure within the confines of legal discourse not only distort the strictures of jurisprudence, but also privilege a comforting distance over painful intimacy. Fetishistic invocation of genocide becomes a substitute for meaningful engagement. The appropriation of hierarchical abstractions as a form of recognition, and fierce contests over who "owns" genocide in the arena of competitive suffering – both eclipse the enormity of the challenge in confronting radical evil. By reducing genocide to legal definition, by banishing perpetrators to a remote island outside our moral realm, by refusing to implicate ourselves as bystanders, we engage in a self-purification constructed not through critical self-examination, but by invoking the alterity – the radical otherness – of evil.

Through such devices, we avoid implicating our "civilized" self in our support of the Khmer Rouge when it was politically expedient, in our furnishing weapons to Saddam Hussein as he gassed Kurdish civilians, in our triumphant *post-histoire* complicity in Bosnia's "ethnic

---

[34] Koskenniemi, "Faith, Identity, and the Killing of the Innocent," 497.
[35] Aristotle, *Politics* (as cited in Francis A. Allen, *The Habits of Legality, Criminal Justice and the Rule of Law* [New York: Oxford University Press, 1996], 3).

cleansing," in our appalling indifference to the slaughter of a million Rwandan Tutsis, and in our ongoing passivity in the face of the horrors unfolding daily in Darfur.

There is yet another, perhaps more troubling dimension to certain displays of passion in jurisprudence. Beyond the trivialization that an all-embracing reduction of genocide to law represents, overt displays of allegiance to unimpeachable humanitarian axioms may also signify a "non-dialogic" or "one-sided" empathy,[36] a dominating self-affirmation that negates the "other" by disregarding the distinction between the aggrieved survivor and the compassionate human rights advocate; the suffering of the victim is lost in the advocate's self-affirming demonstrations of virtue. In other words, so-called progressive jurisprudence can become a ritual sacrifice at the altar of piety in which the offering is someone else's blood and travail. Far from empowering the dispossessed, such condescending *noblesse oblige* may further reduce the humanity of survivors, whose only worthwhile possession may be their stories. In the thoughtful words of Elizabeth Spelman, suffering is "an arable field, on which some do the difficult work of plowing and planting, and others arrive just in time to enjoy the harvest."[37] The resort to "other people's experience of suffering to make sense of our own" can result in our simply "exploit[ing] their labor: I acknowledge your suffering only to the extent to which it promises to bring attention to my own." Thus, in place of genuine empathy, the relation between "self" and "other" is one in which "[y]ou sow the seeds [and] I pluck the fruits of sorrow."[38] In this confusion between self-affirmation and empathy, emotional connection with the immediate reality of suffering and with the meaning of the struggle for justice is lost. Likewise, the voice of the aggrieved is lost in self-righteous commentary.

Against this backdrop, the postmodern rejection of blind faith in "the rule of law" and its pretensions of "neutrality" and "objectivity" may be viewed in a different light. A critical self-consciousness of the inherent limitations of legal reasoning need not lead to paralysis or despair. On the contrary, such consciousness may help liberate jurisprudence from the onerous burden of a wider closure. Somewhere

---

[36] See Karl Morrison, *"I Am You": The Hermeneutics of Empathy in Western Literature, Theology, and Art* (Princeton: Princeton University Press, 1988), xxvi, 30, 60.

[37] Elizabeth V. Spelman, *Fruits of Sorrow: Framing Our Attention to Suffering* (Boston: Beacon, 1997), 172.

[38] *Ibid.*

between incontestable and indeterminate interpretations, between the objective and the subjective, both the potential and the limitations of the law may be discovered.

In becoming conscious of the limitations of legal discourse when dealing with crimes such as genocide, we also become conscious of the potentialities of mere positive law, through its deliberate silence, as a means of awakening empathy and a feeling of community with the "other."[39] Thus, a self-conscious jurisprudence that concedes the inevitable influence of subjectivity but that deliberately strives for the relative objectivity of positive rules is a means not of suppressing "passion," but of displacing it elsewhere, outside the strictures of legal discourse. Ironically, the self-restraint of positivist jurisprudence becomes the most befitting tribute to suffering, to the ineffable that is ever present yet can never be adequately labeled. In what it leaves unsaid, such jurisprudence demonstrates both the promise and the wisdom of legal reasoning that is self-conscious, disciplined, and probing.

There is another advantage, too, of identifying and surrendering the desire to inflate lawmaking and jurisprudence into meta-legal closure. In other words, a conscious and deliberate understanding of the law's modest ambitions may significantly attenuate the pressures that a well-meaning jurist or human rights advocate may feel when confronted with the enormity of crimes such as genocide. Contrary to expressions of righteous indignation and demonstrations of virtue as sometimes evinced in progressive jurisprudence, justice, as Hannah Arendt puts it, "demands seclusion, it permits sorrow rather than anger, and it prescribes the most careful abstention from all the nice pleasures of putting oneself in the limelight."[40]

When Arendt remarked to Karl Jaspers that the Nazi atrocities "explode the limits of the law," she also exposed the potentialities residing in a conscious banalization of overwhelmingly monstrous crimes through the rituals of legal process. Through acknowledging that the

---

[39] On the interdependence between limitations and potentialities, see, for example, Peter Haidu, "The Dialectics of Unspeakability: Language, Silence, and the Narratives of Desubjectification," in Saul Friedlander, ed., *Probing the Limits of Representation: Nazism and the "Final Solution"* (Cambridge, MA: Harvard University Press, 1992), 277, 278, remarking that "silence is enfolded in its opposite, in language. As such, silence is simultaneously the contrary of language, its contradiction, and an integral part of language. Silence, in this sense, is the necessary discrepancy of language with itself, its constitutive alterity."

[40] Hannah Arendt, *Eichmann in Jerusalem: A Report on the Banality of Evil* (London and New York: Routledge, 1994), 6.

guilt of those who conceived the Final Solution "oversteps and shatters any and all legal systems,"[41] she acknowledged the insurmountable dimensions of evil represented by the Holocaust. In this context,
the closure that legal process could not achieve in capturing the magnitude of suffering became the only befitting expression of its true
gravity. This sensibility was reflected in the *Eichmann* case, where the
enormity of evil was captured by what the court, with full deliberation, *failed* to articulate:

> The scene that unfolded before us in this appeal is one steeped in blood and
> tears, in which the story of the Holocaust of European Jewry is revealed. *No
> human pen, no human tongue can ever succeed in describing the barest outline of the
> suffering of the millions* who were killed – slaughtered and burned in the exter-
> mination camps and gas-chambers by the murderous tools invented and per-
> fected by the "fertile" brain and the perverse fantasy of the Nazi scum.[42]

The judges of the Jerusalem district court – including Holocaust
survivors – well understood that attempting to inflate jurisprudence
into a broader closure was futile and that superfluous commentary
would inescapably drown and devalue the harrowing testimony
of survivors. They understood that, just as the law speaks through
expressions of passionate humanity, so, too, does it speak through its
deliberate silence.

  The silence of the law is not intended to suggest that we move in the
direction of postmodern radical indeterminacy, where "argumentative
oppositions continue to deconstruct the foundations of one another
infinitely."[43] In the quixotic rush to destroy all totalizing tendencies,
such anti-foundational fanaticism imposes yet another single, triumphant truth: its absolute negation of all truth. For our purposes,
though, what is important is that, ironically, such radical critiques
of reason are equally complicit in avoiding genuine emotional connection and empathy, all in the name of rationalism. The tragedy, as
Roberto Unger points out, is that the "planned campaign of social and
cultural criticism … is a dead-end. It tempts the radical indeterminist

41 "Letter to Karl Jaspers," in *Hannah Arendt/Karl Jaspers: Correspondence 1926–1969*, eds.
Lotte Kohler and Hans Saner, trans. Robert Kimber and Rita Kimber (New York:
Harcourt Brace Jovanovich, 1992), 51, 54.
42 *Attorney General of Israel v. Eichmann*, 36 I.L.R. 277, 322 (Supreme Court of Israel, 1962)
(emphasis added).
43 Outi Korhonen, "New International Law: Silence, Defence or Deliverance?," *European
Journal of International Law* 7 (1996): 1, 16–17 (footnotes omitted).

into an intellectual desert, and abandons him there alone, disoriented, disarmed, and, at last, corrupted – by powerlessness."[44]

We must bear in mind the distinction between reverent and repressive silence. As Peter Haidu observes, "Silence is the antiworld of speech, and at least as polyvalent, constitutive, and fragile. The necessary refuge of the poet, the theologian, and the intellectual, it is equally the instrument of the bureaucrat, the demagogue, and the dictator." Thus, silence can signify "courage and heroism or the cover of cowardice and self-interest." The pliability of silence resembles that of words "in that each production of silence must be judged in its own contexts, in its own situations of enunciation. Silence can be a mere absence of speech; at other times, it is both the negation of speech and a production of meaning." At times, silence has to be overcome for the same reason that "the effort is made to index a 'beyond' of language in full recognition of the fact that language is not to be transcended."[45]

In this light, George Steiner's aphorism that the "world of Auschwitz lies outside speech and it lies outside reason"[46] signifies both the limitations and the potentialities of language as a medium. In its attempts to convey meaning, the sphere of the sacred can be touched but not conquered; any pretension that this sphere can be fully rationalized and captured betrays a misapprehension of its intrinsically elusive nature. Just as crimes such as genocide "defy comprehension and escape human conventions for making sense and meaning of life,"[47] a consciousness of the inadequacy of legal constructs opens the way to appreciating the magnitude of suffering – a surrender to the transcendent empathy that it demands. Confronted by the ineffable, our limited subjective universe momentarily falls into the embrace of the infinite, the beyond where self and other merge in a communion of shared, but unknowable, spiritual essence, where seeking justice becomes an embodiment of humanity's inextricable oneness. Far from the silence that is a deceptive "cover of cowardice and self-interest,"[48] this transcendence is the starting point of an eternal conversation, between presence and absence, being and nonbeing, silence and words. It calls to

---

[44] Roberto M. Unger, *What Should Legal Analysis Become?* (London and New York: Verso, 1996), 121.
[45] Haidu, "The Dialectics of Unspeakability," 278.
[46] George Steiner, "K," in Steiner, *Language and Silence* (London: Faber & Faber, 1966), 123.
[47] Martha Minow, *Between Vengeance and Forgiveness* (Boston: Beacon, 1998), 147.
[48] Haidu, "The Dialectics of Unspeakability," 278.

mind the thirteenth-century Sufi mystic, Rumi, who conveyed silence in his enchanting words:

If you want peace and purity,
tear away your coverings.

This is the purpose of emotion,
to let a streaming beauty flow through you.

Call it spirit, elixir, or the original agreement
between yourself and God.

Opening into that gives peace, a song of being empty,
pure silence.[49]

---

[49] *Say I Am You: Rumi*, trans. John Moyne and Coleman Barks (Athens, GA: Maypop, 1994), 52.

Index

Aboriginal rights, Canadian violations of, 121–23
actus reus criteria, genocide as, 30n.12, 49–52
Adorno, Theodor, 102
affirmative prevention principle, 64
Africa Action, 135
Agos (newspaper), 1
Agranat, Simon, 117, 118–19
Akayesu, Jean-Paul, 8
Akayesu case, 45, 45n.81, 50–51, 52–55, 83, 115, 144–53
Akçam, Taner, 2
Alito, Samuel, 20
American Jewish Congress, 95
Amnesty International, Georgia genocide charges and, 6
Andenæs, Johannes, 25, 26n.51, 64
Annan, Kofi, 8
Annett, Kevin, 121
anti-Semitism, Holocaust as crime of, 115–20
Arendt, Hannah, 10, 104, 117–18, 179
armed conflict
    no nexus with crimes against humanity, 35–37
    war crimes nexus with, 31–32
Armenian massacre, 1–2, 91–92, 126
Army of Republika Srpska, 57
attack, nexus with, crimes against humanity standard and, 35
Axis Rule in Occupied Europe (Lemkin), 6–7, 90, 93–95

Bahá'í minority, persecution in Iran of, viii, 132, 169
Barthes, Roland, 140
Al-Bashir, Omar, 9, 46, 48n.95, 136
Bassiouni, M. Cherif, 87n.122

Bauer, Yehuda, 126
Beć, Janja, 137
Bing Bing Jia, 74
biological destruction
    forcible transfer of children as, 52n.23
    genocide as, 50–52
blameworthiness, sentencing criteria and, 76, 78
Blaškić case, 28, 54
The Body in Pain (Scarry), 170
Booker, Salih, 135
Bosnia v. Serbia, genocide charges in case of, 9, 137–38
Bosnian Muslims
    discriminatory intent mass-murder of, 159–68
    mass-murder in Srebrenica of, vii, viii, 33, 49, 137–38, 153–68
Brčko, mass-murder of Muslims in, 153–68
Brennan, William J., 18
Browning, Christopher, 108
Buddhist minority, Cambodian genocide against, 133–35
Burger, Warren, 19
Bush, George W., inaction on genocide by, 2–3

Cambodia
    Extraordinary Chamber in the Courts of Cambodia, ix, 9
    genocide in, ix, 132n.47, 133–35
    Khmer Rouge, ix, 133–35
    United Nations General Assembly Group of Experts on Cambodia, 134
Canada, Aboriginal rights violations in, 121–23
Canadian Indian residential school system, 122–23

Hohenberg, John, 89
Holocaust
  Arendt's comments on, 10
  crimes against humanity criteria in
    wake of, 41–42
  Eichmann trial as judicial narrative of,
    116
  Genocide Convention in wake of,
    111–15
  as genocide paradigm, vii, 6, 28, 155
  legal ritual of prosecutions involving,
    102–20
  Lemkin's personal experience of, 96–98,
    100
  Lemkin's warnings concerning, 93–95
  "naming" and labeling of, 102
  "Nuremberg view" of, 108
  Queen v. Finta case and, 24
  survivors of, 171
  "uniqueness" of, 124–32, 125n.13
hors de combat. See protected person status
Human Rights Watch, Georgia genocide
    charges and, 6
humanitarian law
  protected person status and, 32–33
  "scope of application," 32
Humphrey, John, 89
Hutu tribe, Rwandan genocide and, 148

ICC. *See* International Criminal Court
ICJ. *See* International Court of Justice
ICTR. *See* International Criminal Tribunal
    for Rwanda
ICTY. *See* International Criminal Tribunal
    for the Former Yugoslavia
"'If I Look at the Mass I Will Never Act':
    Psychic Numbing and Genocide"
    (Slovic), 172–73
Ignatieff, Michael, 129
ILC. *See* International Law Commission
in abstracto, war crimes, 79–81
"in whole or in part" criteria for genocide,
    48–49
incapacitation, punishment and, 14n.10
individual circumstances criteria,
    sentencing principles and, 59–66
individual rehabilitation, sentencing
    principles and, 65
"inherent jurisdiction" principle,
    genocide and, 82–83
intent
  discussion in *Jelisić* of, 154n.58
  sentencing criteria and determination
    of, 77–81
"intent to destroy" principle, 44–45, 48–52
International Court of Justice (ICJ)
  actus reus and, 51

Bosnia v. Serbia case, 9, 137–38
Corfu Channel case, 76
Genocide Convention interstate
    enforcement through, 114, 115n.124
genocide criteria, 48
Lemkin's appointment, 99
International Criminal Court (ICC), viii
  classification of crimes by, 28, 28n.7
  Darfur genocide charges and, 135–36
  Elements of Crimes as tool of, 34,
    34n.29, 39–42, 45–48
  genocide statute of, 82–83, 146n.29
  gravity of crime and individual
    circumstances as factors in
    sentencing, 59–66
  hierarchy of crimes in, 72–73
  intent standard for genocide, 45
  lack of genocide prosecutions in, 9
  nexus requirement lifted in crimes
    against humanity rulings, 36
  persecution statute, 43
  prosecutorial strategy of, 155
  Rwandan genocide jurisprudence and,
    146–47
  Sudanese crisis and, 4
  widespread/systematic attack standard
    for crimes against humanity, 37–39
international criminal jurisdiction,
    Genocide Convention references to,
    114
international criminal law
  legacy of criminal tribunals, 32
  Lemkin's advocacy for, 95, 97
International Criminal Tribunal for
    Rwanda (ICTR), ix
  Akayesu case, 45, 50–51, 52–55, 148
  armed conflict-war crimes nexus
    requirement, 32, 36–37
  civilian population terminology of, 74,
    75n.80
  genocide criteria of, 8, 9, 28n.7, 43n.72,
    83
  gravity of crime and individual
    circumstances as factors in
    sentencing, 59–66
  hierarchy of international crimes,
    ambiguity concerning, 83
  "intent to destroy" terminology of,
    44–45
  jurisprudence of, 144–53
  Kambanda case and, 54, 83, 97n.49
  Kayishema case and, 150–51
  legacy of, 32
  mens rea in crimes against humanity
    and, 39–42
  sentencing criteria for, 60n.15, 66–87
  special intent under, 44

Powell, Lewis F., 19
Power, Samantha, 2–3, 36
A Problem from Hell: America in the Age of Genocide (Power), 2–3
progressive jurisprudence, 178
proportionality
  core international crimes, 27–31
  criminal law principles relating to, 76–81
  purposes of punishment and, 13–17
  sentencing criteria of international tribunals and, 66–87
  stigma in punishment and, 22–26
proprio motu principle
  in genocide trials, 58
  in *Jelisić* case, 156–57, 164
prosecutorial strategy
  of International Criminal Court, 155
  in *Jelisić* trial, 159–68
  with low-ranking perpetrators, 153–54
protected person status, in war crimes, 32–33, 75n.80
Prunier, Gérard, 148–53
psychic numbing and genocide, 172–73
psychological status, as defense in *Jelisić* case, 159–68
psychology of healing, recovery from genocide and, 169–70
Pulitzer, Joseph, 105
punishment
  as deterrence, 14–15
  proportionality and purposes of, 13–17
  purposes of, in international criminal law, 62–66
  rehabilitation and incapacitation and, 14n.10
  retribution as, 16–17
  stigma and proportionality in, 22–26
  wrongdoing and culpability principles and, 16–17
Putin, Vladimir, 5

qualitative criteria for genocide, 48
quantitative criteria for genocide, 48
Queen v. Finta, 24
Quo Vadis (Sienkiewicz), 91

racial discrimination, genocide terminology applied to, 130
rape
  death penalty for, 12, 18–22
  fair labeling principle, 22–23
  as genocide, 29, 52–55
  in hierarchy of crimes, 70–71
rationalism, genocide and, 141–43, 174–82
rehabilitation, punishment and, 14n.10

Rehnquist, William, 19
religious discrimination, genocide terminology applied to, 130
retribution/retributive theory
  deterrence vs., 25
  hierarchy of crimes and, 17–22
  punishment as, 16–17
  sentencing criteria and, 76
Romani Holocaust (*Porrajmos*), 125
Rome Conference, ICC intent standard for genocide adopted at, 45
Rome Statute, 87n.122
Rorty, Richard, 173
Rosenthal, A. M., 90
rule of law, postmodern rejection of, 178
Russell, Bertrand, 132–33
Russell Tribunal, 132–33
Russia, invasion of Georgia by, 5–6
Rwanda. *See also* International Criminal Tribunal for Rwanda
  Akayesu case and genocide in, 144–53
  travaux préparatoires in genocide jurisprudence, 151–52
  Tutsi genocide in, ix, 8, 9, 131
  U.S. inaction regarding genocide in, 3, 139, 139n.75

Samast, Ogun, 1
Samphan, Khieu, 134
Sartre, Jean-Paul, 132, 132n.47
Sary, Ieng, 134
"scale and gravity" threshold, crimes against humanity, 35
Scarry, Elaine, 170
Schabas, William, 83, 85, 135
Scheffer, David, 114
Schulhofer, Stephen, 77–81
Schwelb, Egon, 41–42
"scope of application" of humanitarian law, 32
Scott, Duncan Campbell, 123
sentencing principles
  genocide and, 59–66
  gravity of crime and individual circumstances as factors in, 59–66
  at international criminal tribunals, 60n.15, 66–87
  purposes of punishment in international criminal law, 62–66
  war crimes vs. crimes against humanity, 67–81
sentimental education, Rorty's concept of, 173
Shahabuddeen, Mohamed, 69–71, 73, 75–76
Shawcross, Hartley, 7, 96n.42, 106, 112–14

Lightning Source UK Ltd.
Milton Keynes UK
UKOW05f1007151116

287639UK00001B/30/P